John Henry Walsh

The Dogs of Great Britain, America, and Other Countries

John Henry Walsh

The Dogs of Great Britain, America, and Other Countries

ISBN/EAN: 9783744678704

Printed in Europe, USA, Canada, Australia, Japan

Cover: Foto ©Andreas Hilbeck / pixelio.de

More available books at **www.hansebooks.com**

ENGLISH SETTER, COUNTESS.—See page 9:.

OF

GREAT BRITAIN, AMERICA, AND OTHER COUNTRIES.

Their Breeding, Training, and Management in Health and Disease.

COMPRISING ALL THE ESSENTIAL PARTS OF THE TWO STANDARD WORKS ON THE DOG,

By STONEHENGE.

TOGETHER WITH CHAPTERS BY AMERICAN WRITERS.

NEW AND ENLARGED EDITION.

WITH OVER ONE HUNDRED ILLUSTRATIONS.

NEW YORK:
ORANGE JUDD COMPANY,
1906

CONTENTS.

BOOK I.
THE NATURAL HISTORY, ZOOLOGICAL CLASSIFICATION, AND VARIETIES OF THE DOG.

CHAPTER I.
PAGE
Origin; General Characteristics; Habitats; Varieties; F. Cuvier's Divisional Arrangement; Arrangement adopted by Stonehenge - 17

CHAPTER II.
Wild and half-reclaimed Dogs, hunting in Packs; The Dingo; The Dhole; The Pariah; The Wild Dog of Africa; The South-American Dog; The North American Dog; Other Wild Dogs - - 27

CHAPTER III.
Domesticated Dogs Hunting Chiefly by the Eye and the Nose, and Killing their Game for Man's use; The Rough Scotch Greyhound and Deerhound; The Smooth or English Greyhound; The Irish Greyhound, or Wolf-dog; The French Matin; The Hare-Indian Dog; The Albanian Dog; The Grecian Greyhound; The Turkish Greyhound; The Persian Greyhound; The Russian Greyhound; The Italian Greyhound; The Bloodhound; The Foxhound; The Harrier; The Beagle; The Otterhound; The Terrier; The Duchshund - 32

CHAPTER IV.
Domesticated Dogs, finding game by scent, but not killing it, being chiefly used in aid of the gun; The Modern English Pointer; The Portuguese Pointer; The French Pointer; The Dalmatian and Danish Dogs; The English and Irish Setters; The Russian Setter; The Ordinary Field Spaniel, including the Springer (Clumber, Sussex, and Norfolk breeds), and the Cocker (Welsh and Devonshire); The Water Spaniel (English and Irish); The Chesapeake Bay Dog - - - - - - - - 88

CHAPTER V.
Pastoral Dogs, and those used for the purposes of draught; The English Sheep-Dog; The Colley; The German Sheep-Dog; Pomeranian or Spitz Dog; The Newfoundland and Labrador Dogs; The Esquimaux Dog; The Greenland Dog. - - - - 124

CHAPTER VI.
Watch Dogs; House Dogs, and Toy Dogs; Bulldog; English Mastiff; Mount St. Bernard; Thibet Dog; Poodle; Maltese Dog; Lion Dog; Shock Dog; Toy Spaniels; Toy Terriers; The Pug Dog; Italian Greyhound. - - - - - - - 141

CHAPTER VII.
Crossed Breeds.—Retriever; Bull-Terrier - . . . - 163

BOOK II.

THE BREEDING, REARING, BREAKING, AND MANAGEMENT OF THE DOG, IN-DOORS AND OUT.

CHAPTER I.

Breeding.—Principles of Breeding; Axioms for the Breeder's Use; Crossing and Crossed Breeds; Importance of Health in both Sire and Dam; Best Ages to Breed From; in-and-in Breeding; Best Time of Year; Duration of Heat; Management of the Bitch in Season; The Bitch in Whelp; Preparations for Whelping, Healthy Parturition; Destruction or Choice of Whelps at Birth - 173

CHAPTER II.

Rearing.—Management in the Nest; Choosing; The Foster-Nurse; Feeding before Weaning; Choice of Place for Whelping; Removal of Dew-Claws, etc.; Weaning; Lodging; Feeding; Exercise; Home Rearing vs. Walking; Food; General Management; Cropping, Branding, and Rounding · · 187

CHAPTER III.

Kennels and Kennel Management.—Greyhound Kennels; Foxhound Kennels; Pointer Kennels; Kennels for Single Dogs; House Dogs · · · · · · · - 206

CHAPTER IV.

Breaking and Entering.—The Entering of the Greyhound and Deerhound; Of Foxhounds and Harriers; Breaking the Pointer and Setter; The Retriever (Land and Water); The Spaniel; The Vermin Dog · · · · · · · · · - 215

CHAPTER V.

The Use of the Dog in Shooting.—Grouse and Partridge (Quail) Shooting; Snipe and Woodcock Shooting; Wild Fowl Shooting: Shoal-water Fowl; Deep-water Fowl; Hare Hunting; Deer Hunting; Game in the Far West · · · · · - 243

BOOK III.

THE DISEASES OF THE DOG AND THEIR TREATMENT.

CHAPTER I.

Peculiarities in the Anatomy and Physiology of the Dog.—The Skeleton, including the Teeth; The Muscular System; The Brain and Nervous System; The Digestive System; The Heart and Lungs; The Skin · · · · · · · - 287

CHAPTER II.

The Remedies Suited to the Dog, and the Best Means of Administering them.—Alteratives; Anodynes; Antispasmodics; Aperients; Astringents; Blisters; Caustics; Charges; Cordials; Diuretics; Embrocations; Emetics; Expectorants; Fever Medicines; Clysters; Lotions; Ointments; Stomachics; Styptics; Tonics; Worm Medicines; Administration of Remedies · · 292

CONTENTS. VII

CHAPTER III.
Fevers, and their Treatment.—Simple Ephemeral Fever, or Cold;
Epidemic Fever, or Influenza; Typhus Fever, or Distemper;
Rheumatic Fever; Small-Pox; Sympathetic Fever - - - 309

CHAPTER IV.
Inflammations.—Definition of Inflammation; Symptoms and Treatment of Rabies, Tetanus, and Turnside; Of Inflammation of the Eye, Ear (canker), Mouth, and Nose; Of the Lungs; Of the Stomach; Of the Bowels; Of the Liver; Of the Kidneys and Bladder; Of the Skin - - - - - - - 123

CHAPTER V.
Diseases Accompanied by Want of Power.—Chorea; Shaking Palsy;
Fits; Worms; General Dropsy or Anasarca - - - - 347

CHAPTER VI.
Diseases Arising from Mismanagement or Neglect.—Anæmia; Rickets; Indigestion - - - - - 359

CHAPTER VII.
Diseases and Accidents Requiring Surgical Aid.—Tumors; Cancer;
Encysted Tumors; Abscesses; Unnatural Parturition; Accidents and Operations - - - - - - - - 361
New York Annual Bench Shows, ... 367

LIST OF ILLUSTRATIONS.

Frontispiece......(Countess.)..	
Fetching Game.................	7
Outwitting the Dog............	10
Group of Dogs.................	11
Pointing a Grouse.............	12
Flushing Birds................	14
The Wolf......................	17
English Pointer, Drake *Full page*	21
Head of Wild Dog..............	26
The Dingo.....................	27
Head of Retriever.............	31
Deerhound.....................	32
Greyhound.....................	35
" Pair of..............	36
Setters, Pair of......*Full page*.	39
Deer at Bay...................	48
Hare-Indian Dog...............	49
Greyhound, Persian............	51
Greyhounds, Italian, Pair of....	52
Hound, Head of................	54
Bloodhound, Head of...........	55
Foxhound......................	57
Beagles, American.............	64
" Rabbit................	66
English Terrier...............	69
Dandie Dinmont Terriers.......	72
Irish Setter, Rover..*Full page*..	109
Skye Terrier..................	77
Fox Terrier...................	79
Yorkshire Terrier.............	81
Head of Terrier...............	82
Fox Terrier.........*Full page*..	73
Dachshunds....................	85
Dalmatian Dog.................	91
Gordon Setter, Lang.*Full page*..	93
Setter at Work................	95
Shepherd Dogs.....*Full page*,.	125
Spaniel, Clumber..............	113
" Sussex................	114
" Cocker................	115
" Head of...............	117
" Irish Water...........	118
Dachshund.........*Full page*..	83
Spaniel and Woodcock..........	123
Chesapeake Bay Dog............	121
Colley Dog, Scotch............	128
Sheep Dog, Head of............	130
Spitz Dog.....................	131
Newfoundland Dog..............	134
Esquimaux Dogs, Heads of.	186–137
Esquimaux Dog....*Full page*..	139
Bull Dogs.....................	142
" " Head of........	145
Mastiff, English..............	146
St. Bernard, Rough............	148
" Smooth............	150
" Head of...........	151
Poodle Dog....................	152
Bull Dog and Spaniel..........	153
Maltese Dog...................	154
Spaniel, King Charles.........	156
" Blenheim.............	157
Pug Dogs, A Pair of...........	159
Dog and Crow..................	160
Terriers, Toy.................	161
Retrievers......*Full page*..	165
Bull Terrier..................	169
Terrier and Cat...............	170
Dachshund and Pups............	186
Group of Dogs.................	205
Kennel, Plan of...............	207
" Elevation of..........	208
" Bench for.............	211
" Ventilating Shaft.....	212
Hound, Head of................	217
Plan of Quartering Ground.....	228
Puzzle Peg....................	231
Pointer, Daisy....*Full page*..	237
Head of Skye Terrier..........	247
Snipe............*Full page*..	253
Woodcock.........*Full page*..	259
American Hare.....*Full page*,.	273
Deer at Salt Lick....*Full page*..	277
Coursing Deer.................	280
Buffalo Hunters.....*Full page*..	281
Teeth of Dogs, 4 Figures......	289
Head of Sick Dog..............	291
Dog in Trouble................	308
Paper Carrier.................	322
Puppy.........................	346
Maw Worm......................	351
Tape Worm.....................	352
Tape Worm, Head of............	352
Kidney Worm...................	354
Shepherd Dog and Flock........	358
A Sudden Encounter............	366
Bloodhound, Head of...........	381
Colburn's Dash................	382

FULL PAGE ILLUSTRATIONS.

1. Frontispiece, COUNTESS, the celebrated English setter belonging to Mr. Purcell Llewellyn. Stonehenge regards her as an absolutely perfect dog. For her complete pedigree, see pages 96-97.

2. DRAKE, (page 21), a distinguished pointer in his day. He belonged to Mr. R. J. Lloyd Price, of North Wales, and is fully described on page 90.

3. FLORA and NELLY, (page 39), two well-known American setters exhibited at a recent New York Bench Show, the former by W. C. Waters, of New York, and the latter by Milo Seagears, an eminent shot and trainer of Florida, Orange County, N. Y. NELLY, the under dog in the illustration, was the stanchest little setter we ever shot over; she was unfortunately drowned not long since in a vat, to the great regret of many sportsmen.

4. ROVER (page 109), a majestic Irish setter, belonging to Mr. Macdona. He is by BEAUTY out of the Rev. R. Callaghan's GROUSE, and is own brother to PLUNKET. He is referred to page 110.

5. FOX TERRIER (page 73). This breed of dogs is becoming very popular as companions. They are fully described, page 78. The English Terrier BELCHER, whose portrait is given on a previous page (69), has taken many prizes. He now belongs to Mr. T. B. Swinburne, of Great Britain, and is considered the most perfect specimen of the breed extant.

6. LANG (page 90), an elegant Gordon setter belonging to Mr. Coath, of Great Britain. He has taken numerous prizes at Birmingham and elsewhere, and is fully described, page 106. The Dalmatian dog CAPTAIN, of which an engraving is given on a previous page, (91), belongs to Mr. Fowdry, of Great Britain, and since 1875 has taken several first prizes at London, Birmingham, and other important Dog Shows in England.

7. SHEPHERD DOGS (page 125), or SCOTCH COLLEYS. The group belong to Mr. Francis Morris, of Philadelphia, Pa. These dogs have a most tenacious memory, whereby they are enabled to recognize every sheep in the flock. The breed is described, page 126.

8. DACHSHUND (page 80). This is an engraving of a dog belonging to Mr. Raab, of Hoboken, N. J. Ten years ago there were very few Dachshunds in the United States in addition to Mr. Raab's small pack. They are now becoming quite popular, as they already have been on the European Continent. The breed is described, page 85.

9. ESQUIMAUX OR WOLF DOG (page 139). This engraving represents the breed of North American dogs, which, having many of the characteristics of the wolf, were frequently taken for the latter animal by Dr. Kane. They are described, page 135.

10. WAVY-COATED RETRIEVERS, *Paris* AND *Melody* (page 165). These two beautiful animals belong to Mr. G. Brewis, of Great Britain. The

breed is now much employed in England, though as yet comparatively little used in the United States, their work being performed by our setters and pointers. They are described, page 164.

11. POINTER, DAISY (page 237). This pointer, belonging to Dr. A. R. Strachan, of New York City, took the first prize of her class in a recent New York Bench Show. She is small, but finely formed, and beautiful both in color and action.

12. AMERICAN SNIPE (page 259). Though commonly called English Snipe, and formerly supposed to be identical, this is an American bird, the differences first having been ascertained and designated by Dr Alexander Wilson, the celebrated Ornithologist. The bird in the engraving was shot on the Hackensack Meadows, and owing to its size and beauty, preserved for illustration. Snipe shooting is described. page 253.

13. WOODCOCK, (page 259). The engraving represents the American Woodcock. Though smaller than the English bird, it is fully as handsomely marked and held in equal estimation by epicures of both countries. The bird described flew from its feeding ground across a village street in Bergen, New Jersey, and dashing through the window of a drug store broke its neck against the stove.

14. AMERICAN HARE (page 273). Suggestions regarding the hunting of hares in the United States are given, page 275.

15. SHOOTING DEER AT A SALT-LICK (page 277). The engraving represents a favorite and successful mode of hunting deer in the United States, and is described, page 280.

16. BUFFALO HUNTERS' CAMP (page 281). This scene, representing buffalo hunters, curing the hides of the animals, was sketched in Southern Kansas by one of the contributors to this volume. The present ranges of the buffalo are described, page 283.

17. COLBURN'S DASH (page 382). This celebrated dog, belonging to George C. Colburn, of this city, combines the English, Irish, and Gordon strains, and has sired some of our best prize and field winners.

PUBLISHERS' PREFACE.

For fifty years, "Stonehenge," by which name Mr. J. H. Walsh is known in both Continents, has made the dog a constant study. More than twenty years ago the Messrs Longman, of London, selected him to revise Mr. Youatt's work. Since then his voluminous writings in the "Field," and elsewhere, have revealed such thorough knowledge of the subject as to constitute him the undisputed authority on all matters pertaining to the dog. Blaine, Daniel, Hill, Mayhew, Richards, Youatt, and other authors, take rank far below him, while "Idstone," who, perhaps, stands next to him, frankly alludes in his work to "Stonehenge" as "without doubt the first of living authorities," "the most experienced and scientific of writers," etc. He is so regarded to-day in America, as well as in Europe. The writings on which "Stonehenge's" reputation and present popularity mainly rest are contained in the two works "The Dog in Health and Disease," (1872), and "The Dogs of the British Islands," (1878). The high cost of these works has placed them, with few exceptions, beyond the reach of would be buyers in the United States, where there is a very general curiosity and desire to procure them. Such being the case, we have incorporated all the essential features of both works into one, at a cost to the reader of less than one-fifth the amount charged for the two imported works. The new volume may be correctly described as Stonehenge's writings, omitting minor details of merely local interest, and following the original text, except in the reconstruction of sentences for the sake of perspicuity and simplicity. Such additional matter as has been deemed desirable for an American book is contributed, among others, by Mr. David W. Judd, whose annual three months' hunting trips for many years, have discovered choice hunting grounds in the Middle and Western States and Territories; by Mr. Henry Stewart, whose long studies in animal life have produced several successful volumes, and by Mr. F. R. Ryer, whose familiarity with dog lore has so frequently been verified in controversial papers. The engravings have been executed by Mr. Charles Hinkle, whose known experience with dogs enables him to successfully bring out the required points in his subject. The full page illustrations are distributed without regard to the text, but to add to the general effect of the volume. Lists of prize winners in Dog Shows, down to 1887, are given.

INTRODUCTORY.

Every lover of the dog has hailed with lively satisfaction the reproduction of Stonehenge's Great Works in the United States. Mr. Walsh does not always express himself in the smoothest terms, but what he writes is to the point. The reader feels that he is explaining or advising what he knows to be true from actual experience, that he can safely purchase one animal or administer medicine to another in accordance with his directions. The composition of his latest book, the "Dogs of the British Islands," shows a marked improvement over that of "The Dog in Health and Disease," though the directions for breeding, rearing, etc., and for the treatment of the diseases, are fuller and more satisfactory in the latter. The present volume very properly, therefore, combines descriptions of dogs selected from both works, while the matter pertaining to the breeding of dogs, management in disease, etc., is reproduced almost bodily from Stonehenge's first book. The Illustrations are much the superior in the latest work, and are therefore selected from that for reproduction. Portraits of several well known American dogs are added.

The rapidly increasing interest manifested in Dog Shows bears evidence to the growing regard and care in the United States for the canine species. Of all animals, the dog possesses the most intelligence, and, with proper effort and training, can be educated up to a point next to human. We have plenty of books on the dog, but none furnishing the desired information and instruction which are presented in Stonehenge's combined works.

Time devoted to the animal creation is by no means lost. Not to speak of the practical results, it has an ameliorating effect upon humanity. He who is kind to his brutes does not himself become a brute. If the disposition to treat them with consideration is cultivated, it is carried into his daily walk and conversation, with humanity. He who practices profanity and physical abuse upon his animals, all the more readily berates his family. However degraded, the man who loves his dog is not wholly lost. There is yet considerable humanity about him, which may, perhaps, be sooner or later successfully appealed to. The dog is a valuable factor in society. Cuvier styles the domestic dog "the most useful conquest that man has gained in the animal world." The Shaggy Esquimaux which draws its heavy sled over weary roads; the faithful Colley, "without which," says the Ettrick Shepherd, "the whole of the open mountainous land in Scotland would not be worth a sixpence"; the noble Newfoundland which protects and rescues life; the sturdy Mastiff which guards well the home from all intruders; the Pointer or Setter which, with its unerring scent, contributes to the delicacy of the table, and in the "season" swells may be his masters slender income; the lively Terrier which rids the house of vermin; the ever alert Skye, whose shrill night bark betokens danger—one and all enact an important part for mankind. When we take into account the very many valuable services performed for us by the various species, we can not so much wonder, perhaps, that the untutored savage thinks his dog follows him straight to the spirit land, or that the ancient Egyptians freshly shaved themselves as a mark of grief every time a dog died in the family, or that a tribe of Ethiopia once set up a dog for their king, and accepted the wags of his tail as heavenly divinations. He is certainly one of the noblest and most useful of animals.

BOOK I.

THE NATURAL HISTORY, ZOOLOGICAL CLASSIFICATION, AND VARIETIES OF THE DOG.

Fig. 1.—THE WOLF.

CHAPTER I.

ORIGIN. — GENERAL CHARACTERISTICS. — HABITAT. — VARIETIES. — F. CUVIER'S DIVISIONAL ARRANGEMENT.—ARRANGEMENT ADOPTED BY "STONEHENGE."

From the earliest times we have reason to believe that the dog has been the faithful companion and assistant of man in all parts of the world, and his fidelity and attachment are so remarkable as to have become proverbial. Before the introduction of agriculture, it was by means of the hunting powers of this animal that man was enabled to support himself by pursuing the wild denizens of the forest; for though now, with the aid of gunpowder, he can in great measure dispense with the services of his assistant, yet, until the invention of that destructive agent, he was, in default of the dog, reduced to the bow and arrow, the snare, or the pitfall. The dog was also of incalculable service in guarding the flocks and herds from the depredations of the *Carnivora*, and even man himself was often glad to have recourse to his courage and strength in resisting the lion, the tiger, or the wolf.

Much has been written on the origin of the dog, and Pennant, Buffon, and other naturalists have exhausted their powers of research and invention in attempting to discover the parent stock from which all are descended. The subject, however, is wrapped in so much obscurity as to baffle all their efforts, and it is still a disputed point whether the shepherd's dog, as supposed by Buffon and Daniel, or the wolf, as conjectured by Bell, is the progenitor of the various breeds now existing. Anyhow, it is a most unprofitable speculation, and, being unsupported by proof of any kind, it can never be settled upon any reliable basis. We shall not, therefore, waste any space in entering upon this discussion, but leave our readers to investigate the inquiry, if they think fit, in the pages of Buffon, Linnæus, Pennant, and Cuvier, and our most recent investigator, Professor Bell. It may, however, be observed that the old hypothesis of Pennant that the dog is only a domesticated jackal, crossed with the wolf or fox, though resuscitated by Mr. Bell, is now almost entirely exploded; for while it accounts somewhat ingeniously for the varieties which are met with, yet it is contradicted by the stubborn fact that, in the present day, the cross of the dog with either of these animals, *if produced*, is incapable of continuing the species when paired with one of the same crossed breed. Nevertheless, it may be desirable to give Mr. Bell's reasons for thinking that the dog is descended from the wolf, which are as follows:—

"In order to come to any rational conclusion on this head, it will be necessary to ascertain to what type the animal approaches most nearly, after having for many successive generations existed in a wild state, removed from the influence of domestication, and of association with mankind. Now we find that there are several different instances of the existence in dogs of such a state of wildness as to have lost even that common character of domestication, variety of color, and marking. Of these, two very remarkable ones are the Dhole of India, and the Dingo of Australia. There is, besides, a half-reclaimed race amongst the Indians of North America, and another, also partially tamed in South America, which deserve attention. And it is found that these races in different degrees, and in a greater degree as they are more wild, exhibit the lank and gaunt form, the lengthened limbs, the long and slender muzzle, and the great comparative strength which characterize the wolf; and that the tail of the Australian dog, which may be considered as the most remote from a state of domestication, assumes the slightly bushy form of that animal.

"We have here a remarkable approximation to a well-known wild animal of the same genus, in races which, though doubtless descended from domesticated ancestors, have gradually assumed the wild condition; and it is worthy of especial remark that the anatomy of the wolf, and its osteology in particular, does not differ from that of the dog in general, more than the different kinds of dogs do from each other. The cranium is absolutely similar, and so are all, or nearly all, the other essential parts; and, to strengthen still further the probability of their identity, the dog and wolf will readily breed together, and their progeny is fertile. The obliquity of the position of the eyes in the wolf is one of the characters in which it differs from the dog; and, although it is very desirable not to rest too much upon the effects of habit on structure, it is not perhaps straining the point to attribute the forward direction of the eyes in the dog to the constant habit, for many successive generations, of looking forward to his master, and obeying his voice."*

Such is the state of the argument in favor of the original descent from the wolf, but, as far as it is founded upon the breeding together of the wolf and dog, it applies also to the fox, which is now ascertained occasionally to be impregnated by the dog; but in neither case we believe does the progeny continue to be fertile if put to one of the same cross, and as this is now ascertained to be the only reliable test, the existence of the first cross stands for

---

* Bell's British Quadrupeds, pp. 196-7.

nothing. Indeed, experience shows us more and more clearly every year, that no reliance can be placed upon the test depending upon fertile intercommunion, which, especially in birds, is shown to be liable to various exceptions. Still it has been supported by respectable authorities, and for this reason we have given insertion to the above extract.

GENERAL CHARACTERISTICS.

In every variety the dog is more or less endowed with a keen sight, strong powers of smell, sagacity almost amounting to reason, and considerable speed, so that he is admirably adapted for all purposes connected with the pursuit of game. He is also furnished with strong teeth, and courage enough to use them in defence of his master, and with muscular power sufficient to enable him to draw moderate weights, as we see in Kamtschatka and Newfoundland. Hence, among the old writers, dogs were divided into *Pugnaces*, *Sagaces*, and *Celeres;* but this arrangement is now superseded, various other systems having been adopted in modern times, though none perhaps much more satisfactory. Belonging to the division *Vertebrata*, class *Mammalia*, order *Feræ*, family *Felidæ*, and sub-family *Canina*, the species is known as *Canis familiaris*, the sub-family being distinguished by having two tubercular teeth behind the canines on the upper jaw, with non-retractile claws, while the dog itself differs from the fox with which he is grouped, in having a round pupil in the eye instead of a perpendicular slit, as is seen in that animal.

The attempt made by Linnæus to distinguish the dog as having a tail curved to the left, is evidently without any reliable foundation, as though there are far more with the tail on that side than on the right, yet many exceptions are to be met with, and among the pugs almost all the bitches wear their tails curled to the left. The definition, therefore, of *Canis familiaris caudâ* (*sinistrorsum*) *recurvatâ*, will not serve to separate the species from the others of the genus *Canis*, as proposed by the Swedish naturalist.

POINTER, DRAKE.—*See page* 90.

HABITAT.

In almost every climate the dog is to be met with, from Kamtschatka to Cape Horn, the chief exception being some of the islands in the Pacific Ocean; but it is only in the temperate zone that he is to be found in perfection, the courage of the bulldog and the speed of the greyhound soon degenerating in tropical countries. In China and the Society Islands dogs are eaten, being considered great delicacies, and by the ancients the flesh of a young fat dog was highly prized, Hippocrates even describing that of an adult as wholesome and nourishing. In a state of nature the dog is compelled to live on flesh which he obtains by hunting, and hence he is classed among the *Carnivora ;* but when domesticated he will live upon vegetable substances alone, such as oatmeal porridge, or bread made from any of the cereals, but thrives best upon a mixed diet of vegetable and animal substances; and, indeed, the formation of his teeth is such as to lead us to suppose that by nature he is intended for it, as we shall hereafter find in discussing his anatomical structure.

VARIETIES OF THE DOG.

The varieties of the dog are extremely numerous, and, indeed, as they are apparently produced by crossing, which is still had recourse to, there is scarcely any limit to the numbers which may be described. It is a curious fact that large bitches frequently take a fancy to dogs so small as to be incapable of breeding with them; and in any case, if left to themselves, the chances are very great against their selecting mates of the same breed as themselves. The result is, that innumerable nondescripts are yearly born, but as a certain number of breeds are described by writers on the dog, or defined by "dog-fanciers," these "mongrels," as they are called from not belonging to them, are generally despised, and, however useful they may be, the breed is not continued. This, however, is not literally true, exceptions being made in favor of certain sorts which have been improved by admixture with others, such as the cross of the bulldog with the greyhound; the foxhound with the Spanish pointer; the bulldog with the terrier, etc., etc., all of which are now recognized and admitted into the list of valuable breeds, and not only are not considered mongrels, but, on the contrary, are prized above the original strains from which they are descended. An attempt has been made by M. F. Cuvier to arrange these varieties under three primary divisions, which are founded upon the shape of the head and the length of the jaws, these being supposed by him to vary in accordance with the degree of cunning and scenting powers, which the animal possessing them displays. The following is his classification, which in the main is correct, and I shall adhere to it, with trifling alterations, in the pages of this book.

F. Cuvier's Divisional Arrangement.

I. MATINS.

Characterized by head more or less elongated; parietal bones insensibly approaching each other; condyles of the lower jaw placed in a horizontal line with the upper molar teeth, exemplified by—

SECT. 1. *Half-reclaimed dogs*, hunting in packs; such as the Dingo, the Dhole, the Pariah, etc.

SECT. 2. *Domesticated dogs*, hunting in packs, or singly, but using the eye in preference to the nose; as, for instance, the Albanian dog, Deerhound, etc.

SECT. 3. *Domesticated dogs*, which hunt singly, and almost entirely by the eye. Example: the Greyhound.

II. SPANIELS.

Characteristics.—Head moderately elongated; parietal bones do not approach each other above the temples, but diverge and swell out, so as to enlarge the forehead and cavity of the brain.

SECT. 4. *Pastoral dogs*, or such as are employed for domestic purposes. Example: Shepherd's Dog.

SECT. 5. *Water dogs*, which delight in swimming. Examples: Newfoundland Dog, Water-Spaniel, etc.

SECT. 6. *Fowlers*, or such as have an inclination to chase or point birds by scenting only, and not killing. Examples: the Setter, the Pointer, the Field-Spaniel, etc.

SECT. 7. *Hounds*, which hunt in packs by scent, and kill their game. Examples: the Foxhound, the Harrier, etc.

SECT. 8. *Crossed breeds, for sporting purposes.* Example: the Retriever.

III. HOUSE DOGS.

Characteristics.—Muzzle more or less shortened, skull high, frontal sinuses considerable, condyle of the lower jaw extending above the line of the upper cheek teeth. Cranium smaller in this group than in the first and second, in consequence of its peculiar formation.

SECT. 9. *Watch dogs*, which have no propensity to hunt, but are solely employed in the defence of man, or his property. Examples: the Mastiff, the Bulldog, the Pug dog, etc.

As before remarked, this division is on the whole founded on natural laws, but there are some anomalies which we shall endeavor to remove. For instance, the greyhound is quite as ready to hunt in packs as any other hound, and is only prevented from doing so by the hand of his master. The same restraint keeps him from using his nose, or he could soon be nearly as good with that organ as with the eye. So also Cuvier defines his sixth section as "having an inclination to chase and point *birds*," whereas they have as great, and oftener a greater, desire for hares and rabbits. Bearing therefore in mind these trifling defects, we shall consider the dog under the following heads:

CHAP. I. Wild and half-reclaimed dogs, hunting in packs.

CHAP. II. Domesticated dogs, hunting chiefly by the eye, and killing their game for the use of man.

CHAP. III. Domesticated dogs, hunting chiefly by the nose, and both finding and killing their game.

CHAP. IV. Domesticated dogs, finding game by scent, but not killing it; being chiefly used in aid of the gun.

CHAP. V. Pastoral dogs, and those used for the purposes of draught.

CHAP. VI. Watch dogs, House dogs, and Toy dogs.

CHAP. VII. Crossed breeds, Retrievers, etc.

Fig. 2.—THE DINGO.

CHAPTER II.

WILD AND HALF-RECLAIMED DOGS HUNTING IN PACKS.—THE DINGO.—THE DHOLE.—THE PARIAH.—THE WILD DOG OF AFRICA.—THE SOUTH-AMERICAN DOG.—THE NORTH-AMERICAN DOG.—OTHER WILD DOGS.

THE DINGO.

It is upon the great similarity between these wild dogs and the wolf or fox, that the supposition is founded of the general descent of the domesticated dog from either the one or the other. After examining the portrait of the dingo, it will at once be seen that it resembles the fox so closely in the shape of its body, that an ordinary observer could readily mistake it for one of that species, while the head is that of the wolf. The muzzle is long and pointed, the ears short and erect. Hight about 24 inches, length 30 inches. His coat is more like fur than hair, and is composed of a mixture of silky and woolly hair, the former being of a deep yellow, while the latter is grey. The tail is long and bushy, and resembles that of the fox, excepting in carriage, the dingo curling it over the hip, while the fox trails it along the ground.* While in his unreclaimed state this dog is savage and unmanageable, but is easily tamed, though even then he is not to be trusted, and when set at liberty will endeavor to escape. Many dingoes have been crossed with the terrier, and have been exhibited as hybrids between the dog and fox, which latter animal they closely resemble, with the single exception of the pendulous tail. Whenever, therefore, a specimen is produced which is said to be this hybrid, every care must be taken to ascertain the real parentage without relying upon the looks alone.

THE DHOLE.

The native wild dog of India, called the Dhole, resembles the Dingo in all but the tail, which, though hairy, is not at all bushy. The following is Captain Williamson's description, extracted from his "Oriental Field Sports," which is admitted to be a very accurate account by those who have been much in India. "The dholes are of the size of a small greyhound. Their countenance is enlivened by unusually brilliant eyes. Their body, which is slender and deep-chested, is thinly covered by a coat of hair of a reddish brown or bay color. The tail is dark towards its extremity. The limbs are light, compact, and strong, and equally calculated for speed and power. They resemble many of the common pariah dogs in form, but the singularity of their color and marks at once demonstrate an evident distinction. These dogs are said to be perfectly harmless if unmolested. They do not willingly approach persons, but, if they chance to meet any in their course, they do not show any particular anxiety to escape. They view the human

---

* The engraving of the Dingo was taken from an animal in confinement, in which state the tail is seldom curled upwards.

race rather as objects of curiosity than either of apprehension or enmity. The natives who reside near the Ranochitty and Katcunsandy passes, in which vicinity the dholes may frequently be seen, describe them as confining their attacks entirely to wild animals, and assert that they will not prey on sheep, goats, etc.; but others, in the country extending southward from Jelinah and Mechungunge, maintain that cattle are frequently lost by their depredations. I am inclined to believe that the dhole is not particularly ceremonious, but will, when opportunity offers, and a meal is wanting, obtain it at the expense of the neighboring village.

"The peasants likewise state that the dhole is eager in proportion to the animal he hunts, preferring the elk to any other kind of deer, and particularly seeking the royal tiger. It is probable that the dhole is the principal check on the multiplication of the tiger; and although incapable individually, or perhaps in small numbers, to effect the destruction of so large and ferocious an animal, may, from their custom of hunting in packs, easily overcome any smaller beast found in the wilds of India." Unlike most dogs which hunt in packs, the dholes run nearly mute, uttering only occasionally a slight whimper, which may serve to guide their companions equally well with the more sonorous tongues of other hounds. The speed and endurance of these dogs are so great as to enable them to run down most of the varieties of game which depend upon flight for safety, while the tiger, the elk, and the boar diminish the numbers of these animals by making an obstinate defence with their teeth, claws, or horns, so that the breed of dholes is not on the increase.

THE PARIAH.

This is the general name in India for the half-reclaimed dogs which swarm in every village, owned by no one in particular, but ready to accompany any individual on a hunting excursion. They vary in appearance in different districts, and can not be described very particularly; but the type of the pariah may be said to resemble the dhole in general characteristics, and the breed is most probably a cross with that dog and any accidental varieties of domesticated dogs which may have been introduced into the respective localities. They are almost always of a reddish brown color, very thin and gaunt, with pricked ears, deep chest, and tucked up belly. The native Indians hunt the tiger and wild boar, as well as every species of game, with these dogs, which have good noses and hunt well, and though they are not so high-couraged as our British hounds, yet they often display considerable avidity and determination in "going in" to their formidable opponents.

THE EKIA, OR WILD AFRICAN DOG.

The native dogs of Africa are of all colors, black, brown, and yellow, or red; and they hunt in packs, giving tongue with considerable force. Though not exactly wild, they are not owned by any individuals among the inhabitants, who, being mostly Mahometans, have an abhorrence of the dog, which by the Koran is declared to be unclean. Hence they are complete outcasts, and obtain a scanty living either by hunting wild animals where they abound, or, in those populous districts where game is scarce, by devouring the offal which is left in the streets and outskirts of the towns. The *Ekia*, also called the *Deab*, is of considerable size, with a large head, small pricked ears, and round muzzle. His aspect in general resembles that of the wolf, excepting in color, which, as above remarked, varies greatly, and in the tail, which is almost always spotted or variegated. These dogs are extremely savage, probably from the constant abuse which they meet with, and they are always ready to attack a stranger on his entrance into any of the villages of the country. They are revolting animals, and unworthy of the species they belong to.

THE NORTH AND SOUTH AMERICAN DOGS.

A great variety of the dog tribe is to be met with throughout the continent of America, resembling in type the dingo of Australia, but appearing to be crossed with some of the different kinds introduced by Europeans. One of the most remarkable of the South-American dogs is the *Alco*, which has pendulous ears, with a short tail and hog-back, and is supposed to be descended from the native dog found by Columbus; but, even allowing this to be the case, it is of course much intermixed with foreign breeds. The North-American dogs are very closely allied to the dingo in all respects, but are generally smaller in size, and are also much crossed with European breeds. In some districts they burrow in the ground, but the march of civilization is yearly diminishing their numbers throughout the continent of America.

OTHER WILD DOGS.

Many other varieties of the wild dog are described by travellers, but they all resemble one or other of the above kinds, and are of little interest to the general reader.

Fig. 3.—DEERHOUND, BRAN.

CHAPTER III.

DOMESTICATED DOGS HUNTING CHIEFLY BY THE EYE, AND KILLING THEIR GAME FOR MAN'S USE.

THE ROUGH SCOTCH GREYHOUND AND DEERHOUND.—THE SMOOTH OR ENGLISH GREYHOUND.—THE GAZEHOUND. — THE IRISH GREYHOUND, OR WOLF-DOG.—THE FRENCH MATIN—THE HARE-INDIAN DOG—THE ALBANIAN DOG.—THE GRECIAN GREYHOUND.—THE TURKISH GREYHOUND.—THE PERSIAN GREYHOUND—THE RUSSIAN GREYHOUND.—THE ITALIAN GREYHOUND.

THE ROUGH SCOTCH GREYHOUND AND DEERHOUND.

This breed of dogs is, I believe, one of the oldest and purest in existence, but it is now rapidly becoming extinct, being supplanted in public estimation, for coursing purposes, by the English greyhound, or by a cross between the two. The rough greyhound is identical in shape and make with the pure deerhound, and the two can only be distinguished by their style of running when at work or play; the deerhound, though depending on his nose, keeping his head much higher than the greyhound, because he uses this attitude in waiting to pull down his game. By some people it is supposed that the smooth variety of the greyhound is as old as the rough; but, on carefully examining the description given by Arrian, no one can doubt that the dog of his day was rough in coat, and in all respects like the present Scotch dog. In shape, the Scotch greyhound resembles the ordinary smooth variety, but he is rather more lathy, and has not quite the same muscular development of loin and thigh, though, the bony frame being more fully developed, this is perhaps more apparent than real.

In spite of the external form being the same in the rough Scotch greyhound used for coursing hares, and the deerhound, there can be no doubt that the two breeds, from having been kept to their own game exclusively, are specially adapted to its pursuit by internal organization, and the one cannot be substituted for the other with advantage. Generally speaking, the deerhound is of larger size than the greyhound, some being 28 inches high, though this size is not very uncommon in the greyhound, and dogs of 26½ or 27 inches are frequently seen. Mr. Scrope, the author of "Deer-stalking," gives the following description of Buskar, a celebrated deerhound belonging to Captain McNeill of Colonsay, viz.: hight, 28 inches; girth round the chest, 32 inches; running weight, 85 lbs.; color, red or fawn, with black muzzle. Bran, whose portrait is given at the head of this chapter, and which showed all the points of the deerhound, was by Mr. Stewart Hodgson's Oscar, of the breed of Mr. McKenzie, of Ross-shire, Scotland. The measurement of this noble animal was as follows: from nose to setting on of the tail, 47 inches; tail, 22 inches; hight, 32 inches; length of head, 12 inches; circumference of head, 17½ inches; round the arm at the elbow, 9½ inches; girth at chest, 33½ inches; girth at loin, 24 inches; round the thigh, 17½ inches; round lower thigh hock, 7 inches; knee, 7 inches. To these external qualifications were added great speed and strength, combined with endurance and courage, while the sagacity and docility of the dog made him doubly valuable. He was used for coursing the deer, but his nose was good enough for hunting, even a cold scent, as was the case with all of his breed. Whether or not the deerhound can now be procured in a state of purity, I am not prepared to say, but that they are extremely rare, is above dispute, though there are numberless animals resembling them in form, but all more or less crossed with the foxhound, bloodhound, bulldog, etc., and consequently not absolutely pure. Mr. Scrope himself, with all his advantages, could not succeed in obtaining any, and had recourse to the cross of the greyhound with the foxhound, which, he says, answered particularly well; as, according to his experience, "you get the speed of the greyhound with just enough of the nose of the foxhound to answer your purpose....In point of shape, they resemble the greyhound, but they are larger in the bone and shorter in the leg. Some of them, when in slow action, carry the tail over the back like the pure foxhound; their dash in making a cast is most beautiful, and they stand all sorts of rough weather." He advises that the first cross only should be employed, fearing that, as in some other instances, the ultimate results of breeding back to either strain, or of going on with the two crosses, would be unsatisfactory. "Maida," the celebrated deerhound belonging to Sir Walter Scott, was a cross of the greyhound with the bloodhound, but some distance off the latter. The bulldog infusion has the disadvantage of making the deerhound thus bred, attack the deer too much in front, by which he is almost sure to be impaled on the horns, so that, in spite of the high courage of the breed, it is from this cause quite useless in taking deer.

The rough Scotch greyhound, as used for coursing, averages about 26 inches in the dog, and 22 or 23 inches in the bitch; but as above remarked, its use is almost abandoned in public, and those which are still bred are either used in private, or are kept entirely for their ornamental properties, which are very considerable, and, as they resemble the deerhound, they are very commonly passed off for them. They are of all colors, but the most common are fawn, red, brindled (either red and black mixed, or fawn and blue), grey, and black. The coat is harsh, long, and rough, especially about the jaws, where the hair stands out like that of a Scotch terrier. In speed they are about equal to the smooth greyhound, but they do not appear to be quite so stout, though of late we have had no opportunities of judging, as a rough greyhound in public is rare in the extreme. Mr. A. Graham, who formerly was celebrated for his breed of these dogs, has now abandoned their use, excepting when largely crossed with the smooth greyhound, for which purpose they seem well suited, when the former are too small or too delicate for the work they have to do. But as these are now bred of a much more hardy kind than formerly, so that they will stand cold and wet almost as well as the Scotch dog, there is little necessity for resorting to the cross, and it is accordingly abandoned by almost all the breeders of the animal. Nevertheless, some of the best dogs of the present day have a strain of the rough dog in them, but it is gradually dying out as compared with ten or twenty years ago. It is alleged, and I fancy with some truth, that the rough dog runs cunning sooner than the smooth, and hence the cross is objected to; and certainly many litters of greyhounds bred in this way within the last few years have been remarkable for this objectionable vice.

The points, or desirable external characteristics of this breed, with the exception of the rough coat, are so similar to those of the smooth greyhound, that the two may be considered together.

Fig. 4.—PAIR OF SMOOTH GREYHOUNDS—RIOT AND DAVID.

THE SMOOTH GREYHOUND.

This elegant animal appears to have existed in Britain from a very early period, being mentioned in a very old Welsh proverb, and a law of King Canute having precluded the commonalty from keeping him. Numberless hypotheses have been brought forward relative to the origin of the greyhound, Buffon tracing him to the French nation, and some other writers fancying that they could with more probability consider him as the descendant of the bulldog or the mastiff. But as I believe that it is impossible to ascertain with any degree of certainty the origin of the species Canis, so I am quite satisfied with the conclusion that no long-standing variety can be traced to its source. We must, therefore, be content to take each as we find it, and rest content with investigating its present condition; perhaps in some cases extending our researches back for fifty or a hundred years, and even then we shall often find that we are lost in a sea of doubt.

Until within the last twenty-five years public coursing was confined to a very limited circle of competitors, partly owing to the careful retention of the best blood in the kennels of a chosen few, but chiefly to the existing game laws, which made it imperative that every person coursing should not only have a certificate, but also a qualification, that is to say, the possession of landed property to the value of one hundred pounds per annum. Hence the sport was forbidden to the middle classes, and it was not until 1831 that it was thrown open to them. From that time to the present the possession of the greyhound has been coveted and obtained by great numbers of country gentlemen and farmers in rural districts, and by professional men as well as tradesmen in our cities and towns, so that the total number in Great Britain and Ireland may be estimated at about fifteen or twenty thousand. Of these about five or six thousand are kept for public coursing, while the remainder amuse their owners by coursing the hare in private.

Various explanations have been offered of the etymology of the prefix grey, some contending that the color is implied, others that it means Greek (*Graius*), while a third party understand it to mean great. But as there is a remarkable peculiarity in this breed connected with it, we need not, I think, go farther for the derivation. No other breed, I believe, has the blue or grey color prevalent; and those which possess it at all have it mixed with white, or other color; as, for instance, the blue-mottled harrier, and the blotched blue and brown seen in some other kinds. The greyhound, on the contrary, has the pure blue or iron grey color very commonly; and although this shade is not admired by any lovers of the animal for its beauty, it will make its appearance occasionally. Hence it may fairly be considered a peculiarity of the breed, and this grey color may, therefore, with a fair show of probability, have given the name to the greyhound.

In describing the greyhound it is usual, and indeed almost necessary, to consider him as used for the two purposes already mentioned, that is to say,—1st, as the private, and 2ndly, as the public, greyhound; for though externally there is no difference whatever, yet in the more delicate organization of his brain and nerves there is some obscure variation, by which he is rendered more swift and clever in the one case, and more stout and honest in the other. In the horse the eye readily detects the thoroughbred, but this is not the case here: for there are often to be met with most beautifully formed greyhounds of private blood, which it would be impossible to distinguish from the best public breeds by their appearance, but which in actual trial would be sure to show defective speed and sagacity. This being the case, I shall first describe the general characteristics of both, and afterwards those in which they differ from one another.

The points of the greyhound will be described at length, because as far as speed goes, he may be taken as the type to which all other breeds are referred; but, before going into these particulars, it will be interesting to examine the often-quoted doggrel rhymes, which are founded upon a longer effusion originally published by Wynkyn de Worde in 1496, and to institute a comparison between the greyhound of the fifteenth and nineteenth centuries. In the former of these periods it was said that this dog should have—

> " The head of a snake,
> The neck of the drake,
> A back like a beam,
> A side like a bream,
> The tail of a rat,
> And the foot of a cat."

Now, although the several points herein mentioned may be enlarged upon, it is scarcely possible to dissent from any one of them; but, as all my readers may not exactly know the form which is meant to be conveyed by the side of a bream for instance, it is necessary to explain it in more intelligible language.

1st. The HEAD, it is said, should be snake-like, but this is not to be taken literally, as that of the snake differs considerably from the head of any specimen of the greyhound which has ever come under my observation. Every snake's head is flat and broad, with the nose or snout also quite compressed, while the head of the greyhound, though flat at the top, is comparatively circular in its transverse section, and the nose is irregularly triangular. There is no doubt that the greyhound of former days, before the cross of

AMERICAN SETTERS. FLORA AND NELLY.—*See page 9.*

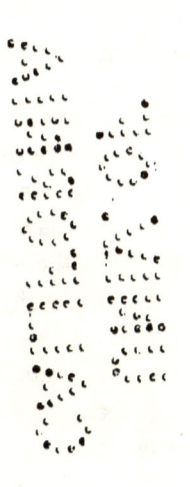

the bulldog was introduced, had a much smaller head than that which is now seen; and I also believe that some breeds at present existing may be ascertained to be free from this cross, by their small brain-cases; but, still, none have the perfectly flat head of the reptile in question. The tyro, therefore, who looks for a literal interpretation of the first line of the rhyme will be disappointed. My own belief is that a full development of brain gives courage and sagacity, but leads to such a rapid acquirement of knowledge relative to the wiles practised by the hare, as to make the dog possessing it soon useless for anything but killing his game, which he is often able to do with absolute certainty. Hence it is important to bear this in mind, and to take care not to overdo this characteristic. In all cases, the more the development is increased behind the ears, the higher will be the courage; and if this can be obtained without a corresponding increase in the diameter in front of those organs, there will be no attendant disadvantage, as the intellectual faculties no doubt reside in the anterior part of the brain. The best average measurement opposite the ear in dogs of full size is about 15 inches, and for bitches, 14 or 14¼. The jaw should be very lean, and diminishing suddenly from the head, not gradually falling off in one uniform line. The teeth are of great importance, as, unless they are strong and good, the hare cannot be seized and held. They should be white, strong, and regular, showing strength of constitution, as well as being useful in the course. As a rule, the incisor teeth meet each other, but some dogs are underhung like the bulldog, and others the reverse, like the pig; that is to say, one or other set of teeth overlaps those above or below, as the case may be. The former is not of much consequence, unless very much marked, when it diminishes the chance of holding the hare; but the latter is certainly prejudicial, and a "pig-jawed" greyhound should never be selected, though I have known one or two good killers with this formation. The eye should be bright and tolerably full, the color varying with that of the coat. The ears are generally recommended to be soft and falling, and pricked ears are despised, as being terrier-like, but some good breeds possess them, nevertheless, probably deriving them from the bulldog. I cannot, therefore, lay any great stress upon this point in the formation of the head.

The NECK also, though compared to that of a drake, is a long way from being as thin, but, nevertheless, it may be said that it should be as drake-like as possible. The object of this is to enable the greyhound to stoop and bear the hare without being put out of his stride. The proper average length of the neck is about equal to that of the head.

The beam-like BACK is all-important, for without strength in this department, though high speed may be obtained for a short distance, it is impossible to maintain it, and then we have a flashy animal, who is brought up at the end of a quarter of a mile. What is meant by the comparison to the beam is not only that it shall be strong, but that the back shall have the peculiar square form of that object. There is a long muscle which runs from the hip forwards to be attached to the angles of the ribs, and this, if well developed, gives great power in turning, so that it is a very essential point, and upon the size of it the squareness mainly depends. Without width of hip no back can be strong, since the muscles have no possibility of attachment in sufficient breadth, and the same may be said of the ribs. In examining, therefore, a dog out of condition, the experienced eye often detects the probability of the future development of a good back, even though there is no appearance of muscle at the time; because, the bones being of good size and breadth, there is every reason to expect, with health and good feeding, that they will be covered by their usual moving powers, and will then show the substance which is desired. It is also desirable to have depth of back from above downwards, by which the whole body is "buckled and unbuckled" with quickness and power, as is required in the gallop. The muscles of the abdomen may draw the chest towards the hind legs powerfully, but the action is too slow, and for quick contraction those of the under side of the back are essential.

By the SIDE is to be understood the chest, which is composed of the two sides combined. The bream-like form of this part depends upon the width at the angles of the ribs, where they curve towards the backbone, and upon which, as I before observed, the size of the back depends. Very round ribs like a barrel are not so desirable as the squared form which I have alluded to, for several reasons which will be given under the anatomical description of this part. Great depth of chest is apt to prevent the dog stooping on rough ground, as he strikes it against high ridges or large stones, but a moderately deep chest is a valuable point, giving plenty of "bellows' room" as it is popularly called. This, however, is provided for better by breadth than depth, and the former should be insisted on more than the latter, provided there is not that round tub-like form of the ribs which interferes with the action of the shoulder-blades, and often accompanies low-breeding.

A rat-like TAIL is insisted upon, not as of absolute use in any way, but as a sign of high breeding, without which it is well known the greyhound is comparatively valueless. But it must be understood that it is only in the size of the bones that the similarity should be insisted on, for many good breeds have a considerable quantity of hair upon the tail, though this never ought to be in a bushy form. A slight fan-like distribution of hair is not therefore to be considered objectionable, and in puppies is a mark of hardihood.

Cat-like FEET are much insisted on, and this point has been so much attended to that some breeds have been produced remarkable for having their feet even more round than those of the cat. Their toes seem to be the only parts touching the ground, the pad appearing as if it was not in contact with it. This form I believe to be an exaggeration of a good point, as all dogs so provided are very apt to draw their nails, or break their toes, both of which accidents it is of great importance to avoid. The most essential point, therefore, is such a form of foot as will prevent the toes spreading, taking care that the knuckles are well up, by which a good foothold is secured. But beyond this it is necessary to provide for the wear and tear which the sole of the foot incurs, and hence a thick pad well covered with hard skin is to be insisted on. If the greyhound has this he will stand his work, while its absence renders him at all times liable to become footsore, and incapable of doing it.

The HIND QUARTER is entirely overlooked in the rhymes above-mentioned, but it is of the greatest importance nevertheless, being the chief element of progression. First of all, we should insist upon a good framework, which, presenting the levers acted on by the muscles, must be in proper form, and of sufficient length and strength. Thus it is usual in examining puppies for selection to extend them to their full length, and then the one which stretches over the greatest distance is supposed to be the best in this point, and (other things being equal) very properly so. Thus, then, we arrive at the conclusion that the hinder limbs should be made up of long bones; but they must be united by well-formed joints, and in order that the dog shall not stand too high they should be well bent, though if the fore part of the dog is lower than the hind, there is no necessity for the presence of this form, as it comes to the same thing in reality. Strong bony stifle-joints and hocks, with great length between them and from the stifle to the hip, united with a short leg, constitute the perfection of form in the hind quarter, if, as is almost always the case, the muscles covering them are strong enough to put them in action.

The FORE QUARTER is composed of the shoulder, the upper arm (between it and the elbow), the fore-arm (below the elbow), the knee, the leg, and the foot. The shoulder should be oblique, well covered with muscles, and moving freely on the ribs, which it seldom does if the two blades are kept wide apart at their upper edges by the tub-like form of the chest, described under that head. Hence we should examine, and anxiously look for, length of shoulder-blade, which cannot exist without obliquity; freedom of play, without which the fore quarter is not protruded in the gallop as it ought to be; and muscular development to bear the shocks to which this part is subject. The arm also should be long, so as to raise the point of the shoulder high enough to make the blade lie at an angle of 45° with the horizon, and to throw the elbow well back to take the weight of the body. With regard to the elbow itself, the joint must be placed in the same plane as the body; that is to say, the point of the elbow should not project either inwards or outwards. In the former case, the feet are turned out, and then there is a want of liberty in the play of the whole shoulder, because the elbow rubs against the ribs, and interferes with the action. This is called being "tied at the elbow," and is most carefully to be avoided in selecting the greyhound, as well as all other breeds. The arm should be straight, long, and well clothed with muscle. The knee should be bony, and not bent too much back, which is an element of weakness, though seldom to such an extent as to be prejudicial to real utility. The leg, or bones below the knee, should be of good size, the stopper (or upper pad) well united to it, and firm in texture, and supported upon a foot of the formation recommended under that head.

The COLORS commonly met with among high-bred greyhounds, are black, blue, red, fawn, brindled, and white, variously mixed. There are also sometimes seen cream, yellow, brown, dun, and grey dogs. When a plain color is speckled with small white marks, the dog is said to be ticked. The black, red, and fawn are the most highly prized by most coursers, especially when the last two have black muzzles. Some people are partial to blue dogs, of which several good specimens have been met with, as may also be said of the brindled color, but, as before remarked, the general opinion is in favor of black, red, and fawn. I believe that black, red, and white, may be considered as the primary colors, and that the others arise out of their mixture in breeding. Thus a black dog and a white bitch will produce either blacks, whites, black and whites, blues, or greys; while a red dog and white bitch will have red, white, fawn, red and white, yellow, or cream puppies. Black and red united together make the red with black muzzle or the black brindle, while the blue and fawn give rise to the blue brindle; or sometimes we see the black or blue tanned color, as we meet with commonly enough in the setter, spaniel, and terrier. Mr. Thacker was of opinion, with some of the early writers on the greyhound, that the brindle was a mark of the descent from the bulldog; but, as nothing is known of the time when the color first appeared, no reliance can be placed on the hypothesis.

The texture of the COAT is the last point upon which any reliance is placed, but, as far as my experience goes, there is little to be gained from it. Nevertheless, I should always discard a very soft woolly coat as being an evidence of a weak constitution, unable to bear exposure to weather, and, on that account, unfit for the purposes of the courser. The old breeds were, many of them, very bald about the cheeks and thighs, and this used to be considered a mark of good blood; but, since the intermixture of the rough greyhound, most of our best sorts have been free from this peculiarity, and many of them have had hard rough coats, quite unlike the fine and thin hair, which was formerly so highly prized. My own impression is in favor of a firm, glossy, and somewhat greasy-feeling, coarse coat, which stands wetting well, and at the same time looks healthy and handsome to the eye.

The relative value of these several points varies a good deal from those of dogs whose breeding can chiefly be arrived at by external signs—*e.g.*, the stern, color, and coat in the pointer and setter. Here the pedigree is well known for many generations; and therefore, although the breeding may be guessed at from the appearance of the individual, it is far better to depend upon the evidence afforded by the *Coursing Calendar*, or if that is not forthcoming, to avoid having anything to do with breeding from the strain. I quote:

"In measuring a dog, I should take only the following points, which should be nearly of the proportions here given in one of average size:

"Principal points: Hight at the shoulder, 25 in.; length from shoulder point to apex of last rib, 15 in.; length of apex of last rib to back of buttock, 13 in. to 15 in.; length from front of thigh round buttock to front of other thigh, 21 in.

"But to be more minute, it is as well to measure also the subordinate points as under: Circumference of head between eyes and ears, 14¼ in. to 15 in.; length of neck, 9 in. to 10 in.; circumference of chest, 28 in. to 30 in. in condition; length of arm, 9 in.; length of knee to the ground, 4½ in.; circumference of the loin, 18 in. to 19 in., in running condition; length of upper thigh, 10½ in.; lower thigh, 11 in.; and leg from hock to ground, 5¼ in. to 6 in.

"In taking these measurements, the fore legs should, as nearly as possible, be perpendicular, and the hind ones only moderately extended backwards."

The specimens selected for illustrations are Riot and David, which were perhaps the best greyhounds for all kinds of ground which ever ran, not even excepting the two treble winners of the Waterloo Cup, as they were not tried over the downs. Riot was the property of Mr. C. Randell, of Chadbury, and was not only the winner of seventy-four courses in public, with the loss of only ten, but she was also the dam of several good greyhounds. David had also the same double distinction, but was not quite so celebrated in the coursing field as the bitch. He had, however, the advantage at the stud, as might be expected from his sex, and a goodly list of winners are credited to him.

In the CHOICE OF A GREYHOUND I have already observed that we must be guided by other considerations besides make and shape, depending greatly upon the precise object which the intending possessor has in view, since, although the high-bred and low-bred greyhounds are alike externally, yet there is in their internal structure some difference beyond the ken of our senses. But, as it is found by experience that in this particular "like produces like," it is only necessary to be assured that the parents possessed this internal formation, whatever it may be, in order to be satisfied that their descendants will inherit it. Thus we arrive at the necessity for "good breed," or "pure blood," as the same thing is called in different language, both merely meaning that the ancestors, for some generations, have been remarkable for the possession of the qualities most desired, whatever they may be. Hence, in selecting greyhounds to breed from, the pedigree for many generations is scrutinized with great care, and if there is a single flaw it is looked at with suspicion, because the bad is almost sure to peep out through any amount of good blood.

The modes of breeding, managing, breaking, and using the greyhound, will be described later on in the volume.

THE IRISH GREYHOUND, OR WOLF-DOG.

This fine animal is now, I believe, extinct, though there are still some gentlemen who maintain that they possess the breed in all its pristine purity of blood. They are much larger than the deerhound, some of them being 35 or even 38 inches high, but resembling that dog in shape, being generally of a fawn color, with a rough coat and pendent ears. They were formerly used for the purpose of hunting the wolf.

THE MATIN.

The French mâtin is not a very distinct dog, comprehending an immense variety of animals, which in England would be called lurchers, or sheep dogs, according to the uses to which they are put. The head has the elongated form of this division of the dog, with a flat forehead; the ears stand up, but are pendulous towards the tip, and the color varies from red to fawn. He is about 24 inches high, has strong muscular action, and is very courageous, being employed in hunting the wild boar and wolf. This dog is said, by F. Cuvier, to be the progenitor of the greyhound and deerhound; but Pennant, on the contrary, considers him to be descended from the Irish wolf-dog.

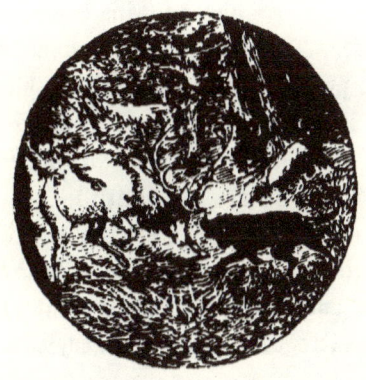

Fig. 5.—THE HARE-INDIAN DOG.

THE HARE-INDIAN DOG.

The Hare-Indian dog inhabits the country watered by the Mackenzie River and the Great Bear Lake of America, where it is used to hunt the moose and reindeer by sight, aided occasionally by its powers of scent, which are by no means contemptible, but kept in abeyance by disuse. The feet are remarkable for spreading on the snow, so as to prevent them from sinking into it, and to enable the dog to bound lightly over a surface which the moose sinks into at every stride. The hight is about 25 inches, combined with great strength. The ears are broad at the base, and pointed towards the tips, being perfectly erect. The tail is thick, bushy, and slightly curved, but not so much so as in the Esquimaux dog. The hair is long and straight; the ground color being white, marked with large, irregular patches of greyish black, shaded with brown.

THE ALBANIAN DOG.

The Albanian dog is said to stand about 27 or 28 inches high, with a long pointed muzzle, powerful body, strong and muscular limbs, and a long bushy tail, carried like that of the Newfoundland dog. His hair is very fine and close, being of a silky texture, and of a fawn color, variously clouded with brown. He is used for hunting the wild boar and wolf, as well as for the purpose of guarding the sheep-fold from the latter; but the accounts of this dog vary greatly, and are not much to be relied on.

THE GRECIAN GREYHOUND.

This elegant animal is somewhat smaller than the English dog. The hair is longer and slightly wavy, the tail also being clothed with a thin brush of hair. This is supposed to be the same breed as the greyhound of Xenophon, the Athenian.

THE RUSSIAN GREYHOUND.

This variety of the greyhound hunts well by scent, and, being at the same time fast and stout, he is used for the destruction of the wolves and bears which inhabit the Russian forests, and also for coursing the deer and the hare. For this latter sport he is well adapted; but, being somewhat deficient in courage and strength, he is hardly a match for the wolf and bear, excepting in packs.

The Russian greyhound is about 26 or 27 inches high, with short pricked ears, turned over at the tips; he is rather thin and weak in the back and loins, and long on the leg. The coat is thick, but not long, excepting the hair of the tail, which is fanlike, with a spiral twist of a peculiar form. The color is dark brown or grey. I am not aware of any undoubted specimen of this breed having been imported into England, nor of a correct portrait having been painted; so my readers must depend upon description alone.

THE TURKISH GREYHOUND.

A small and almost hairless dog, of the greyhound kind, is met with in Turkey, but it is not common in that country, and I have never seen a specimen or even a good portrait of it.

THE PERSIAN GREYHOUND

Is an elegant animal, beautifully formed in all points, and resembling the Italian in delicacy of proportions. In Persia he is used for coursing the hare and antelope, as well as sometimes the wild ass. When the antelope is the object of the chase, relays of greyhounds are stationed where the game is likely to resort to, and slipped each in their turn as the antelope passes.

The Persian greyhound is about 24 inches high. The ears are pendulous like those of the Grecian dog, and hairy like those of the English setter, but in other respects he resembles the English smooth greyhound, with the exception of the tail, which may be compared to that of a silky-coated setter. Several portraits of this dog have appeared at various times in the "Sporting Magazine," and elsewhere, but I am told they do not well represent his appearance.

52 DOMESTICATED HUNTING-DOGS.

Fig. 6.—ITALIAN GREYHOUNDS, BISMARK AND CRUCIFIX.

THE ITALIAN GREYHOUND.

This little dog is one of the most beautifully proportioned animals in creation, being a smooth English greyhound in miniature, and resembling it in all respects but size. It is bred in Spain and Italy in great perfection, the warmth of the climate agreeing well with its habits and constitution. In England, as in its native country, it is only used as a pet or toy dog, for though its speed is considerable for its size, it is incapable of holding even a rabbit. The attempt, therefore, to course rabbits with this little dog has always failed, and in those instances where the sport (if such it can be called) has been carried out at all, recourse has been had to a cross between the Italian greyhound and the terrier, which results in a strong, quick, little dog, quite capable of doing all that is required.

The chief points characteristic of the Italian greyhound are shape, color, and size.

In shape, he should as nearly as possible resemble the English greyhound, as described elsewhere. The nose is not usually so long in proportion, and the head is fuller both in width and depth. The eyes, also, are somewhat larger, being soft and full. The tail should be small in bone, and free from hair. It is scarcely so long as that of the English greyhound, bearing in mind the difference of size. It usually bends with a gentle sweep upwards, but should never turn round in a corkscrew form.

The color most prized is a golden fawn. The dove-colored fawn comes next; then the cream color, and the blue fawn, or fawn with blue muzzle, the black-muzzled fawn, the black-muzzled red, the plain red, the yellow, the cream-colored, and the black; the white, the blue, the white and fawn, and the white and red. Whenever the dog is of a whole color, there should be no white whatever on the toes, legs, or tail; and even a star on the breast is considered a defect, though not so great as on the feet.

The size most prized is when the specified weight is about six or eight pounds; but dogs of this weight have seldom perfect symmetry, and one with good shape and color, of eight pounds, is to be preferred to a smaller dog of less perfect symmetry. Beyond twelve pounds the dog is scarcely to be considered a pure Italian, though sometimes exceptions occur, and a puppy of pure blood, with a sire and dam of small size, may grow to such a weight as sixteen pounds.

I have never yet seen an Italian greyhound more nearly approaching perfection than Mr. Pim's Bismark, a considerable prize-winner at Bristol and in Ireland, although he has recently been twice unnoticed, beyond a high commendation at Birmingham and the Alexandra Park Shows. These defeats were, however, mainly owing to the excellence of the bitches amongst which he was classed; for at Birmingham there were four of that sex only a trifle behind the celebrated Molly in shape and color, while at the Alexandra Park there were nearly as many. Bismark is, nevertheless, a very neat dog, and, barring his round head and his color, which has a shade of blue in the fawn, he is very little behind the first-class bitches of his day. His pedigree

3

is unknown, so that it is not possible to trace these defects to their cause; but I have little doubt that, at some time more or less remote, a terrier cross in his pedigree would creep out. At all events, he is the best dog exhibited of late years, and as such I have selected him for illustration. Crucifix, his companion in the engraving, was, like him, passed over at the above shows, obtaining only a second prize at the shows recently held at Birmingham and Alexandra Palace. My own opinion, however, was strongly in her favor at both of these shows; and, in spite of the high authority of Messrs. Hedley and Handley (the respective judges), I have accordingly selected her for portraiture. Her beautiful golden-fawn color is even superior to Molly's dove-color, and her general shape and symmetry are nearly equal; but no doubt in head Molly has the advantage, and if the two were shown together, both in their prime, the latter would weigh down the scale considerably. Like Bismark, she has had more honor in her own country than at Birmingham and London, having been awarded the first prize at Manchester in two dog shows, and also at Glasgow in two other years. She is by Bruce's Prince out of his Beauty; Prince by Old Prince—Speed; Beauty by Chief—Tit.

Fig. 7.—HEAD OF BLOODHOUND.

THE BLOODHOUND.

The name given to this hound is founded upon his peculiar power of scenting the blood of a wounded animal, so that, if once put on his trail, he could hunt him through any number of his fellows, and would thus single out a wounded deer from a large herd, and stick to him through any foils or artifices which he may have recourse to. From this property he has also been used to trace human beings; and as his nose is remarkably delicate in hunting, even without blood, he has always been selected for that purpose, whether the objects of pursuit were slaves, as in Cuba, or sheep-stealers, as in England.

At present there are, as far as I know, no true bloodhounds in England for this purpose, or indeed for any other, as I believe the breed to be extinct; but several gentlemen possess hounds commonly called bloodhounds, though only partially resembling the veritable animal, and use them for hunting fallow-deer, especially those which are only wounded with the rifle, and not killed outright. This dog is also kept for his fine noble appearance; and as his temper is generally less uncertain than the genuine old bloodhound, and his taste for blood not so great, though still sometimes beyond all control, he is not unfitted to be the constant companion of man, but must always be regarded with some degree of suspicion. Bloodhounds, more or less purely bred, are still plentiful in the Southern States, where formerly considerable packs were kept for hunting both deer and fugitive slaves.

The following are the distinctive marks of this dog, which should make their appearance even when one only of the parents is thorough-bred:—Hight, from 24 to 25 or even 26 inches; peculiarly long and narrow forehead: ears from 8 to 9, and even 10, inches long; lips loose and hanging; throat also loose, and roomy in the skin; deep in the brisket, round in the ribs, loins broad and muscular, legs and feet straight and good, muscular thighs, and fine tapering and gracefully waving stern; color black-tan, or deep and reddish fawn (no white should be shown but on just the tip of the stern); the tongue loud, long, deep, and melodious, and the temper courageous and irascible, but remarkably forgiving, and immensely susceptible of kindness. The illustration is a portrait of the fine head of a dog owned by Mr. Reynold Ray, an old and well-known breeder, and a prize-winner at various shows.

THE FOXHOUND.

Fig. 8.—FOXHOUND, BLUECAP.

THE FOXHOUND.

The modern foxhound is one of the most wonderful animals in creation, which is probably owing to the great pains that have been bestowed upon him for the last two or three centuries. Numerous instances have occurred where forty or fifty thousand dollars a year have been spent for a long time together upon a fox-hunting establishment, and therefore, when this outlay has been united with the great judgment which has been displayed in the most celebrated kennels of the present century, it can scarcely occasion surprise that the combination has resulted in the most complete success. In breeding cattle and sheep, one man has, in more than one instance, during his single life, effected a complete revolution in the animal he was engaged in improving; and therefore, when a number of gentlemen combine for one purpose, and spare neither time, money, nor trouble, we ought to expect the fulfilment of their wishes. In no department of rural sports has so much been written as on fox-hunting, and this not only of late years, but for the last three centuries, during which Markham, Somerville, and Beckford may be instanced as examples of truthful as well as clever writing on the subject. Beckford, who wrote in the latter part of the last century, his first letter being dated 1779, is, however, the father of the modern school, and, with slight exceptions, the hound described by him is still that selected by our best masters, though perhaps they carry out his principles to a greater extent than he ever expected they would go. Much has been written, it is true, since his time, but I am not aware that any one has deviated from his description without doing wrong, and therefore, as I like to give credit where credit is due, I shall extract his description entire, as contained in his third letter to his friend.

"You desire to know what kind of hound I would recommend. As you mention not for any particular chase or country, I understand you generally; and shall answer that I most approve of hounds of the middle size. I believe all animals of that description are strongest, and best able to endure fatigue. In the hight as well as the color of hounds, most sportsmen have their prejudices; but in their shape, at least, I think they must all agree. I know sportsmen who boldly affirm that a small hound will oftentimes beat a large one; that he will climb hills better, and go through cover quicker; whilst others are not less ready to assert that a large hound will make his way in any country, will get better through the dirt than a small one, and that no fence, however high, can stop him. You have now their opinions: and I advise you to adopt that which suits your country best. There is, however, a certain size best adapted for business, which I take to be that between the two extremes, and I will venture to say that such hounds will not suffer themselves to be disgraced in any country. Somerville I find is of the same opinion:

> 'But here a mean
> Observe, nor a large hound prefer, of size
> Gigantic; he, in the thick-woven covert,
> Painfully tugs, or in the thorny brake,
> Torn and embarrass'd, bleeds: but, if too small,
> The pigmy brood in every furrow swims;
> Moil'd in the clogging clay, panting, they lag
> Behind inglorious; or else shivering creep,
> Benumb'd and faint, beneath the sheltering thorn.
> Foxhounds of middle size, active and strong,
> Will better answer all thy various ends,
> And crown thy pleasing labors with success.'

I perfectly agree with you that to look well they should be all nearly of a size; and I even think that they should all look of the same family,

> 'Facies non omnibus una,
> Nec diversa tamen, qualem decet esse sororum."

"If handsome without they are then perfect. With regard to their being sizeable, what Somerville says, is so much in your own way that I shall send it you:

> 'As some brave captain, curious and exact,
> By his fix'd standard, forms in equal ranks
> His gay battalion: as one man they move,
> Step after step; their size the same, their arms,
> Far gleaming, dart the same united blaze;
> Reviewing generals his merit own;
> How regular! how just! And all his cares
> Are well repaid if mighty GEORGE approve:
> So model thou thy pack, if honor touch
> Thy gen'rous soul, and the world's just applause.'

"There are necessary points in the shape of a hound which ought always to be attended to by a sportsman, for if he be not of a perfect symmetry, he will neither run fast nor bear much work He has much to undergo, and should have strength proportioned to it. Let his legs be straight as arrows, his feet round and not too large; his shoulders back; his breast rather wide than narrow; his chest deep; his back broad; his head small; his neck thin; his tail thick and brushy; if he carry it well, so much the better. Such hounds as are out at the elbows, and such as are weak from the knees to the foot, should never be taken into the pack.

"I find that I have mentioned a small head as one of the necessary requisites of a hound; but you will understand that it is relative to beauty only, for as to goodness, I believe large-headed hounds are in no wise inferior. The color I think of little moment, and am of opinion with our friend Foote, respecting his negro friend, that a good dog, like a good candidate, cannot be of a bad color.

"Men are too apt to be prejudiced by the sort of hound which they themselves have been most accustomed to. Those who have been used to the sharp-nosed foxhound, will hardly allow a large-headed hound to be a foxhound; yet they both equally are; speed and beauty are the chief excellencies of the one, while stoutness and tenderness of nose in hunting are characteristic of the other. I could tell you that I have seen very good sport with very unhandsome packs, consisting of hounds of various sizes, differing from one another as much in shape and look as in their color; nor could there be traced the least sign of consanguinity amongst them. Considered separately the hounds were good; as a pack of hounds they were not to be commended; nor would you be satisfied with anything that looked so very incomplete. You will find nothing so essential to your sport as that your hounds should run well together; nor can this end be better attained than by confining yourself, as near as you can, to those of the same sort, size, and shape."

Thus then as to points, it will be evident from the above extract that Beckford was fully aware of all which are considered essential to the foxhound, except the depth of the back ribs, in which the modern hound differs from both of his supposed progenitors (the greyhound and old-fashioned hound), and which has been established by carefully breeding from sires and dams peculiar for this development. It is upon this formation that stoutness, and the capability of bearing work day after day, mainly depend; and hence all good judges both of the hunter and the hound insist so strongly upon it. Nimrod (Apperley) also remarks that Beckford has omitted to particularize "the length of thigh discernible in first-rate hounds, which, like the well-let-down hock of the horse, gives them much superiority of speed, and is also a great security against laming themselves in leaping fences, which they are more apt to do when they become blown and consequently weak." It may also be remarked, that though Beckford insists upon a middle size, he does not define what he means by the term, but as foxhounds vary from 23 inches to 20, I should say 23 to 25 inches for doghounds, and 21 to 23 for bitches, would be about the hight meant by him. In open countries, with thin fences or walls, a large hound may perhaps suit best; but in woodlands, the small size, if not too small and delicate, has many advantages, and will always beat the larger and heavier hound, who tires himself in driving through the runs, which will readily admit the small dog or bitch. Nimrod fixed the hight at "21 to 22 inches for bitches, and 23 to 24 for doghounds;" but I have given a little more latitude in the above estimate. The speed of the foxhound may be estimated from the well known match over the Beacon course, at Newmarket, which is 4 miles 1 furlong and 132 yards, and which was run by Mr. Barry's "Bluecap" (the winner) in eight minutes and a few seconds, Mr. Meynell's hounds being not far behind; and only twelve out of sixty horsemen who started with them being with them to the end. Colonel Thornton's bitch, "Merkin," is even said to have run the same course in seven minutes and half a second. This speed is accounted for by the greyhound descent, if it really exists ; and that it does so I have little doubt, as it is quite clear that the old hound was deficient in those points which the greyhound alone would be able to give; but as this is only conjecture I have not insisted upon it.

The small rounded ear of the foxhound is due to the rounding irons of the huntsman, who removes a large portion of the pup's ears in order to save them from the tears and scratches which they would inevitably encounter in "drawing," if allowed to remain on. The portion left is sufficient to protect the passage to the internal organ, but for which necessity it would be better to crop them closely, as is practised with dogs intended for fighting; just as the wrestler and the pugilist have their hair cropt as close to their heads as possible.

The prevailing colors of foxhounds in the present day are as follows, placing them in the order of their frequency :—(1.) Black and white with tan; (2.) The mixed or blended colors, known as "pies," as red pie, blue pie, yellow pie, grey pie, lemon pie, hare pie, and badger pie, the last three very handsome; (3.) Tan; (4.) Black; (5.) White; (6.) Red; (7.) Blue; each being more or less mixed with white. Foxhounds are often slightly ticked, but rarely mottled, the "blue mottled hound," according to Mr. Apperley, being a true harrier or beagle, and most probably descended from the southern hound, which was often of this color.

It must be remembered that the foxhound is always to be looked at as part of a pack, and hence it is of no use to breed an exceptionally high or otherwise well made hound if it will make him run in a different style to his companions. Hence it is necessary to keep to such a model as can be produced in number sufficient to form the pack, which is another argument in favor of a medium size; and hence, in looking at a pack, together or separately, the lover of the foxhound is always on the look-out for "suitiness," or the resemblance to another in size and shape, which Beckford alludes to in describing a good-looking pack of hounds as appearing "all of one family."

In his work the foxhound is peculiar for dash, and for always being inclined to cast forwards, instinctively appearing to be aware that the fox makes his point to some covert different from that in which he was found. On the other hand, the harrier casts back, from a knowledge, instinctive or acquired, that hare has a tendency to return to the place from which she started, and will be almost sure to do so if she has time enough given her.

THE HARRIER.

The true harrier is a dwarf southern hound, with a very slight infusion of the greyhound in him. Hence he is more throaty than the foxhound, and has also more ear, with a broader head, more fully developed flews, and altogether a heavier and less active frame. The hight is usually at present under 20 inches, averaging about 18 ; but in the old times, when t e dwarf foxhound was never used for the purpose, harriers were often 22 and sometimes 23 inches high, because even with that size they dwelt on the scent so long that they were not too fast for sport. But it is in tongue and in style of hunting that true harriers are chiefly remarkable, the former being melodious in the extreme, and a pack in full cry being heard for miles; while the latter is distinguished by excessive delicacy of nose, and by an amount of patience in working out the doubles of the hare which the old-fashioned hare-hunter considered perfection. Mr. Yeatman has, however, introduced a different style, and according to his system the hare is driven so fast that she is compelled to abandon her cunning devices, and to trust to her speed alone. But as, following his example, most of the modern packs of harehounds are dwarf foxhounds, it is unnecessary to dwell upon the old-fashioned animal, and the modern harrier may therefore be described as a foxhound in shape, but of a size averaging about 18 or 19 inches, and kept to hare with great care, so that in some instances packs are known to refuse to own the scent of the fox; but these are rare exceptions, as most huntsmen will be ready to hunt one whenever they have the opportunity, and many regularly finish their season by shaking down a bag-fox, or by trying for one in some covert where they have permission. The fashion of the day is to demand pace in all kinds of hunting, and for this reason these dwarf foxhounds are selected, taking care to unite with it as fine and delicate a nose as possible, but altogether regardless of the music, which used to be a sine quâ non with masters of harriers.

One chief beauty in hare-hunting is the proper packing of the hounds, and as this can not be done without having all nearly of the same size, shape, and breed, masters of harriers are very particular in keeping the whole of their kennel of one strain; and when they cross their hounds it should be with great care, so as to avoid the introduction of blood very different to that which they already possess.

Fig. 9.—AMERICAN BEAGLES.

THE BEAGLE.

The true beagle, like the old harrier, is now almost entirely displaced by dwarf specimens of the foxhound, or by crosses with it in varying proportions. Still there are some packs left, and a good many gentlemen also possess one or two couple which they use for covert shooting, though even here this breed is giving way to the spaniel.

In external form the beagle resembles the southern hound, but is much more compact and elegant in shape, and far less throaty in proportion to its size, though still possessing a considerable ruff. There are three or four varieties, however, which differ a good deal among themselves in shape and make, and also to some degree in style of hunting.

The medium-sized beagle may be taken as the type of the others of the same name, and somewhat resembles a small old-fashioned harrier in shape, but with a larger body and shorter legs in proportion to it. The head is very wide and round, with a short square nose, very full and soft drooping ears, good feet, and not much hair on the body, but with a slight brush on the tail. Their tongues are most musical, and their noses extremely delicate, being even more so than the harrier, but hunting in the same style, with the same tendency to dwell on the scent. In size they may be described as averaging about 12 or 14 inches.

The rough beagle is apparently a cross between the above little hound and the rough terrier, though by many people he is supposed to be a distinct breed, and as much so as the Welsh harrier, which he resembles in all but size. His origin is, however, lost in obscurity, and can only be conjectured. One chief reason why I have supposed him to arise from the above cross is, that he has lost in great measure the beagle tongue, and squeaks like the terrier, though not quite so much as that dog.

The Kerry or Laune (Irish) Beagles are distinguished for speed, strength, size, endurance, and keen nose. These characteristics admirably adapt them for deer hunting. The first of this strain, Towler, was imported to the United States by Dr. Lewis A. Sayre, of New York City, in 1879. In October, 1881, Towler died. Dr. Sayre, however, still has left Doxey and Lightfoot, which, together with Towler, were presented to him by a grandson of John O'Connell. The New York "Turf, Field and Farm," of Nov. 18, 1881, contains a detailed and interesting description of this rare strain of dogs, together with engravings of Doxey and Lightfoot.

The dwarf or rabbit beagle is a very small and delicate little hound, but with an excellent nose, and much faster than he looks. Some sportsmen have carried their predilection for small dogs to such an extent, as to use a pack of these beagles which might be carried about in the shooting pockets of the men; and in this way have confined their duties to the hunting alone, so that they were not tired in trailing along the road from the kennel to the hunting-field and back again. The average hight of these may be taken at 10 inches, but their bodies are disproportionately lengthened Patience and perseverance are stil' more necessary in these hounds than in their larger brethren, and without them they soon lose their hare, as they must be content to hunt her at a pace with which a man can readily keep up on foot, horses being quite out of place with such a diminutive pack.

A pack of rabbit-beagles, the property of Mr. Crane, of South-over House, England, we believe to contain the best "patterns" we have ever known. We have seen them on a cold bad scenting

Fig. 10.—RABBIT BEAGLES, GIANT AND RINGLET.

day work up a rabbit and run him in the most extraordinary manner, and although the nature of the ground compelled the pack to run almost in Indian file, and thus to carry a very narrow line of scent, if they threw it up, it was but for a moment. Mr. Crane's standard is 9 in., and every little hound is absolutely perfect. We saw but one hound at all differing from his companions, a little black-tanned one. This one on the flags we should have drafted but when we saw him in his work we quite forgave him for being of a conspicuous color. Giant (see portrait) was perhaps the very best of the pack, a black-white-and-tanned doghound, always at work, and never wrong. He has a capital tongue, and plenty of it. The bitch, Ringlet, has the most beautiful points we have ever seen, and is a fit companion for her mate, Giant. Damper, Dutch man, and Tyrant, are also all of them beautiful models. We give the measurement of Damper: hight, 9 in.; round the chest, 16 in. across the ears, 12 in.; extreme length, 2 ft. 4 in.; eye to nose, 2½ in.

THE OTTERHOUND.

No hound which is now kept in Great Britain resembles the southern hound so much as this. the difference being only in the rough, wiry coat, which has been obtained by careful breeding, to enable them to resist the ill effects of the rough weather which the breed have to encounter, whether in the chase of the hare, for which they were originally employed in Wales, or for that of the otter, to which they are now almost exclusively restricted. If, therefore, the reader turns to the description of the southern hound, and adds to it a rough, wiry coat, with a profusion of rough whisker, he will at once understand the form and nature of the otterhound, alias the Welsh harrier. It is a disputed point whether this roughness is obtained by crossing, or whether it is attributable to careful selection only. We are inclined to think that as the full melodious note of the hound is retained, there is no cross of the terrier or of the deerhound, which two breeds divide between them the credit of bestowing their coats upon the otterhound. Anyhow, it is a distinct breed in the present day; and, with the shape I have described, it unites all the characteristics of the old southern hound, in dwelling on the scent, in delicacy of nose, and in want of dash. Whether the power of swimming has been obtained by any cross with the water-spaniel, is also a disputed point; but as I do not believe in any peculiar swimming power inherent in that breed, I am not inclined to attribute that of the otterhound to a cross with it, especially as the foxhound swims equally well.

As these hounds have to compete with a very savage and hard-biting animal, they must of necessity be fearless and hardy; and as, for their specific purposes, those which are not so, have been rejected, it happens that the breed has become unusually savage, and that they are constantly fighting in kennel. Indeed, instances are common enough of more than half being destroyed in a single night, in the bloody fight which has been commenced by perhaps a single couple, but soon ending in a general scrimmage No dog bites more savagely; and, unlike the bulldog, the hold is not firmly retained, but the teeth are torn out with great force the instant the hold is taken. The usual hight of the otterhound is from 22 to 25 inches in the dogs, the bitches being somewhat lower.

The points of the otterhound are like those of the bloodhound, except as to the coat, which should be composed of hard and long hair, somewhat rough in its lying, and mixed with a short, woolly under-coat, which serves to keep the body warm even when wetted by long immersion. The color differs also, in not being confined to black-and-tan or tan—the former, however, being often met with.

THE TERRIER.

The terrier, as used for hunting, is a strong, useful little dog, with great endurance and courage, and with nearly as good a nose as the beagle or harrier. From his superior courage, when crossed with the bulldog, as most vermin-terriers are, he has generally been kept for killing vermin whose bite would deter the spaniel or the beagle, but would only render the terrier more determined in his pursuit of them. Hence he is the constant attendant on the rat-catcher, and is highly useful to the gamekeeper, as well as to the farmer who is annoyed with rats and mice. Formerly it was the custom to add a couple of terriers to every pack of foxhounds, so as to be ready to aid in bolting the fox when he runs into a drain, or goes to ground in any easily accessible earth; the stoutness of the terrier enabling him, by steadily following on the track, to reach the scene of operations before it would be possible to obtain any other assistance. This aid, however, in consequence of the increased speed of our hounds, is now dispensed with, and the old fox-terrier is out of date, or is only kept for the purpose of destroying ground vermin, such as the rat or the weasel, or as a companion to man, for which purpose his fidelity and tractability make him peculiarly fitted. Terriers are now usually divided into eight kinds:—1st, the old English Terrier; 2d, the Scotch; 3d, the Dandie Dinmont; 4th, the Skye; 5th, the Fox

Fig. 11.—ENGLISH TERRIER, BELCHER.

Terrier; 6th, the Bedlington; 7th, the Halifax Blue Tan; and 8th, the Modern Toy Terriers of various kinds.

The *English Terrier* is a smooth-haired dog, weighing from about 6 to 10 lbs. His nose is very long and tapering neatly off, the jaw being slightly overhung, with a high forehead, narrow flat skull, strong muscular jaw, and small bright eye, well set in the head; ears when entire are short and slightly raised, but not absolutely pricked, turning over soon after they leave the head. When cropped they stand up in a point, and rise much higher than they naturally would. The neck is strong, but of a good length; body very symmetrical, with powerful short loins, and chest deep rather than wide. Shoulders generally good, and very powerful, so as to enable the terrier to dig away at an earth for hours together without fatigue, but they must not be so wide as to prevent him from "going to ground." Fore legs straight and strong in muscle, but light in bone, and feet round and hare-like. Hind legs straight but powerful. Tail fine, with a decided down carriage. The color of these dogs should be black and tan, which is the only true color; many are white, slightly marked with black, red, or sometimes, but very rarely, blue. The true fox-terrier was generally chosen with as much white as possible, so that he might be readily seen, either coming up after the pack, or when in the fox's earth, in almost complete darkness; but these were all crossed with the bull dog. Those which are now kept for general purposes are, however, most prized when of the black and tan color, and the more complete the contrast, that is, the richer the black and tan respectively, the more highly the dog is valued, especially if without any white. In all cases there should be a small patch of tan over each eye; the nose and palate should always be black. The toes should be pencilled with black reaching more or less up the leg. In the first volume of the stud book, which chronicles the principal shows for fourteen years, he was simply and properly described as the black and tan terrier, "English" of course being understood; but since 1874 they have added to his title, "or *Manchester Terrier.*" The reason for this change I do not know, as the records of their own stud book do not disclose many names of eminent Manchester breeders or exhibitors besides Mr. Samuel Handley, who bred and exhibited some of the best that have been shown, and who is still generally recognized as one of the best judges of them; and, however great an honor it may be to be "Manchester," it is a greater honor to be English, and, so far as I can see, the change in name was useless and uncalled for, and derogatory to the breed. In addition to Mr. Handley, there were years ago the following celebrated Lancashire breeders: Mr. James Barrow, Mr. Joseph Kay, and Mr. William Pearson, all now dead; but the crack dogs now met with at our shows have generally been bred by unknown people, and brought out by astute judges and spirited exhibitors. In the early days of shows Birmingham took the lead in this breed, and Mr. G. Fitter, of that town, who had a good strain, held the first position for several years with his exceptionally good dog Dandy. Of late years the most successful exhibitors have been Mr. George Wilson, Huddersfield; the late Mr. Martin, Manchester; and, more so than either, Mr. Henry Lacy, of Hebden Bridge.

This breed is not such a general favorite with the public as it deserves to be, for it has many excellent qualities to recommend it to those who like a nice pet that does not need nursing, an affectionate, lively, and tractable companion, not given to quarrelling, very active and graceful in his actions, and with pluck enough and a keen zest for hunting and destroying such vermin as rats that infest houses and outbuildings; for with larger vermin, such as the fox, badger, etc., (with exceptional cases), he has not the hardness to cope with or to stand their bites, nor has he the strength even of other terriers of his own weight, as he is formed more for nimbleness than work requiring power. His most ardent admirers cannot claim for him the courage and obduracy of attack and defence that characterize less pure terriers. As a house dog he is unexcelled, always on the alert, and quick to give alarm.

The *Scotch Terrier* closely resembles the English dog in all but his coat, which is wiry and rough, and hence he is sometimes called the wire-haired terrier, a name perhaps better suited to a dog which has long been naturalized in England, and whose origin is obscure enough. Beyond this difference in externals, there is little to be said distinctive of the one from the other, the colors being the same, but white being more highly prized in the southern variety, and the black and tan when more or less mixed with grey, so as to give the dog a pepper and salt appearance, being characteristic of the true Scotch terrier; but there are numberless varieties in size, and also in shape and color. This is a very good vermin dog, and will hunt anything from a fox to a mouse; but while he may be induced to hunt feather, he never takes to it like fur, and prefers vermin to game at all times.

The *Dandie Dinmont* breed of terriers, now so much celebrated, was originally bred by a farmer of the name of James Davidson at Hindalee, in Roxburghshire, who, it is generally believed, got his dogs from the head of Coquet Water. There was also a good strain at Ned Dunn's at Whitelee, near the Carter Bar.

Those who have investigated the subject are inclined to think that the Dandie Dinmont is a cross between the Scotch terrier and

Fig. 12.—DANDIE DINMONTS, DOCTOR AND TIT-MUMPS.

the otterhound, or, as I believe, the Welsh harrier, which is identical with the latter.

The most celebrated strains are those belonging to the Duke of Buccleugh (presented by James Davidson); Stoddart, of Selkirk; Frain, of the Trows; McDougall, of Cessford; F. Somners, of Kelso; Sir G. Douglass, of Springwood Park; Dr. Brown, of Melrose; J. Aitken, of Edinburgh; and Hugh Purves, of Leaderfoot, who is the principal hand in having kept up the breed. So much were the Dandies in vogue some years ago, that Mr. Bradshaw Smith, of Dumfriesshire, bought up every good dog he could lay his hands on, and as a consequence his breed is now well known.

FOX TERRIER.

The Dandie is represented by two colors of hair, which is sometimes rather hard, but not long; one entirely a reddish brown, and called the "mustard," the other grey or bluish-grey on the back, and tan or light brown on the legs," and called the "pepper;" both have the silky hair on the forehead. The legs are short, the body long, shoulder low, back slightly curved, head large, jaws long and tapered to the muzzle, which is not sharp; ears large and hanging close to the head; eyes full, bright, and intelligent; tail straight and carried erect, with a slight curve over the back (houndlike); the weight, 18 to 24 lbs., varying according to the strain, but the original Dandie was a heavy dog. Occasionally in a litter there may be some with the short, folding ear of a bull-terrier, and also with some greater length of the legs; these are not approved of by fanciers, but nevertheless are pure, showing a tendency to cast back. Sir W. Scott, I believe, preferred the small ear.

The following letter from Mr. E. Bradshaw Smith to the Editor of the "London Field" is of interest:

"Sir—If not trespassing too much on your valuable space I may here be allowed to show how I first became possessed of this historic breed.

"During my residence in Roxburghshire my fancy was greatly taken by several specimens I saw of this game little animal. In 1841, I bought the first Dandie I ever possessed, and since that date I have no hesitation in stating that more Dandie Dinmonts have passed through my hands than through those of any half dozen of fanciers. I feel myself competent, therefore, to give a decided opinion on the article penned by 'Stonehenge,' although it be at variance with his remarks.

"In the first place, it seems to me an entire mistake on his part that the Dandie Dinmont of the present day is longer in the body than formerly. My observation tends rather in the opposite direction.

"Secondly, a strong characteristic of the breed has ever bee tenacity of purpose, and I have only known two of my dogs which could be taught at command to leave the trail of either fox or rat bit; certainly it would be a hopeless task to prevent a Dandie Dinmont from engaging with a fox were an opportunity to offer. I consider the animal as naturally good-tempered, but when once roused, he is ready to seize hold of anything within reach. When I first kept these dogs, I was ignorant of their extremely excitable nature, and had many killed from time to time in fights, either in the kennels or at the entrance of rabbit holes; in short, when once their blood is fairly up they become utterly unmanageable. On this account, for years past (though I keep a number) I do not allow more than one dog and one bitch in a kennel, but sometimes a dog and two bitches if very harmonious. The first I had worried, many years ago, was a beautiful little fellow 14 lb. weight, bred by Mr. Kerss (Bowhill), from a sister of Stoddart's old Dandie and his own old Pepper. He was killed in the night time by another of my dogs, to my great annoyance. When I mentioned the circumstance to Mr. Kerss, he informed me that during the time the little animal belonged to him, he had worried some of his, amongst the number a Newfoundland pup six months old. Yet it is by no means always the most excitable and pugnacious animal that stands the severe test, viz., to face alone two badgers at once, and fasten upon one of them while the other in turn attacks him, as I have known very many do. For my part, I prefer the dog who encounters his antagonist coolly and without any fuss.

"In conclusion, I annex a list of the kennels I purchased, viz., that of Mr. Somner (including his crack dog Shem), those of Messrs. Purves, Frain, M'Dougald (including his famous Old Mayday), J. Stoddart (who sold to me his celebrated Old Dandie), and many other Dandies from Mr. Milne, of Faldonside, bred from his famous Old Jenny, from Mr. Jas. Kerss (Bowhill), and likewise from the Haining, near Selkirk. From these ancestors my dogs are purely and lineally descended.

"Apologizing for having occupied so much of your columns,
"E. Bradshaw Smith.

"Zürich, Switzerland."

The illustration is a portrait of Mr. Locke's Doctor, which has been established as one of the favorites of the various experts employed to judge this breed, and, as I think, deservedly, until the last Brighton show, where naturally enough the immediate descendants of Shamrock had the best of it under the fiat of his owner.

The *Skye Terrier* is remarkable for his long weasel-shaped body, and for his short, fin-like legs, added to which he has a long rather than a wide head, and also a neck of unusual dimensions, so that when measured from tip to tail the entire length is more than three times his hight. The nose is pointed, but so concealed in the long

Fig. 13.—SKYE TERRIER.

hair which falls over his eyes, that it is scarcely visible without a careful inspection; eyes keen and expressive, but small as compared with the spaniel. The ears, if falling, are large and slightly raised, but turning over; in the prick-eared variety, which is by many in the north preferred, the ears stand up like those of the fox; tail long, but small in bone, and standing straight backwards, that is, not curved over the back, but having only a very gentle sweep, to prevent touching the ground. Fore legs slightly bandy, yet this is not to be sought for, but to be avoided as much as possible, though always more or less present. The dew-claws are entirely absent, and if present may be considered a mark of impurity. The colors most in request are steel-grey, with black tips; fawn with brown tips to ears and tail; black, fawn, or blue, especially a dark, slaty blue; the slightest trace of white is carefully avoided. The hair is long and straight, hard, and not silky, parted down the back, and nearly reaching the ground on each side, without the slightest curl or resemblance to wool. On the legs and on the top of the head it is lighter in color than on the body, and is softer and more silky. This dog is little used as a sporting or vermin dog, being chiefly reserved for the companionship of man, but he is sometimes employed as a vermin-killer, and is as game as the rest of the terriers, when employed for that purpose. His weight is from 10 to 18 lbs., averaging about 14. But the variations in this particular, as indeed in almost all the points of the Skye terrier, are numerous beyond description. Thus there are, first of all, two if not three kinds of the pure Skye; one rather small in size, with long soft hair; another considerably larger, and with hard, wiry hair; while again, between these two, a third may, by hair-splitters, be readily made out. Then there is also a cross between the Skye and Dandie, which partakes in nearly equal proportions of the characteristics of each; and, lastly, most of the Skye terriers about London are crossed with the spaniel, giving them that silky coat and jet black color which are admired by the ladies, but mark impurity of blood. This cross is detected by the worn-out appearance of the hair on the face, up to the brow. The Skye is a very good vermin dog, and will hunt anything. The portrait of the prick-eared variety given is that of a dog belonging to Mr. H. Martin, of Glasgow.

The *Fox Terrier* was originally kept as an addition to every pack of foxhounds, being always so handy as to be up within a very few minutes of running to ground. Now hounds are so fast that he would be left many miles behind in a run, and dependence is therefore placed upon any chance terrier at hand when one is wanted. But in proportion as he has ceased to be used in the hunting-field, he has attained popularity as the most fashionable companion for young men, and of late years the classes of fox-terriers at our dog shows have been the most numerous and generally interesting.

The points are as follows: Head flat, and narrow between the eyes, but wider between the ears,—these are set rather back but lie close to the cheek, and are small and thin; jaw strong, mouth level, and teeth strong; eyes small and keen; nose black; shoulders straight, not too wide; chest full and round, but not deep; neck light and coming beautifully out of the shoulder; back pow-

Fig. 14.—FOX TERRIER, BITTERS.

erful, and thighs well bent and strong; legs and feet straight and strong; color white, with black, or black and tan, or tan markings about the head; coat fine, but hard and not silky; weight not exceeding 16 lbs.

At the present time the most noted show fox terriers are Mr. Burbidge's Bitters, Nimrod, Royal, Nettle, and Dorcas, Mr. Abbott's Moslem, Mr. Hyde's Buffett, Mr. Murchison's Forceps, Olive, Natty, and Whisky, Mr. Gibson's Boxer and Joe, Mr. Fletcher's

Rattler, and Mr. Whittle's Yorick. The most successful breeders of these have been Mr. Luke Turner and Mr. Gibson, the former having bred Nettle, Olive, and Joe, besides the first bitch puppy at the Lillie Bridge show, while the latter has bred Dorcas, Buffett, Natty, and Boxer.

I have selected for the engraving, as the best specimen, the dog Bitters, he being, I believe, the nearest of any of the dogs to the requirements of a fox terrier. Bitters won his first prize (under the name of Jock) at Epworth in 1872, and has altogether won nine first and nine second prizes.

The *Bedlington Terrier* has long been prized in the north of England, but until lately it has not been known out of that district. It is a very quarrelsome dog, and is said to be of high courage. The body is not very long, the general appearance being somewhat leggy; head high and narrow, and crowned with a tuft of silky hair like the Dandie; eyes small, round, and rather sunk; ears filbert-shaped, long, and hanging close to the cheek; neck long and slender; legs rather long, but well formed and straight; color liver or sandy, or dark blue,—in the two former cases with a cherry nose, in the latter with a black one.

The *Yorkshire Blue Tan, silky coated Terrier*, is a modern breed altogether, having been almost unknown beyond the neighborhood of Halifax until within the last few years. Excepting in color and coat this dog resembles the old English rough terrier, as well as the Scotch, but the silky texture of his coat and his rich blue tan color are the result of careful selection and probably of crossing with the Maltese. The ears are generally cropped, but if entire should be fine, thin, and moderately small. The coat should be long, silky in texture, and well parted down the back. The beard is peculiarly long and falling, being often several inches in length, and of a rich golden tan color. The color must be entirely blue on the back and down to the elbows and thighs, without any mixture of tan or fawn. The legs and muzzle should be a rich golden tan; the ears being the same, but of a darker shade. On the top of the skull it becomes lighter and almost fawn. The weight varies from 10 lbs. to 18 lbs.

THE TERRIER. 81

Visitors to our dog shows who look out for the beautiful as well as the useful, cannot fail to be attracted by this little exquisite, as he reclines on his cushion of silk or velvet, in the center of his little palace of crystal and mahogany, or struts round his mansion, with the consequential airs of the dandy that he is; yet, with all

Fig. 15.—YORKSHIRE TERRIER, LADY GIFFARD'S KATIE.

his self-assertion of dignity, his beard of approved cut and color, faultless whiskers of Dundreary type, and coat of absolute perfection, without one hair awry, one cannot help feeling that he is but a dandy after all.

Although so very modern, it is difficult to trace satisfactorily the pedigree of this breed; indeed, pedigree he may be said at present to have none, and it is hard to say out of what materials he was manufactured; but the warp and woof of him appear to have been the common long-coated black and tan, and the lighter-colored specimens of what is known as the Glasgow or Paisley Skye terrier, the former of no certain purity, and the latter an admitted mongrel; and from which I think the Yorkshire gets the softness and length of coat due to Maltese blood. In shape this dog is in the proportion of hight to length between the Skye and English terrier—rather nearer to the latter; a long back is objected to. As they are always shown in full dress, little more than outline of shape is looked for; the eye, except when the hair is tied up, is invisible; the tail is shortened, and the ear is generally cut; when uncut it must be small, and is preferred when it drops slightly at the tip, but this is a trival point, and sinks into insignificance before coat and color; the coat must be abundant over the whole body, head, legs, and tail, and artificial means are used to encourage its growth; length and straightness, freedom from curl and waviness, being sought for; the body color should be clear, soft, silvery blue, of course varying in shade, with this is preferred a golden tan head, with darker tan about the ears, and rich tan legs. The style in which the coat is arranged for exhibition is beautifully shown in the sketch of Katie; but that stage of perfection is not attained without much time, trouble, and patience. When the pups are born, they are black in color, as are pepper Dandie Dinmonts and others; at an early age the tip of the tail is nipped off to the desired length, the ears, if cut at all, not until the age of six to eight months, and before this the coat will be changing color, getting gradually lighter. To prevent the hair being scratched and broken, little or no meat is given.

DACHSHUND.—See page 9.

(83)

Fig. 16.—PAIR OF DACHSHUNDS.

THE DACHSHUND, OR GERMAN BADGER DOG.

The Dachshund is perhaps one of the most ancient forms of the domesticated dog. The fact is that he has for centuries represented an isolated class between the hound and the terrier, without being more nearly connected with the one than the other. His obstinate, independent character, and his incapacity to be trained or broken to anything beyond his inborn, game-like disposition, are quite unrivalled among all other races of the dog. Regarding his frame, he differs from the hound, not only by his crooked fore legs and small size, but by the most refined modification of all parts of his body, according to his chief task—to work underground. It is not possible to imagine a more favorable frame for an "earth dog" than the real dachshund type. Some of our high-bred dachshunds are near perfection, according to German points; they do not want much improvement, but propagation, for they are seldom met with even in northern Germany.

The desire for "hound-like type" in dachshunds would never have originated if the natural vocation of this breed (underground work) had not been overlooked. The consequence of this erroneous idea will be that well-bred dachshunds will be regarded as a "terrier cross," and that it will be next to impossible for many dog fanciers to get a clear idea of the real type of the dachshund.

Having concentrated all varieties of the badger dog to one single class—the crook-legged, short-haired dog, with head neither hound nor terrier-like, weight from 8 lbs. to 20 lbs., color black-tan and its variations—we shall still meet here many varying forms. With some attention we shall soon distinguish the common breed and the well or high-bred dachshund. The first is a stout, strong-boned, muscularly built dog, with large head and strong teeth; the back not much arched, sometimes even straight; tail long and heavy; fore legs strong and regularly formed; the head and tail often appear to be too large in the dog; the hair is rather coarse, thick-set, short, and wiry, lengthened at the underside of the tail, without forming a brush or feather, and covering a good deal of the belly. These dogs are good workmen, and are less affected by weather than high-bred ones; but they are very apt to exceed 18 lbs. and even 20 lbs. weight, and soon get fat if not worked frequently. From this common breed originates the well and high-bred dog, which may at any time be produced again from it by careful selection and in-breeding without any cross. The well and high-bred dog is smaller in size, finer in bone, more elegantly built, and seldom exceeds 16 lbs. to 17 lbs. weight; the thin, slight, tapering tail is only of medium length; the hair is very short, glossy like silk, but not soft; the under part of the body is very thin-haired, rendering these nervous and high-spirited dogs rather sensitive to wet ground and rain.

In hunting above ground the dachshund follows more the track than the general scent (*witterung*) of the game; therefore he follows rather slowly, but surely, and with the nose pretty close to the ground. His noise in barking is very loud, far sounding, and of surprising depth for a dog of so small a frame; but, in giving tongue while hunting, he pours forth from time to time short, shrill notes, which are quickened as the scent gets hotter, and, at sight of the game the notes are often resolved into an indescribable scream, as if the dog were being punished in a most cruel manner.

Though not a pack hound, the dachshund will soon learn to run in couples; and two or three of these couples, when acquainted with one another, or forming a little family, will hunt pretty well together. They do not frighten their game so much as the larger hounds, and, when frequently used, they will learn to stay when arrived at the line of the shooters, not by obedience to their master, but because they are intelligent enough as to see that it is quite useless to run longer after the game.

For tracking wounded deer or a roebuck a dachshund may be used when no bloodhound is to be had; but they must be accustomed to collar and line for this purpose, and then they are rather troublesome to lead in rough ground or coverts. They retrieve better by running free or slipped, but must carry a bell, for they are apt to keep silence when they find their game dead; and, beginning to lick at the wound where the ball has gone into the body, they will slowly advance to tearing and to eating their prey.

Dachshunds are very headstrong and difficult to keep under command; and, as they are at the same time very sensitive to chastisement, it is next to impossible to force them to do anything against their will. Many good badger dogs have been made cowards for their whole life by one severe whipping. They must be taken as they are—with all their faults, as well as their virtues. When treated always kindly, the dachshund is very faithful to his master, and not only a useful, but a most amusing dog—a very humorist among the canine family. In spite of his small frame, he has always an air of consequence and independence about him; but, at the same time, he is very inquisitive, and always ready to interfere with things with which he has no concern. He seems to have an antipathy to large dogs, and, if they object to be domineered over, the dachshund will certainly quarrel with them. When his blood is up, he will care neither for blows nor for wounds, and is often bitten dreadfully in such encounters. Therefore dachshunds should not be kept in kennels with larger dogs. When kept in houses and accustomed to children, they will make good pets, for they are clean, intelligent, and watchful, without being noisy, though often snappish with strangers. First introduced into the United States about twelve years ago, they are now becoming quite numerous.

CHAPTER IV.

DOMESTICATED DOGS, FINDING GAME BY SCENT, BUT NOT KILLING IT, BEING CHIEFLY USED IN AID OF THE GUN.

THE MODERN ENGLISH POINTER. — THE PORTUGUESE POINTER. — THE FRENCH POINTER. — THE DALMATIAN AND DANISH DOGS. — THE ENGLISH AND IRISH SETTERS.—THE RUSSIAN SETTER.—THE ORDINARY FIELD SPANIEL, INCLUDING THE SPRINGER (CLUMBER, SUSSEX, AND NORFOLK BREEDS), AND THE COCKER (WELSH AND DEVONSHIRE).—THE WATER SPANIEL (ENGLISH AND IRISH).—THE CHESAPEAKE BAY DOG.

THE MODERN ENGLISH POINTER.

This is now one of the most beautiful of all our sporting dogs, dividing with the setter the admiration of all those who enjoy the pleasures attending on the use of the gun.

The points desirable in the pointer are, a moderately large head, wide rather than long, with a high forehead, and an intelligent eye of medium size. Muzzle broad, with its outline square in front, not receding as in the hound. Flews manifestly present, but not pendent. The head should be well set on the neck, with a peculiar form at the junction only seen in the pointer. The neck itself should be long, convex in its upper outline, without any tendency to a dewlap or to a "ruff," as the loose skin covered with long hair round the neck is called. The body is of good length, with a strong loin, wide hips, and rather arched ribs, the chest being well let down, but not in a hatchet shape as in the greyhound, and the depth of the back ribs being proportionately greater than in that dog. The tail, or "stern" as it is technically called, is strong at the root, but suddenly diminishing it becomes very fine, and then continues nearly of the same size to within two inches of the tip, when it goes off to a point looking as sharp as the sting of a wasp, and giving the whole very much the appearance of that part of the insect, but magnified as a matter of course. This peculiar shape of the stern characterizes the breed, and its absence shows a cross with the hound or some other dog. The shoulders are points of great importance in the pointer, as unless they are well-formed he cannot last throughout the day, and, moreover, he can neither stop himself nor turn quickly in his work as he ought to do. Hence, a long, slanting, but muscular blade is of vast importance, united to a long upper arm, which again requires for its existence an elbow well let down below the chest, and a short fore arm. This low position of the elbow is not generally sufficiently insisted on, but in pointers and setters it is all-important, and it will be seen to be particularly well shown in the portrait, page 21. Plenty of bone in the leg, well clothed with muscle and tendon, a strong knee, full-sized ankle, and round strong foot, provided with a thick sole, are also essential to the wear and tear of the fore quarter, while the hind requires muscular haunches and thighs, strong well-bent stifles, large and strong hocks, and the hind feet of the same character as those described for the fore feet. The color should be principally white, in order that the dog may readily be seen either among heather, or in clover or turnips, as the case may be. Liver-colored or black pointers look very handsome, but it will be found that great inconvenience attaches to them, as they will often be lost sight of when pointing in either of the above kinds of beat. White, with black, liver, yellow, or lemon-colored heads, are the most prized; and of these my prejudice is in favor of the last from having had and seen so many good dogs of that color. A spot or two on the body, and any number of ticks, are not considered objectionable, particularly the latter, which are generally admired. Some breeds are distinguished by having numerous white ticks in the color, especially when there are large patches on the body, the marks on the head being usually free from them. Black and white pointers have sometimes also the tanned spots over the eye, and the edges of the black on the cheeks tinged with tan; but this is supposed to indicate a cross of the foxhound, and no doubt in many cases with truth; yet I fancy that if a yellow and white pointer is put to a black and white one, the tan will show itself occasionally without any admixture with the hound. The coat of the high-bred pointer is short and soft to the touch; but for hard work, especially on the moors, a dog with rather a wiry coat, and well clothed with hair on the legs and feet, should be preferred; but these will show rather more hair on the stern than is thought to be characteristic of high breeding; yet let the stern be ever so hairy, there ought to be the same small bone and pointed tip as in the engraving

Among pointers there are no national divisions corresponding with those of the setters. There are, however, two distinct varieties, strongly marked by color, viz., the lemon and white, and the liver and white, besides the black and white, the whole liver, and the whole black strains; but these last are not common in the present day, and the appearance of one on the show bench is almost as rare as a black swan. Among the liver and whites, the dogs are often too heavy for much speed or endurance—a remarkable exception being the celebrated Drake (see page 21), bred by Sir R. Garth, and sold by him at a high figure in his seventh season to Mr. R. J. Lloyd Price, of Wales, at which advanced age he went as fast, and showed as good a nose, as most puppies even of high class. This dog was in his day the fastest and most wonderful animal that ever quartered a field, and his race up to a brace of birds at Shrewsbury in the field trials of 1868, when the ground was so dry as to cause a cloud of dust to rise on his dropping to their scent, was a sight which will probably never be seen again. He was truly a phenomenon among pointers. His extraordinary pace compelled his dropping in this way, for otherwise he could not have stopped himself in time, but when he had lost pace in his seventh season, he began frequently to stand up, as represented. In appearance, he is not taking, having a plain head with a somewhat throaty neck; but his frame is all through good, and there is no lumber about him.

THE PORTUGUESE POINTER

Resembles the Spanish in general form, but is furnished with a bushy stern, and looks like a cross with the old-fashioned spaniel.

Fig. 17.—DALMATIAN DOG, CAPTAIN.

THE DALMATIAN AND DANISH DOGS.

The *Dalma'ion dog* is a handsome, well-formed dog, standing about 24 or 25 inches high, and resembling the pointer in his shape, but usually having his ears cropped, as shown in the engraving. He is beautifully spotted with black on a white ground, his chief merit consisting in the nearly uniform size of the spots (which should be from about an inch in diameter), and in their distinctness from the white in which they are imbedded; and being remarkably fond of horses, and of road-work with them, he has been long employed in England to accompany our carriages as an ornamental appendage; but this fashion has of late years subsided. Hence he is commonly known as the "Coach Dog;" but in his native country he is used as a pointer in the field, and is said to perform his duties well enough.

The small *Danish dog* is smaller than the Dalmatian; but, being spotted in the same way, and characterized by the same fondness for horses, they are generally confounded under the term "Coach Dog."

SETTERS.

THE ENGLISH SETTER.—THE BLACK AND TAN OR GORDON SETTER.—THE IRISH SETTER.

The setter is, without doubt, either descended from the spaniel, or both are offshoots from the same parent stock. Originally— that is before the improvements in the gun introduced the practice of "shooting flying,"—it is believed that he was merely a spaniel taught to "stop" or "set" as soon as he came upon the scent of the partridge, when a net was drawn over the covey by two men. Hence he was made to drop close to the ground, an attitude which is now unnecessary; though it is taught by some breakers, and notably to very fast dogs, who could not otherwise stop themselves quickly enough to avoid flushing. Manifestly, a dog prone on the ground allowed the net to be drawn over him better than if he was standing up; and hence the former attitude was preferred, an additional reason for its adoption being probably that it was more easily taught to a dog like the spaniel, which has not the natural cataleptic attitude of the pointer. But when "shooting flying" came into vogue, breakers made the attempt to assimilate the attitude of the setting spaniel, or "setter" as he was now called, to that of the pointer; and in process of time, and possibly also by crossing with that dog they succeeded, though, even after the lapse of more than a century, the cataleptic condition is not so fully displayed by the setter as by the pointer. In the present day, as a rule, the standing position is preferred, though some well known breakers, and notably George Thomas, Mr. Statter's keeper, have preferred the "drop," which certainly enables a fast dog to stop himself more quickly than he could do by standing up. It is,

GORDON SETTER, LANG.—(*Page* 104.)

however, attended with the disadvantage that in heather or clover a "dropped" dog cannot be seen nearly so far as if he was standing, and on one occasion, at the famous Bala trials, the celebrated Ranger was lost for many minutes, having "dropped" on game in a slight hollow, surrounded by heather. As a rule, therefore, the standing position is the better one, but in such fast dogs as Ranger and Drake, "dropping" may be excused. At the above meeting, however, after a long and evenly balanced trial between Mr. Macdona's Ranger and Mr. R. J. Ll. Price's Belle, the latter only won by her superior attitude on the point, and Ranger again suffered the penalty for dropping at Ipswich.

THE ENGLISH SETTER.

Since the first publication of the articles on the various breeds on dogs in *The Field*, during the years 1865-6, the strain of English setters known by the name of "Laverack," from the gentleman who bred them, has carried all before it, both on the show bench and in the public field trials which have been annually held. For this high character it is greatly indebted to the celebrated Countess, who was certainly an extraordinary animal, both in appearance and at work; for until she came out the only Laverack which had shone to advantage was Sir R. Garth's Daisy, a good average bitch. Though small, Countess was possessed of extraordinary pace, not perhaps quite equal to that of the still more celebrated pointer Drake, but approaching so closely to it that his superiority would be disputed by many of her admirers. On referring to her portrait (see frontispiece), it will be seen that her frame, though on short legs, is full of elegance, and her beautiful head and neck are absolutely perfect.

The most remarkable feature in the Laverack breed of setters is the extraordinary extent to which in-breeding has been carried, as shown in the pedigree of Countess, given by Mr. Laverack in his book on the setter. By examining this carefully, it will be seen that every animal in it, is descended from Ponto and Old Moll, which were obtained by Mr. Laverack in 1825 from the Rev. A. Harrison, who lived near Carlisle, and who had kept the breed pure for thirty five years. Four names only besides these two are found in the right hand column, and these four are all descended from Ponto and old Moll, as will be seen at a glance by referring to the names in italic in the middle of the table. Thus it appears that they alone formed Mr. Laverack's breed, though he often stated that he had tried the introduction of alien blood, but finding it not to answer, he had abandoned the produce, and resorted again to the original stock. This has led to the belief that the pedigree is incorrect, but he was very positive in his statement. If correct, it certainly is the most remarkable case of breeding-in-and-in I ever met with.

THE ENGLISH SETTER. 97

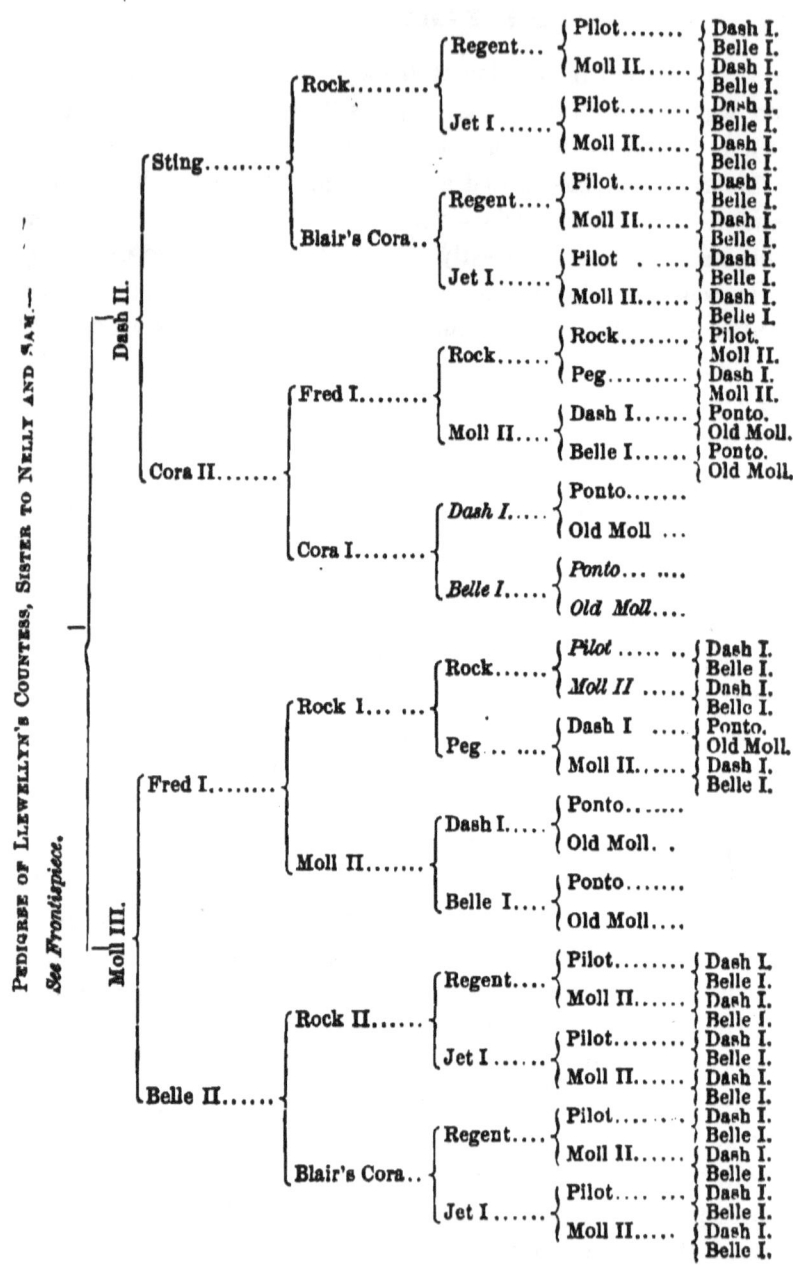

A great many different strains of English setters might be adduced from all parts of the country, but notably from the north of England, with claims superior to those of Mr. Laverack's strain, up to the time of the institution of field trials. Among these were the Graham and Corbet breeds, those of the Earl of Tankerville, Lord Waterpark, Mr. Bishop, Mr. Bayley, Mr. Lort, Mr. Jones (of Oscott), Major Cowan, Mr. Withington, Mr. Paul Hackett, and Mr. Calver, the last two being a good deal crossed with Gordon blood. None of these strains were, however, so generally known beyond the immediate circle of their owners' friends as to have gained a universal reputation; and it was not until the public appearance of Mr. Garth's Daisy, and afterwards that of Mr. Purcell Llewellyn's Countess and Nelly, that the Laverack strain attained its present high reputation. Before Daisy came out, Mr. Garth had produced a brace of very bad ones at Stafford in 1867; and it was with considerable prejudice against them that the above celebrated bitches first exhibited their powers, in spite of the high character given of them by Mr. Lort, Mr. Withington, and other well-known sportsmen who had shot over them for years. It is Mr. Lort's opinion that Mr. Withington possessed better dogs than even Countess; but it must not be forgotten that private trials are generally more flattering than those before the public.

I come now to consider the value of Mr. Llewellyn's "field trial" strain, as they are somewhat grandiloquently termed by their "promoters," or as I shall term them, the "Dan-Laveracks," being all either by Dan out of Laverack bitches, or by a Laverack dog out of a sister to Dan. As a proof of the superiority of this cross to the pure Laveracks, "Setter" states, that during the last two years ten of this breed " (Laveracks), "and ten of the Duke-Rhœbe and Laverack cross, have been sent to America; the former including Petrel, winner of the champion prize at Birmingham, Pride of the Border, Fairy, and Victress; the latter including Rock, Leicester, Rob Roy, Dart, and Dora, the same men being owners of both sorts. At the American Shows both sorts have appeared, and the Rhœbe blood has always beaten the Laverack. At field trials no Laverack has been entered; but, first, second, and third prizes were gained at their last field trials, in the champion stakes, by dogs of the Rhœbe blood, all descended from Mr Llewellyn's kennel." I confess that, in my opinion, this does not indicate any superiority in the one over the other, as far as regards field trials, since they were not tested together; and in reference to the superiority of the Dan-Laveracks on the show bench, it is of little interest to my present inquiry, but I unhesitatingly state, that, as far as my judgment and opportunities for forming it go, "Setter" is quite correct. Dan himself was a very fine upstanding and handsome dog, and his stock might therefore be expected to resemble him, while the Laverack dogs are nearly all heavy and lumbering, and the bitches, though very elegant, too small and delicate for perfection.

The points of the English setter may be described as follows:

1. The skull has a character peculiar to itself, somewhat between that of the pointer and cocker spaniel, not so heavy as the former's, and larger than the latter's. It is without the prominence of the occipital bone so remarkable in the pointer, is also narrower between the ears, and there is a decided brow over the eyes.

2. The nose should be long and wide, without any fullness under the eyes. There should be in the average dog setter at least four inches from the inner corner of the eye to the end of the nose. Between the point and the root of the nose there should be a slight depression—at all events, there should be no fullness—and the eyebrows should rise sharply from it. The nostrils must be wide apart and large in the openings, and the end should be moist and cool, though many a dog with exceptionally good scenting powers has had a remarkably dry nose, amounting in some cases to roughness like that of shagreen. In all setters the end of the nose should be black, or dark liver-colored, but in the very best bred whites or lemon and whites pink is often met with, and may in them be pardoned. The jaws should be exactly equal in length, a "snipe nose," or "pig jaw," as the receding lower one is called, being greatly against its possessor.

3. Ears, lips, and eyes. With regard to ears, they should be shorter than the pointer's and rounded, but not so much so as

those of the spaniel. The "leather" should be thin and soft, carried closely to the cheeks, so as not to show the inside, without the slightest tendency to prick the ear, which should be clothed with silky hair little more than two inches in length. The lips also are not so full and pendulous as those of the pointer, but at their angles there should be a slight fullness, not reaching quite to the extent of hanging. The eyes must be full of animation, and of medium size, the best color being a rich brown, and they should be set with their angles straight across.

4. The neck has not the full rounded muscularity of the pointer, being considerably thinner, but still slightly arched, and set into the head without that prominence of the occipital bone which is so remarkable in that dog. It must not be "throaty," though the skin is loose.

5. The shoulders and chest should display great liberty in all directions, with sloping deep shoulder blades, and elbows well let down. The chest should be deep rather than wide, though Mr. Laverack insists on the contrary formation, italicising the word wide in his remarks at page 22 of his book. Possibly it may be owing to this formation that his dogs have not succeeded at any field trial, as above remarked; for the bitches of his breed, notably Countess and Daisy, which I have seen, were as narrow as any setter breeder could desire. I am quite satisfied that on this point Mr. Laverack is altogether wrong. I fully agree with him, however, that the "ribs should be well sprung behind the shoulder," and great depth of the back ribs should be especially demanded.

6. Back, quarters, and stifles. An arched loin is desirable, but not to the extent of being "roached" or "wheel-backed," a defect which generally tends to a slow up-and-down gallop. Stifles well bent, and set wide apart, to allow the hind legs to be brought forward with liberty in the gallop.

7. Legs, elbows, and hocks. The elbows and toes, which generally go together, should be set straight; and if not, the "pigeon-toe" or in-turned leg is less objectionable than the out-turn, in which the elbow is confined by its close attachment to the ribs. The arm should be muscular and the bone fully developed, with strong and

broad knees, short pasterns, of which the size in point of bone should be as great as possible (a very important point), and their slope not exceeding a very slight deviation from the straight line. Many good judges insist upon a perfectly upright pastern, like that of the foxhound; but it must not be forgotten that the setter has to stop himself suddenly when at full stretch he catches scent, and to do this with an upright and rigid pastern causes a considerable strain on the ligaments, soon ending in "knuckling over;" hence a very slight bend is to be preferred. The hind legs should be muscular, with plenty of bone, clean strong hocks, and hairy feet.

8. The feet should be carefully examined, as upon their capability of standing wear and tear depends the utility of the dog. A great difference of opinion exists as to the comparative merits of the cat and hare foot for standing work. Foxhound masters invariably select that of the cat, and, as they have better opportunities than any other class of instituting the necessary comparison, their selection may be accepted as final. But, as setters are specially required to stand wet and heather, it is imperatively necessary that there should be a good growth of hair between the toes, and on this account a hare foot, well clothed with hair, as it generally is, must be preferred to a cat foot naked, as is often the case, except on the upper surface.

9. The flag is in appearance very characteristic of the breed, although it sometimes happens that one or two puppies in a well-bred litter exhibit a curl or other malformation, usually considered to be indicative of a stain. It is often compared to a scimitar, but it resembles it only in respect of its narrowness, the amount of curl in the blade of this Turkish weapon being far too great to make it the model of the setter's flag. Again, it has been compared to a comb; but as combs are usually straight, here again the simile fails, as the setter's flag should have a gentle sweep; and the nearest resemblance to any familiar form is to the scythe with its curve reversed. The feather must be composed of straight silky hairs, and beyond the root the less short hair on the flag the better, especially towards the point, of which the bone should be fine, and the feather tapering with it.

10. Symmetry and quality. In character the setter should display a great amount of "quality," a term which is difficult of explanation, though fully appreciated by all experienced sportsmen. It means a combination of symmetry, as understood by the artist, with the peculiar attributes of the breed under examination, as interpreted by the sportsman. Thus, a setter possessed of such a frame and outline as to charm an artist would be considered by the sportsman defective in "quality" if he possessed a curly or harsh coat, or if he had a heavy head with pendent bloodhound-like jowl and throaty neck. The general outline is very elegant, and more taking to the eye of the artist than that of the pointer.

11. The texture and feather of coat are much regarded among setter breeders, a soft silky hair without curl being considered a sine quâ non. The feather should be considerable, and should fringe the hind as well as the fore legs.

12. The color of coat is not much insisted on among English setters, a great variety being admitted. These are now generally classed as follows, in the order given: (1) Black and white ticked, with large splashes, and more or less marked with black, known as "blue Belton;" (2) orange and white freckled, known as orange Belton; (3) plain orange, or lemon and white; (4) liver and white; (5) black and white, with slight tan markings; (6) black and white; (7) liver and white; (8) pure white; (9) black; (10) liver; (11) red or yellow.

THE BLACK-TAN OR GORDON SETTER.

The black-tan setter, until the institution of shows, was commonly called "Gordon," from the fact that the Dukes of Gordon had long possessed a strain of setters of that color, which had obtained a high reputation. At the first dog show held at Newcastle in June, 1859, Mr. Jobling's (of Morpeth) black and tan Dandy was shown with success in an open class; and in November of the same year Mr. Burdett's Brougham followed suit at Birmingham.

In 1861 Mr. Burdett's Ned (son of Brougham) won the first prize in an open class at Birmingham, after which a special class was made for dogs of that color at Birmingham, London, and other large shows, the breeders of English dogs fancying that the beautiful color of the "Gordons" was too much in their favor.

But, in spite of the above successes, it cannot be denied that the general opinion of good sportsmen in the south has not been in favor of the breed since the institution of field trials, in which it has been brought into competition with the English and Irish setter. Both Rex and Young Kent had shown marvellous powers of scent, but exception was taken to their tiring action, and it must be admitted that six hours' work was enough at one time for either of them, and probably too much for Young Kent. Both dogs also were headstrong, and required severe treatment to keep them under command, and though neither showed the slightest disposition to unsteadiness on the point, yet both were jealous behind, and it was difficult to make them work to hand. Among the numberless specimens of the breed (black-tan) which I have seen at work, not one has shown the solicitude to catch the eye of the shooter which is so essential to the perfect correspondence of man and dog which ensures sport. The pointer or setter ought always to know where his master is, and if put into high covert, such as beans, should raise his head at short intervals above them to ascertain his whereabouts. Now, as far as my experience goes, black-tan setters, and notably the Kents, never do this, and cannot be taken off a scent without very great severity, until they have satisfied themselves of its fallacy.

The points of the black-tan setter are very nearly the same as those of the English dog, the only deviations being as follows:

1. The skull is usually a little heavier than that of the English setter, but in other respects it resembles it.

2. The nose, also, is like the English setters; but it is usually a trifle wider.

9. The flag is usually a trifle shorter than that of the English setter, which it otherwise resembles in shape.

11. The coat is generally harder and coarser than that of the

English or Irish setter, occasionally with a strong disposition to curl, as in the celebrated champions Reuben and Regent.

12. The color is much insisted on. The black should be rich, without mixture with the tan, and the latter should be a deep mahogany red without any tendency to fawn. It is admitted that the original Gordons were often black, tan, and white; but, as in all our shows the classes are limited to black-tan; the long arguments which have been adduced on that score are now obsolete. A little white on the chest, and a white toe or two, are not objected to; but a decided frill is considered by most judges to be a blemish. The red tan should be shown on lips, cheeks, throat, spot over the eyes, fore legs nearly to the elbows, hind legs up to stifles, and on the under side of the flag, but not running into its long hair.

I have selected Mr. Coath's Lang to illustrate this breed, and the engraving, page 93, is a wonderful likeness of this elegant dog. On the show bench he has been very successful since the retirement of his sire Reuben from old age, having won first and champion prizes at Glasgow, Edinburgh, Crystal Palace (twice), Birmingham (thrice), and Alexandra Palace. At the Shrewsbury field trials of 1872 and 1873, he was entered, and showed great pace and a fine style of going; but in the former year his pace was too great for the absence of scent and covert which prevailed there, and he was put out by Mr. Armstrong's Don, in one of those unsatisfactory trials to which owners of dogs have so often been reduced there. In the next year he showed well at first with Mr. Barclay Field's Rake, but was put out from chasing fur. At the same meeting he was bracketed with Mr. Macdona's Ranger in the braces, but not being quite steady behind, they were beaten by Mr. Barclay Field's Bruce and Rose. He is a fine slashing dog, of good size, possessing plenty of bone without lumber, and excellent legs and feet. His pedigree is an excellent one, being as follows:

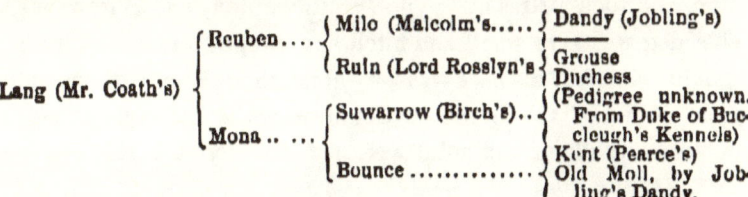

It will be seen that he goes back to Jobling's Dandy, on the side of both sire and dam.

The black and tan setter crosses well with the Irish, and Mr. Salter possesses an excellent specimen of the cross in his Young Rex, winner of the first prize at Brighton in the black and tan class in 1876. This dog is by Rex (son of Kent and Regent), out of Sal, a well-bred bitch descended from Major Hutchinson's Bob, and is a good looking dog, as well as a fine mover. Mr. Purcell Llewellyn has also crossed the Laveracks with it, the result, in 1872, being a very beautiful orange Belton bitch, Flame, out of Carrie, who was by Pilkington's Dash, out of a daughter of Hutchinson's Bob (winner of the champion prize at the Crystal Palace, in 1875); and also a 1st prize winner at the Crystal Palace in 1872, and a 2nd at Birmingham in the same year.

THE IRISH SETTER.

This breed has long been known to sportsmen throughout Great Britain as a good one, especially in point of stamina, and a class was set apart for it at Birmingham in 1860, a year before the black and tans were similarly favored.

There is no reason to suppose that any improvement had taken place in this breed in its native country until very recently, when the institution of local shows seems to have stimulated Irish breeders to fresh exertions; but in the exhibits which have been made in the English shows the chain of progress has been unbroken from Carlo to Dash and Palmerston. In the field trials, the Rev. J. C. Macdona has raised its character by producing his Plunket at Shrewsbury in 1870, after which he was sold to Mr. Purcell Llewellyn, and took prizes at Vaynol, Southampton, and Shrewsbury. This dog was very small and bitch-like in appearance, and rather light in color, but his pace was very great, though not perhaps quite equal to that of the Laverack Countess, while his style of going and his attitude on the point were far superior to hers. He was bred by the Hon. D. Plunket, and combines the blood of that gentleman's kennel with the La Touche and Hutchinson strains. Mr. Purcell Llewellyn purchased him in the hight of his successes, and bred several average dogs from him out of Kate (of the Knight of Kerry's strain), including Kimo, Kite, and Kitty; while another litter, out of Buckell's Min, contained Marvel, May, and Knowing, less successful than the former, both on the bench and in the field. With the solitary exception of Plunket and his daughter Music, who was at Vaynol in 1872, however, no Irish setter has shown anything like high form in the field trials, Mr. Purcell Llewellyn's Samson, who is above the average, being crossed with the Laverack Prince through his dam, Carrie, through both are entered in the Stud Book as Irish setters.

After a great deal of discussion, a separate class has been made in Dublin and elsewhere for "reds" and "white and reds," it being shown that there are two distinct strains of the Irish setter, of these colors respectively. The white and reds stands no chance in the open classes, and yet it was considered hard to debar them from all prizes, especially as by some good judges they are thought to possess better noses than the reds. According to my judgment the rich red, or blood red color as it is described, is made a little too much of, and I should strongly object to the passing over of excellence in shape because the color is too pale; a marked instance of which happened at the Brighton show of 1876.

In points the Irish setter only differs from the English in the following:

1. The skull is somewhat longer and narrower, the eyebrows being well raised, and the occipital prominence as marked as in the pointer.

2. The nose is a trifle longer, with good width, and square at the end; nostrils wide and open, with the nose itself of a deep mahogany or very dark fleshy-color, not pink nor black.

3. Eyes, ears, and lips.—The eyes should be a rich brown or mahogany color, well set, and full of intelligence; a pale or gooseberry eye is to be avoided. Ears long enough to reach within half an inch or an inch of the end of the nose, and, though more

tapering than in the English dog, never coming to a point; they should be set low and close, but well back, and not approaching to the hound's in setting and leather. Whiskers red; lips deep, but not pendulous.

5 and 6. In frame the Irish dog is higher on the leg than either the English or black and tan, but his elbows are well let down nevertheless; his shoulders are long and sloping; brisket deep, but never wide; and his back ribs are somewhat shorter than those of his English brethern. Loin good, slightly arched, and well coupled to his hips, but not very wide; quarters slightly sloping, and flag set on rather low, but straight, fine in bone, and beautifully carried. Breeders are, however, going for straight backs like that of Palmerston, with flags set on as high as in the English setter.

7. Legs very straight, with good hocks, well-bent stifles, and muscular but not heavy haunches.

8. The feet are hare-like, and moderately hairy between the toes.

9. The flag is clothed with a long, straight comb of hair, never bushy or curly, and this is beautifully displayed on the point.

11. The coat should be somewhat coarser than that of the English setter, being midway between that and the black and tan, wavy but not curly, and by no means long. Both hind and fore legs are well feathered, but not profusely, and the ears are furnished with feather to the same extent, with a slight wave, but no curl.

12. The color should be a rich blood red, without any trace of black on the ears or along the back; in many of the best strains, however, a pale color or an occasional tinge of black is shown. A little white on the neck, breast, or toes, is by no means objectionable, and there is no doubt that the preponderance of white, so as to constitute what is called "white and red," is met with in some good strains.

In his work the Irish setter is fast and enduring; his nose is quite up to the average of fast dogs in delicacy, and to those who are limited to a small kennel he is an invaluable aid to the gun. His style of going is very beautiful, with head well up and feeling for the body scent; he has a free action of the shoulders, hind legs brought well under him, and a merry lashing of the flag on the slightest indication of scent—often, indeed, without it. His advocates contend that he is as steady as any other setter when once broken, but, as far as my experience goes, I scarcely think this position can be maintained. Neither Plunket, nor any that I have seen of Mr. Purcell Llewellyn's breeding, nor indeed any of those which I have had out in private, have been always reliable, and I fear that, like almost all other setters of such high courage, it must be admitted that he requires work to keep him in a state of control fit for immediate use with the gun. In this respect, and indeed in delicacy of nose, both the English and Irish setter must yield to the black and tan of the best strains; but to do the same amount of work, at least a double team of the last mentioned must be kept.

Having been charged, by Mr. Adcock, in the case of the bulldog, with selecting inferior specimens for illustration, it is perhaps necessary that I should explain my reasons for choosing a dog without any public reputation to represent the Irish setter in preference to Mr. Hilliard's Palmerston, who has taken all the chief prizes since the last appearance of Dr. Stone's Dash at the Crystal Palace in 1875. As remarked above, no strain but that of the Hon. D. Plunket has been tried in the field; and, as that has done great credit to the breed in the shape of Mr. Macdona's (afterwards Mr. Llewellyn's) Plunket,* his daughter Music, and his sons Marvel and Kite, I prefer a portrait of one of this tried strain to that of any dog not similarly tested. Both Plunket and his daughter Music were too small to serve as a type, while Kite and Marvel have faults which render them equally unfit for that purpose. Fortunately, however, I have been able to meet with a grand specimen of the breed in Rover, an own brother to Plunket, which Mr. Macdona has recently obtained from Ireland, and which has never yet been shown. The faithful portrait of this dog presented on page 109 speaks for itself as to his external shape; but for his performances it is necessary to look to his brother Plunket,

---

* Plunket was purchased by Mr. Llewellyn from Mr. Macdona for $750, and is now in the possession of W. J. Farrar, of Toledo, Ohio.

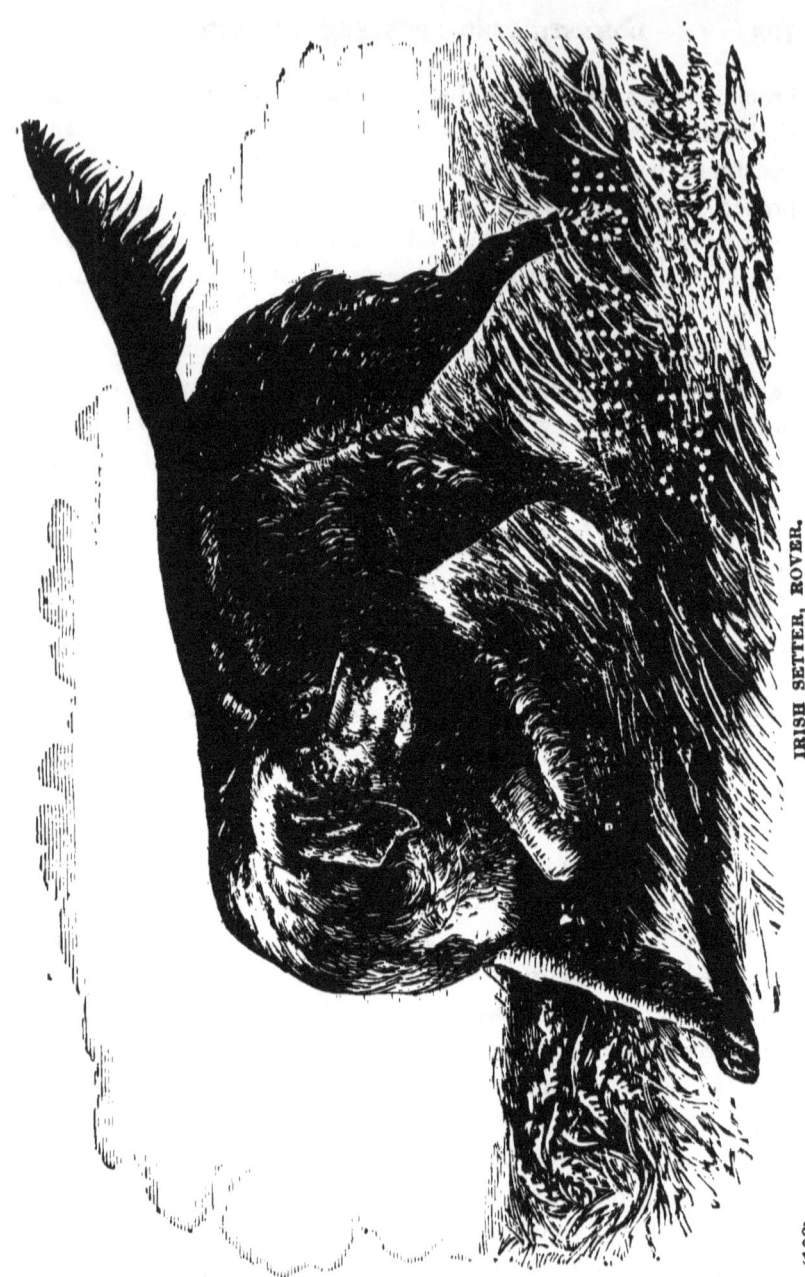

IRISH SETTER, ROVER.

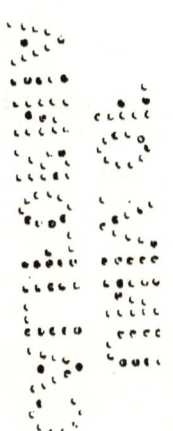

except that I have ascertained on good evidence that in private he has been tried to be first class. In color he is of a beautiful rich red with scarcely any white; while he possesses a frame of great size, symmetry, and substance, with good legs and feet.

THE FIELD SPANIEL.

The field Spaniel is distinguished from the toy dog by his propensity to hunt game, and by his size and strength, which are sufficient to enable him to stand the work which is required in making his way through the briars and thorns of a thick covert, where he is chiefly employed. Although not used for water, where the water spaniel is pre-eminent, his coat must be of such a thick nature as to bear long continued wet, inasmuch as he is generally soaked with it, either from the snow on the briars, or from moisture hanging to them in drops, caused either by rain or dew. Hardihood, therefore, is essential, and though a little dog may possess it, there are few instances of anything under 12 or 14 pounds being able to stand the wet and labor of a day's covert shooting. The nose of the spaniel must be exquisite, or he will be unfit to perform his duties, which require him to follow out the pheasant, woodcock, or hare, to the well-concealed retreat in or under a thick bush, which either of them may have chosen. A good and somewhat musical tongue was, by the old school of sportsmen, considered a desideratum, in order not only to give notice that the dog is on game, but also the particular kind which he is "questing," and which many good spaniels enable their masters to distinguish by a variation in their notes. Formerly this was thought so important, that if a spaniel happened to be mute, he was hunted with a bell round his neck, as is sometimes done with the setter when used in covert. In the present day, a very fashionable breed (the Clumber) is invariably mute; but as these dogs are chiefly used in aid of the battue, there is not the same necessity for them to give notice of their approach, as in the case of spaniels used either in wild-pheasant shooting, or for cocks, hares, or rabbits. It will therefore ap pear, that, for every kind of covert shooting but the battue, we require a strong useful spaniel, capable of bearing exposure to the weather, and neither too large for the runs, nor too small to bear work. Added to these qualities, we want an exquisite nose, and a musical but not noisy tongue, which is all the more valuable if it will distinguish by its note the various kinds of game. These dogs must also be readily kept under command, and must not be inclined to hunt far away from the shooter, or so fast as to prevent his following them. For various purposes a vast number of breeds have been established, more or less resembling each other, and a good many of them being now extinct, in consequence of the diminished demand for their services since the introduction of battues and their attendant preserves, by which, as a matter of course, wild covert shooting is rendered much more scarce. All the spaniels have a marked down carriage of their tails, which they work rapidly when on game, but should never raise above the level of their backs. All these various breeds may, however, be arranged under two leading divisions; one known as the "Springer," and including the Sussex, Clumber, and Norfolk Spaniels, besides several others confined to their respective localities; and the other called "the Cocker," from his being chiefly used for woodcocks, though also good for general purposes. The King Charles and Blenheim originally belonged to the second division, but they are now kept and bred for toy purposes only.

The *Springer* has a most tender and discriminating nose, is very tractable, and therefore easily kept in command. As has been already remarked, some are mute (as the Clumber), while others throw their tongues, as, for instance, the Sussex and the Norfolk. All the springers are heavy and slow as compared with the cockers, and most of them soon tire, three or four hours' work being about a good average day's work. Hence, they are scarcely adapted for beating large and wild woodlands, and for this reason they are seldom used for cock-shooting excepting in small coverts frequented by this bird, and highly valued by the sportsman.

The *Clumber Spaniel*, which for a long time was confined to the Newcastle family, but has lately become very fashionable, is a re-

THE FIELD SPANIEL.

markably long, low, and somewhat heavy dog. In weight he is from 30 to 40 lbs. Hight 18 to 20 inches. The head is heavy, wide, and full, the muzzle broad and square, generally of a flesh color. Nostrils open, and chops full and somewhat pendent. Ears long, and clothed with wavy hair, not too thick. Body very long and strong, the back ribs being very deep, and the chest being very round and barrel-like, the ribs at the same time being so widely

Fig. 18.—CLUMBER SPANIEL, BRUCE.

separated from each other, as to make the interval between them and the hips small in proportion to the great length. Tail bushy, but not at all woolly, the hair being waved only, not curled. It is generally cropped. Shoulders rather heavy and wide apart, arms short but strong, elbows not very well let down, fore arms strong, with plenty of bone, good knees, and strong useful round feet, but not very well up in the knuckles. The legs should be well feathered, and the feet hairy. The hind legs are rather straight, and should, like the fore legs, be short, so that the dog altogether has rather a weasely appearance, but the body being considerably stouter in proportion than that animal's. The coat is very thick, but should be silky and wavy, not curled, except in the featherings, which are long and well marked. Color, yellow and white, or, as is most highly prized, lemon and white. This dog is almost invariably mute. The portrait given of Mr. R. J. Ll. Price's Bruce may be regarded as a good type of the breed.

The *Sussex Spaniel* differs from the Clumber in shape and color, as well as in his "questing," his note being full and bell-like, though sharp. In hight and weight there is not much difference,

Fig. 19.—SUSSEX SPANIEL, GEORGE.

nor is the general character of the head very distinguishable from that of the Clumber; but in length he is not nearly so remarkable as that dog, though still long and low, the body being very round and full, indicating great power. The coat also is pretty nearly the same in quality, being soft and silky, though thick and free from distinct curls; and this dog is also beautifully feathered The head is not quite so heavy about the muzzle, but very square above the eyes, and with an expression of exceeding gravity and intelligence. The ears are full in length, lobe-shaped, but not very thickly covered with hair. Muzzle broad, with the under jaw receding more than in the Clumber, and the point of the nose of a liver-color. The whole body is also of a decided liver-color, but with rather a golden shade, not so puce as that of the Welsh or Devonshire cockers, or the Irish water spaniel. Legs and feet very strong, and well feathered. Tail generally cropped, and well clothed with wavy hair. The bitches are usually smaller than the dogs. All of this breed throw their tongues, and when kept to

Fig. 20.—COCKER SPANIEL, BRUSH.

cocks or pheasants, they readily indicate their scent by a sharper note than usual. The portrait given as a specimen of the breed was bred by the late A. E. Fuller, of Rose Hill, Sussex, England.

The *Cocker* can scarcely be minutely described, inasmuch as there are so many varieties in different parts of Great Britain. He may, however, be said, in general terms, to be a light, active spaniel, of about 14 lbs. weight on the average, sometimes reaching 20 lbs., with very elegant shapes, and a lively and spirited carriage. In hunting he keeps his tail down, like the rest of his kind, and works it constantly in a most rapid and merry way, from which alone he may be known from the springer, who also works his, but solemnly and deliberately, and apparently without the same pleasurable sensations which are displayed by the cocker. The head is round and the forehead raised ; muzzle more pointed than the springer, and the ear less heavy, but of good length, and well clothed with soft wavy hair, which should not be matted in a heavy mass. The eye is of medium size, slightly inclined to water, but not to weep like the toy dog's; body of medium length, and the shape generally resembling that of a small setter. It has long been the custom to crop the tail nearly half off, so as to prevent the constant wearing of it against the bushes, as the dog works his way through them. If left on, it is nearly as long in proportion as that of the setter, but more bushy, and not so closely resembling a fan. These dogs are well feathered, and the work for their feet and legs requires them to be strong and well formed. The coat should be thick and wavy, but not absolutely curled, which last shows the cross with the water spaniel, and that gives too much obstinacy with it to conduce to success in covert shooting. The color varies from a plain liver or black to black and tan, white and black, white and liver, white and red, or white and lemon; and different breeds are noted as possessing some one of these in particular, but I am not aware that any one is remarkable as belonging to a superior race.

The title "cocker" includes every kind of field spaniel except the Sussex and Clumber, and it is therefore necessary to allude to the Norfolk Spaniel as well as to the Welsh and Devon Cocker. The Norfolk spaniel is still to be found scattered throughout the country, and is generally of a liver and white color, sometimes black and white, and rarely lemon and white; usually a good deal ticked with color in the white. Higher on the leg than the Clumber or the Sussex, he is generally more active than either, sometimes almost rivalling the setter in lightness of frame; his ears are long, lobular and heavily feathered, and he is a very useful dog when thoroughly broken, but he is apt to be too wild in his behavior and too wide in his range until he has had a longer drill than most sportsmen can afford, and in retrieving he is often hard mouthed. When thoroughly broken, however, he is an excellent aid to the gun; but he is so intermixed with other breeds, that it is impossible to select any particular specimen as the true type. With regard to the Welsh and Devon cocker of former times, they are now scarcely to be met with in a state of purity and of the regulation size (20 lbs. to 25 lbs.); most of them have been crossed with the springer, or by improved management have been raised in weight to 30 lbs. at the least, which militates against their use in some coverts; and in a vast majority of teams, the modern field spaniel must be regarded as more like the springer than the cocker. The Welsh and Devon cockers are both liver-colored, not of the Sussex golden hue, but of a dead true liver color. Their ears are not too large for work, and on the show bench would by many judges be considered too small; but they are always lobular, without the slightest tendency to a vine shape. Throughout the country there are numberless breeds of cockers of all colors, varying from white, black, or liver to red and white, lemon and white, liver and white, and black and white. Ladybird is nearly all red, but she comes of strains usually all liver or all black. The illustration is a portrait of Mr. W. Gillett's Brush, an excellent representative dog.

The *Blenheim* and *King Charles' Spaniels* will be described under the head of toy dogs, to which purpose alone are they really suited, though sometimes used in covert shooting.

Fig. 21.—IRISH WATER SPANIEL, RAKE.

THE WATER SPANIEL.

Water Spaniels are commonly said to have web-feet, and this point is often made a ground of distinction from other dogs, but the fact is that all dogs have their toes united by membranes in the same way, the only distinction between the water and land dogs being that the former have larger feet, and that the membrane between the toes being more lax, they spread more in swimming, and are thus more useful in the water. Most people would understand, from the stress laid on web-feet in the water dogs, that the toes of the land dogs were nearly as much divided as those of man, but there are none so formed, and, as I before remarked, the toes of all are united throughout by a strong membrane. The coat in all the water dogs is woolly and thickly matted, often curly, and in all more or less oily, so as to resist the action of the water.

This oil is rank in smell, and hence they are all unfit to be inmates of our houses, which is a strong objection even to the poodle as a toy dog. As, therefore, we have no ground for separating the land from the water dogs by this strong line, I have not attempted to do so, but have grouped them according to the divisions under which they naturally fall.

The *Old English water Spaniel* is particularly fond of the water, and will enter it in almost all weathers by choice, while it never is too cold for him when any game is on it. His powers of swimming and diving are immense, and he will continue in it for hours together, after which he gives his coat a shake and is soon dry. Indeed, when he first comes out he does not seem thoroughly wet, his oiled and woolly coat appearing to set at defiance the approach of water. His nose is pretty good, and he is capable of an excellent education; but it takes some time to break him thoroughly, as he is required to be completely under command, and is a very restless dog by nature, whereas his duties demand perfect silence. There are generally said to be two distinct breeds, one larger than the other, but in other respects alike.

His points are as follows:—Head long and narrow, eyes small, and ears of medium length, covered with thick curly hair. Body stout, but elegantly formed, with strong loins, and round barrel-like chest, which is broad across the shoulders. The legs are rather long, but very strong, the bone being of great size, and well clothed with muscle. Feet large and spreading, tail covered thickly with long curly hair, and slightly curved upwards, but not carried above the level of the back.

The *Irish water Spaniel* consists of two distinct varieties, peculiar to the north and south of Ireland. The northern dog has short ears, with little feather either on them or on the legs, but with a considerable curl in his coat. In color he is generally liver, but with more or less white which sometimes predominates, so as to make him decidedly white and liver. The south country Irish water spaniel is, on the contrary, invariably of a puce liver color. Ears long and well feathered, being often two feet from point to point, and the whole coat consisting of short crisp curls. Body long, low, and strong, tail round and carried slightly down; but straight, without any approach to feather. The celebrated breed known as "M'Carthy's" is thus described by that gentleman in a recent communication.

"The present improved and fancy breed, called M'Carthy's breed, should run thus:—Dog from 21 to 22½ inches high (seldom higher when pure bred), head rather capacious, forehead prominent, face from eyes down perfectly smooth, ears from 24 to 26 inches from point to point. The head should be crowned with a well-defined top-knot, not straggling across like the common rough water dog, but coming down in a peak on the forehead. The body should be covered with small crisp curls, which often become draggled in the moulting season: the tail should be round without feather underneath, of the two rather short, and as stiff as a ramrod; the color of a pure puce liver without any white. Though these dogs are generally of very high mettle, I have never found them intractable or difficult to be trained; they readily keep to heel and down-charge, and will find a dead or wounded bird anywhere, either in the open or in covert, but they are not partial to stiff thorny brakes, as the briers catch the curl and trail after them. It is advisable to give them a little training at night, so that in seeking objects they must rely upon the nose alone. For the gun, they should be taught to go into the water like a duck; but when kept for fancy, a good dog of this breed will take a flying jump of from 25 to 35 feet, or more, perpendicular hight, into the water. My old dog Boatswain lived to be about eighteen years old, when, although in good health and spirits, I was obliged to destroy him. When going abroad in 1849, for some years, I gave my breed to Mr. Jolliffe Tuffnell, of Mount-street, Merrion-square, Dublin, son of the late Col. Tuffnell, of Bath. His dog Jack, a son of my dog Boatswain, is known particularly as a sire, to every one in Ireland, and to very many in England. A good well-trained dog of this breed will not be obtained under from $50 to $100, and I have known as much as $200 or $300 to be paid for one. They will not stand a cross with any other breed; the spaniel, setter, Newfoundland dog, and Labrador dog, etc., perfectly destroy coat, ears, tail, and symmetry; added to which, the cross-bred dog is very difficult to dry. If any cross would answer, I should say the bloodhound.—J. M'C."

The portrait on page 118 is from a remarkably good photograph of Mr. Lindoe's celebrated Rake.

Fig. 22.—CHESAPEAKE BAY DOG.

CHESAPEAKE BAY DOG.

The earliest accounts that we have of the above mentioned dog date back to the year 1807, when the ship "Canton," of Baltimore, fell in at sea with an English brig in a sinking condition, bound from Newfoundland to England. The crew were rescued and taken aboard of the "Canton," also two Newfoundland pups, a dog and bitch. The English crew were landed at Norfolk, and the two pups purchased from the English captain for a guinea apiece, and taken to Baltimore. The dog pup, called "Sailor," was given to Mr. John Mercer, of West River; the bitch pup, named "Canton," to Dr. James Stewart, of Sparrow Point. The dog was of a dingy-red color, and the bitch black. They were not large, hair short, but very thick-coated, attained great reputation as water dogs, and were very sagacious, particularly so in all duties pertaining to duck shooting. Gov. Lloyd, for a valuable consideration, succeeded in securing the dog, and took him to his estate on the eastern shore of Maryland, where his progeny may still be known as the Sailor breed. The bitch remained at Sparrow Point, and her progeny are well known to the duck shooters of Patapsco Neck, Gunpowder, etc.

As there now appears to be three types of this dog, the members of the Maryland Poultry and Fancier's Association, at their first show, held at Baltimore, January, 1877, appointed a committee to draw up a standard of points for judging. On the evening of January 3, 1877, they met the members of the club, and made their report, which was adopted. The committee consisted of the following gentlemen (each representing their respective type): Mr. John Stewart, representing the Otter breed, in color a tawny sedge, with very short hair; Mr. O. D. Foulks, the long-haired, or Red Winchester, and Mr. J. J. Turner, Jr., the curly-coated, in color a red-brown—the bitches showing the color and approximating to the points of the class to which they belong, a white spot on the breast in either class not being unusual. The measurements were as follows: from fore toe to top of back, 25 inches; from tip of nose to base of head, 10 inches; girth of body back of fore leg, 33 inches; breast, 9 inches; around fore feet, 6 inches; around fore arm below shoulder, 7 inches; between eyes, $2\frac{1}{4}$ inches; length of ears, 5 inches; from base of head to root of tail, 35 inches; tail, 16 inches in length; around muzzle below the eyes, 10 inches. The writer has one crossed with the pure Irish Water Spaniel, which cannot be excelled as a ducking dog. The illustration page 121 is of the dog "Trip," owned by C. H. Tilghman, of Easton, Md., and awarded the first premium at the Bench Show held in New York in 1877.

CHAPTER V.

PASTORAL DOGS, AND THOSE USED FOR THE PURPOSES OF DRAUGHT.

THE ENGLISH SHEEP-DOG.—THE COLLEY.—THE GERMAN SHEEP-DOG.—POMERANIAN OR SPITZ DOG.—THE NEWFOUNDLAND AND LABRADOR DOGS.—THE ESQUIMAUX DOG.—THE GREENLAND DOG.

THE ENGLISH SHEEP-DOG.

There are so many different breeds of the English Sheep-dog that it is difficult to describe him. He has a sharp muzzle, medium-sized head, with small and piercing eyes; a well-shaped body, formed after the model of a strong low greyhound, but clothed in thick and somewhat woolly hair, which is particularly strong about the neck and bosom. The tail is naturally long and bushy, but, as it has almost invariably been cut off until of late years, its variations can hardly be known. Under the old excise laws the shepherd's dog was only exempt from tax when without a tail, and for this reason it was always removed; from which at last it happened that many puppies of the breed were born without any tails, and to this day some particular breeds are tailless. In almost all sheep-dogs there is a double dew-claw on each hind leg, and very often without any bony attachment. The legs and feet are strong and well formed, and stand road-work well, and the untiring nature of the dog is very remarkable. The color varies greatly, but most are grey, or black, or brown, with more or less white.

Such is the true old English sheep-dog, but a great proportion of those in actual use are crossed with the various sporting dogs, such as the setter, which is very common, or the pointer, or even the hound; and hence we so often find the sheep-dog as good in hunting game as in his more regular duties, while a great many are used as regular poaching dogs by night, and in retired districts by day also.

THE COLLEY.

One of the most beautiful and useful of all dogs is the Scotch sheep-dog or colley, excellent engravings of which are given, pp. 125–128. With a fine muzzle he combines an intelligent-looking and rather broad head, and a clear but mild eye, a pricked and small ear slightly falling at the tip. His body is elegantly formed, and clothed with a thick coat of woolly hair, which stands out evenly from his sides and protects him from all the vicissitudes of the weather, neither wind, rain, nor snow being capable of penetrating it. The legs are well formed and the feet strong and useful. The tail is long, gently curved, and bushy, and the whole outline resembles that of the dingo; but the form is stouter and the limbs stronger. The color is nearly always black and tan, with little or no white; sometimes, however, the whole skin is of one or other of these colors, but then the dog is not considered nearly so valuable. The colley, like the true English sheep-dog, has always one or two dew-claws on each hind leg.

A great deal of discussion has lately taken place in regard to the colley's proper color and general appearance, and various descriptions have been given of what each writer considers the genuine breed, differing in every respect but the one to which I have drawn attention, which in almost all cases has been admitted to be essential. Some gentlemen, however, who have obtained specimens with beautiful but open coats of a glossy black, pointed with tan, have contended that this is the desideratum; and so it is for the dog, considered simply as a companion. Hitherto, however, no one has ventured to propound the theory that he is to be so regarded; and, until I find that a separate class is made at some one or more of our important shows for "toy colleys," I must

SHEPHERD DOGS.

continue to describe the breed from the shepherd's point of view, only—regarding any suspicion of a setter cross, and especially if shown in coat, as injuring his value for the reasons before given. Only those who have seen one or more of the public sheep-dog trials (instituted about four years ago by Mr. Lloyd Price, and many of which have of late years been held in Wales as well as in England), or have privately seen these animals at their usual work, can realize the amount of intelligence displayed by them. In these trials the slightest sign from the shepherd is understood and obeyed, and even the exact amount of driving calculated to make the sheep go quietly forward to the pen without breaking away is regulated to a nicety.

But, irrespective of his obedience to his master's orders, the independent intelligence of the colley is very high, and it is interesting to watch him or some other sheep-dog manage a wild sheep which is to be driven against his will in a certain direction. Very frequently the sheep turns round and stands facing the dog, and the natural expectation on the part of a spectator is that the latter will try by barking to make the sheep turn round and progress somewhere. Not so, however; such a proceeding would inevitably cause a " break away," and the course pursued is to lie quietly down and face the sheep. By this method in a short time the facing is changed to a quiet retreat, or sometimes to a slight backing, when the dog quietly moves a step or two forward and again lies down, till at last, by this kind of coaxing, the weaker animal of the two is quietly managed. In such cases a high degree of intelligence and tact is required which is partly innate and partly acquired from the shepherd by education. As a consequence there must be a due development of brain in the sheep-dog, and there must be a disposition to learn and obey the orders given. So clever is the colley that he will not be imposed on for any purpose not evidently useful, and it is seldom that he can be taught to execute tricks for the gratification of idle spectators, although there is no difficulty in getting him to perform them once or twice to please his master. If exhibited beyond this extent he is apt to sulk and refuse to show off; but when he is wanted to do really useful work, such as is required for the shepherd's purposes, he is untiring, and will go on until utterly exhausted.

No other dog in this country is so constantly with his master engaged in his proper calling—taking the breed as a whole. Occasionally, it is true, pet dogs are as much so, but by no means universally, nor are they even then so frequently employed in carrying out their master's orders. This naturally increases the intelligence of each individual and reacts on the whole breed; so that, independently of the constantly weeding out of puppies rendered

Fig. 23.—SCOTCH COLLEY DOG, TOM RIDLEY.

useless from a want of intelligence, the superiority of the whole variety in mental attributes is easily accounted for. For the same reason, when the pet colley gets old and is submitted to the rebuffs of children or strangers, he is apt to become crusty in temper, and sometimes even savage; but he is always most affectionate to his master, and no dog seems to be more sincerely repentant when he has done wrong.

Within the last ten years the colley has become very fashionable as a pet, and his market price has risen from $15 to $150, or even more for animals good-looking enough to take a prize at our shows. For this kind of colley, beauty of form and a brilliant black coat are the chief requisites, and these are greatly aided by the cross with the Gordon setter; that is to say, without any consideration for the purposes to which this dog was originally bred, and is still extensively used. The pet colley, not being exposed to weather, is quite as useful to his master with an open setter coat and feathered legs; while regarded from an artistic point of view he is more handsome from the superior brilliancy of his color, and from the addition of feather. His ears, when thus bred, are, however, seldom good, being neither pricked like the colley's, nor falling close like the setter's; and this is the chief objection to the cross from the pet dog point of view, though no doubt it is and has been easily bred out by careful selection. Moreover, if a pet is wanted solely as such, the Gordon setter in his purity is a handsomer dog than the colley, with a more pettable disposition, and it would be better to select him accordingly.

In Scotland and the north of England, as well as in Wales, a great variety of breeds is used for tending sheep, depending greatly on the locality in which they are employed, and on the kind of sheep adopted in it. The Welsh sheep is so wild that he requires a faster dog than even the Highlander of Scotland, while in the lowlands of the latter country a heavier, tamer, and slower sheep is generally introduced. Hence it follows that a different dog is required to adapt itself to these varying circumstances, and it is no wonder that the strains are as numerous as they are. In Wales there is certainly, so far as I know, no special breed of sheep-dog, and the same may be said of the north of England, where, however, the colley (often improperly called Scotch), more or less pure, is employed by nearly half the shepherds of that district, the remainder resembling the type known by that name in many respects, but not all. For instance, some show a total absence of "ruff" or "frill;" others have an open coat of a pied black and white color, with a setter shaped body; while others, again, resemble the ordinary drover's dog in all respects. But, without doubt, the modern "true and accepted" colley has been in existence for at least thirty years, as proved by the engraving published in Youatt's bo)k on "The Dog," nearly thirty years ago, which, by permission of his publisher, was accepted by me as the proper type in 1859, in my first treatise on the varieties of the canine race. That portrait was, I believe, copied from a specimen in the gardens of the Zoological Society, which for some years after its formation possessed a most interesting collection of dogs, now unfortunately abandoned. The engraving given on page 99 represents some specimens of good American bred Colleys; that on page 128 is a portrait of Tom Ridley, the first prize dog at the N. Y. Bench Show, 1877, and owned by Mr. F. Bronson, of New York City.

THE GERMAN SHEEP-DOG

Is a small-sized dog, with bushy tail carried over the back, small muzzle, and shaggy coat, which is generally black or light fawn. His manner is brisk and affectionate, and his tractability is great, so that he is most useful in his vocation, and as a companionable dog is not excelled.

THE POMERANIAN OR SPITZ DOG. 131

Fig. 24.—A SPITZ DOG.

THE POMERANIAN OR SPITZ-DOG.

Within the last twenty years this dog has been largely imported from Germany and France into England, in addition to those bred in that country; but, nevertheless, he has not become so general a favorite as was expected, owing in some measure to the fashion of the day tending towards the fox terrier and colley, and also to the temper of the Spitz, which is too short and snappish to make him fit to be trusted with children. It is true that the colley has the same disposition, but not quite to the same extent; and, being a better traveller with horses and carriages, he is more suited to act as a companion in country rides and drives than his more delicate rival.

In his native country, the Pomeranian dog is employed as a

sheep-dog, for which he is fitted by his peculiarly woolly coat and ample frill, rendering him to a great degree proof against wet and cold. Like the colley, he is impatient of control in playing tricks, and, indeed, can seldom be taught to display them even for a time, his intelligence not being of a very high order—at all events, if the attempt is made in any direction but that of his peculiar calling, for which, as far as known, he has never been employed anywhere else. But he is always cheerful in the house, generally free from smell either of coat or breath, and readily taught to be cleanly in all his habits. He has not the fondness for game generally exhibited by the colley, and on that account is more suited to be a ladies' pet, nor is he so pugnacious as that dog, being as a rule inclined to run away rather than fight, when the choice lies between those alternatives. From these peculiarities it may be gathered that he is quite up to the average in his fitness to fill the position of companion.

The specimen selected for illustration is only of average perfection in the shape of body and head, but his coat is highly characteristic of the true breed. He took the first prize at the late Islington Show of the Kennel Club. This variety of dog has become very popular as a house dog in America, but of late has fallen into some disrepute on account of his snappish disposition.

THE NEWFOUNDLAND.

This most valuable animal is of three very different kinds, viz.: 1. The true Newfoundland; 2. The large, loose-made, and long-haired variety, known as the Large Labrador; and 3. The small, compact, and comparatively short-haired dog, known as the St. John's or Lesser Labrador breed. All were originally natives of Newfoundland, and though many are bred in England, fresh specimens are constantly being imported from the island. Many of the naturalized strains are now more or less crossed with the mastiff or setter. They are chiefly used for ornamental purposes and as companions to their masters, the small breed being also crossed with the setter to make the retriever; but in their native country they are used to draw timber over the snow in the winter months, being harnessed to carts and sledges made for the purpose. In intelligence the three breeds are about equal, all being celebrated for their faculty of learning to fetch and carry. This is sometimes developed to such an extent that a well-trained dog will go back for anything which his master has pointed out to him, if it has been handled, when it is only necessary to order him back to seek, and he will find it by the scent.

Both breeds are good water dogs and bear immersion for a long time, but the large variety having a more woolly coat is superior in endurance of wet and cold. Hundreds of anecdotes are told of extraordinary escapes from drowning by means of these dogs, their tendency to fetch and carry being doubly useful here. Children and light small women may be intrusted to them with safety in the water, if they are not bewildered with fear, when they will sometimes cling round the dog's neck, and frustrate all his efforts to restore them to the land by swimming; generally, however, in cases of recovery, the person has fainted, and being then powerless, is towed ashore readily enough. The speed with which the Newfoundland swims is very great, his large legs and feet enabling him to paddle himself with great force. From their great size and strength they are able to beat off most dogs when they are attacked, and their thick coats prevent the teeth of their assailants from doing much damage; but in offensive measures they are of little use, being rather unwieldy, and soon winded in a desperate struggle. Hence they are not useful in hunting the large kinds of game, nor the bear, wolf, or tiger. The nose is delicate enough to hunt any kind of scent, but as they soon tire, they are not used in this way, and it is solely as retrievers on land or water that they are useful to the sportsman, being generally crossed with the setter for the former, and the water spaniel for the latter element.

The characteristic points of the Large Newfoundland are, great size, often being from 25 to 30 inches high; a form proportionally stout and strong, but loosely put together, so that there is a general want of compactness, especially about the loins, which are long and very flexible. The head is not large in comparison to the size, but wide across the eyes; muzzle of average length and width, and without any flews, as in the hounds and pointers; eye and ear both small, the latter falling, and without much hair on it; neck short and clothed with a ruff of hair; tail long, curled on itself slightly, and woolly; legs very strong, but not feathered; feet large and rather flat, bearing the road badly; coat on the body

Fig. 25.—NEWFOUNDLAND DOG, LEO.

long, hairy, shaggy, and shining, without any admixture of wool; the color should be black, but it is sometimes black and white, or white with little black, or liver color, or a reddish dun, or sometimes, but rarely, a dark brindle not very well marked.

The large black Newfoundland is remarkable for his majestic appearance, combined with a benevolent expression of countenance. The latter quality, being really in accordance with his disposition, and frequently displayed by his life-saving capacities in cases of threatened drowning, has made him for many years a great favorite as a companion, especially with those who live near the sea or any great river. With these points in view, judges have naturally made a full size of great importance, since it not only adds to the majestic aspect of the dog, but renders him really more capable of distinguishing himself in the career so beautifully commemorated by Landseer in one of his most popular pictures.

The general opinion now is, that a dog of this breed above 26 inches is almost unknown in Newfoundland; but it is also allowed that puppies bred and reared in England of the pure strains, which in the island never attain a greater hight than 26 inches, will grow to 30 or even 32 inches. Such an animal is Mr. Mapplebeck's Leo, who has recently taken the first prize at Islington in the Kennel Club Show, after distinguishing himself previously at Bath, and other places.

The *Large Labrador* is a more loosely-framed animal, and is never entirely black, being more or less mixed with white. The coat also is longer, more woolly, and curly.

The *St. John's*, or *Smaller Labrador*, or *Newfoundland*, the three names being used indiscriminately, is seldom more than 25 inches high, and often much less. The head is larger in proportion to his size, and the ear also slightly fuller; neck longer; body far more compact, and clothed with shorter hair, shining, and without any woolly texture; tail similar in shape, but the hair less woolly; legs and feet also better adapted for work; color almost always a jet black, rarely liver-colored. This dog is now generally more or less crossed with the setter.

THE ESQUIMAUX DOGS.

These dogs are the only beasts of burden in the northern part of America and the adjacent islands, being sometimes employed to carry materials for hunting or the produce of the chase on their backs. At other times they are harnessed to sledges in teams, varying from 7 to 11, each being capable of drawing a hundred-weight for his share. They are harnessed to a single yoke line by a breast-strap, and, being without any guide-reins, they are entirely at liberty to do what they like, being only restrained by the voice of their master, and urged forward by his whip. A single dog of tried intelligence and fidelity is placed as leader, and upon him the driver depends for his orders being obeyed. In the summer they are most of them turned off to get their own subsistence by hunting, some few being retained to carry weights on their backs. Sledges are then rendered useless by the absence of snow; and, as

Fig. 26.—HEAD OF ESQUIMAUX DOG.

there is a good subsistence for them from the offal of the seal and the walrus which are taken by the men, the dogs become fat at this season of the year. The Siberian and Greenland dogs are nearly similar to those of Kamtschatka, but somewhat larger, and also more manageable, all being used in the same way. The Esquimaux dog is about 22 or 23 inches high, and varies greatly in appearance, having been crossed considerably with the Newfoundland and Labrador species. The illustration, fig. 26, represents a variety used mostly in the region about York Factory, Rupert's Rivers, and Labrador. It is generally of the Newfoundland type. The dog common to the region of the Saskatchewan River and Lake Winipeg is stone-grey, of large and bony build, with large spreading feet and with prick ears. The hair is long and wiry, and lies close to the body. The head of this dog is shown in the engraving, fig. 27, which is from a drawing by Adrian Nelson of Manitoba, who gives the following particulars in a recent letter:

"The black and the yellow Esquimaux dogs are, I believe, pe-

Fig. 27.—HEAD OF ESQUIMAUX DOG.

culiar to the American Esquimaux. These I consider the best sleigh dogs known, especially the black variety. The other variety is found in all shades of yellow, sometimes almost white. A portrait of a white dog of this variety is given on page 139. The following are the measurements of this remarkably fine specimen: Hight at shoulder, 2 ft. 6 in.; length from center between shoulder blades to center between ears, 1 foot; from latter point to end of nose, 11 in.; length from shoulders to setting on of tail, 2 ft. 7 in.; length of tail, 1 foot 4 in.; measurement round head just behind ears, 2 ft.; just above eyes, 1 foot 8 in.; at point of nose, 10 in.; his girth measured fairly tight, not outside the hair, 3 ft.; his weight is 120 lbs. Out of a good many hundred of the black I have not seen a single specimen marked with either white or brown. When skinned it is at once noticed that the skull is unusually flat; this peculiarity is hidden in the live animal by its hair. It has a heavy jaw, very small round ears, which are always erect, and the hair, which is long, hard, and wiry, invariably stands erect off the skin, very similar to that of a bear, to which the whole dog bears a very close resemblance when lying down. All of this breed are fierce, treacherous, and active. A man would be considered a fool who attempted to harness them without his whip, and that whip must have some little bells, thimbles, or pieces of tin attached, so as to constantly jingle. It would be the essence of folly to touch one of these dogs when out of his harness, except with the whip. Approaching the dog, the driver throws the lash, which is about 10 feet long, round the dog's neck, twists it until it almost chokes him, and then drags him to his collar by main strength, grasps his head between his thighs, and then slips the collar, which is very tight, over the head. From that instant the dog is quiet and submissive enough. The whips used are of plaited caribou hide, with from 2 oz. to 8 oz. of small shot woven into them, to give them weight. Besides this, with most strains, it is necessary to carry chains to fasten the dogs at night, and, if travelling on ice, also a spear to picket them to. Mr. Ouyon, of Fort Chippewyan, on Lake Arthabasca, has some splendid dogs of this breed. This post has the reputation of having the finest dogs in the North. A peculiarity in these dogs is that they all have bright, clear, yellow eyes, similar to a cat, with great powers of dilating the pupils. These dogs cannot be purchased, except at a very great expense, a good one being sold for $100, or more.

ESQUIMAUX, OR WOLF DOG.

CHAPTER VI.

WATCH DOGS, HOUSE DOGS, AND TOY DOGS.

BULLDOG.—ENGLISH MASTIFF.—MOUNT ST. BERNARD.—THIBET DOG.—POODLE.—MALTESE DOG.—LION DOG.—SHOCK DOG.—TOY SPANIELS.—TOY TERRIERS.—THE PUG DOG.—ITALIAN GREYHOUND.

The peculiarity of this division is that the dogs composing it are solely useful as the companions or guards of their owners, not being capable of being employed with advantage for hunting, in consequence of their defective noses, and their sizes being either too large and unwieldy, or too small, for that purpose. For the same reason they are not serviceable as pastoral dogs or for draught, their legs and feet, as well as their powers of maintaining long-continued exertion, being comparatively deficient. These dogs nearly all show a great disposition to bark at intruders, and thereby give warning of their approach; but some, as the bulldog, are nearly silent, and their bite is far worse than their bark. Others, as, for instance, the little house dogs, generally with more or less of the terrier in them, are only to be used for the purpose of warning by their bark, as their bite would scarcely deter the most timid. The varieties are as follows:—

THE BULLDOG.

F. Cuvier has asserted that this dog has a brain smaller in proportion than any other of his congeners, and in this way accounts for his assumed want of sagacity. But, though this authority is deservedly high, I must beg leave to doubt the fact as well as the inference, for if the brain is weighed with the body of the dog from which it was taken, it will be found to be relatively above the average, the mistake arising from the evident disproportion between the brain and the skull. For the whole head, including the zygomatic arches and cheek-bones, is so much larger than that of the spaniel of the same total weight of body, that the brain may well look small as it lies in the middle of the various processes intended for the attachment of the strong muscles of the jaw and neck. I have never been able to obtain the fresh brain of a pure bulldog for the purpose of comparison, but, from an examination of the skull, I have no doubt of the fact being as above stated. The mental qualities of the bulldog may be highly cultivated, and

Fig. 28.—BULLDOGS, SMASHER AND SUGAR.

in brute courage and unyielding tenacity of purpose he stands unrivalled among quadrupeds, and with the single exception of the game-cock, he has perhaps no parallel in these respects in the brute creation. Two remarkable features are met with in this breed : First, they always make their attack at the head; and, secondly, they do not bite and let go their hold, but retain it in the most tenacious manner, so that they can with difficulty be removed by any force which can be applied. Instances are recorded in which bulldogs have hung on to the lip of the bull (in the old days of baiting this animal) after their entrails had been torn out, and while they were in the last agonies of death. Indeed when they do lay hold of an object, it is always necessary to choke them off, without which resource they would scarcely ever be persuaded to let go. From confinement to their kennels, they are often deficient in intelligence, and can rarely be brought under good control by education. Owing to the same cause, they show little personal attachment, so that they sometimes attack their friends as well as their enemies when their blood is put up.

But, when differently treated, the bulldog is a very different animal, the brutal nature which he so often displays being mainly attributable to the savage human beings with whom he associates. Although, therefore, I am ready to admit that the bulldog often deserves the character for ferocity which he has obtained, yet I contend that this is not natural to him, any more than stupidity and want of affection, which may readily be proved to be the reverse of his character, if any one will take the trouble to treat him in a proper manner. For the following remarks I am mainly indebted to Mr. Stockdale, who is a celebrated breeder of bulldogs, and has had a long experience of their various attributes. The antiquity of the breed is unquestionable, and it has always been peculiar to the British islands, the Spanish variety having originally been procured from Britain. It is highly probable that the modern bulldog has undergone a change in appearance during the last fifty years, being now decidedly neater in shape than was formerly the case, if we are to judge from the portraits handed down to us. As now exhibited, he is a remarkably neat and compact animal naturally, the deformities sometimes seen being produced principally from the practice of constantly keeping the poor dog tied up with a short chain.

The bulldog has been described as stupidly ferocious, and showing little preference for his master over strangers; but this is untrue, he being an excellent watch, and as a guard unequalled, except, perhaps, by the bull-mastiff, a direct cross from him. Indeed, he is far from being quarrelsome by nature, though the bull-terrier, in many cases undoubtedly is so, and I fancy that some writers have taken their description from this dog rather than from the pure bulldog, which has been at all times rather a scarce animal. If once the pure breed is allowed to drop, the best means of infusing fresh courage into degenerate breeds will be finally lost, except with the addition of extraneous blood, which may not suit them; for it is believed that every kind of dog possessed of very high courage owes it to a cross with the bulldog, and thus the most plucky greyhounds, foxhounds, mastiffs, pointers, etc., may all be traced to this source. Though bull and badger baiting may not be capable of extenuation, to them we owe the keeping up of this breed in all its purity; and though we may agree to discontinue these old-fashioned sports, yet sportsmen will see the bad taste of running down a dog who, with all his faults, is not only the most courageous dog, but the most courageous animal in the world.

The points of a well-bred bulldog are as follows: The head should be round, the skull high, the eye of moderate size, and the forehead well sunk between the eyes, the ears semi-erect and small, well placed on the top of the head, rather close together than otherwise, the muzzle short, truncate, and well furnished with chop; his back should be short, well arched towards the stern, which should be fine, and of moderate length. Many bulldogs have what is called a crooked stern, as though the vertebræ of the tail were dislocated or broken. Some authorities attribute this to in-breeding. The coat should be fine, though many superior strains are very woolly coated; the chest should be deep and broad, the legs strong and muscular, and the foot narrow and well split up, like a hare's.

Many of the old well-known breeders of the bulldog have disappeared from the prize list. In the present day, Mr. G. A. Dawes, of Leamington; Mr. G. Raper, of Stockton-on-Tees; Mr. James Taylor of Rochdale; Mr. Harding Cox; Mr. Adcock, of Wigan; Mr. James Berrie (now one of the oldest and most enthusiastic fanciers), Mr. Layton, Mr. T. H. Joyce, and Mr. Vero Shaw, of London, have many good specimens of the type I have endeavored to describe in the foregoing notes.

The engraving given on page 142 is a portrait of a pair of dogs bred by Mr. Shaw, which show the peculiarities of the breed in a marked degree. The fore-shortened sketch of the dog exhibits the formation of the chest, shoulders, width of skull, and "rose" carriage of ears, peculiar to the breed, while the bitch's side view shows her wonderfully short face and "roached" loin, rarely met with to the same extent. Their pedigrees are as follows: The dog, Smasher, by Master Gully, out of Nettle, by Sir Anthony. The bitch, Sugar (formerly Lily), is by the Abbot out of Mr. J. L. Ashburne's Lola, and was bred by the latter gentleman.

Fig. 29.—ENGLISH MASTIFF, GOVERNOR.

THE MASTIFF.

There is every reason to suppose that this is an indigenous breed, like the bulldog, for though the Cuban mastiff closely resembles it, yet the latter is to all appearances crossed with the bloodhound.

The *English Mastiff* is a fine noble-looking animal, and in temper is the most to be depended on of all the large and powerful dogs, being extremely docile and companionable, though possessed of the highest courage. When crossed with the Newfoundland or bloodhound, they answer well as yard-dogs, but the produce is generally of a savage nature, while the pure breed is of so noble and mild a nature that they will not on any provocation hurt a child or even a small dog, one of their most remarkable attributes being their fondness for affording protection. Mr. Lukey, of Morden, Surrey, has a very fine breed of the pure mastiff. We present an engraving of Governor, the finest of his dogs.

Mr. Lukey began to breed mastiffs rather more than forty years ago, taking a brindled bitch bred by the then Duke of Devonshire as his foundation. Putting her to Lord Waldegrave's celebrated dog Turk, and her puppies to the Marquis of Hertford's Pluto, he obtained a strain with which he stood for some years almost alone as the celebrated mastiff breeder of the day, without any outcross. At length, fearing deterioration by further in-breeding, he resorted to Capt. Garnier's kennel for a sire, the produce being that magnificent dog Governor, by Capt. Garnier's Lion out of his own Countess, a daughter of his Duchess by his Bruce II., who was by his Bruce I. out of his Nell. Of the breeding of his own Lion, and Lord Waldegrave's Turk, Capt. Garnier writes as follows:

"Some time ago I bought of Bill George a pair of mastiffs, whose produce, by good luck, afterwards turned out some of the finest specimens of the breed I ever saw. The dog Adam was one of a pair of Lyme Hall mastiffs, bought by Bill George at Tattersall's. He was a different stamp of dog to the present Lyme breed. He stood $30\frac{1}{2}$ in. at the shoulder, with length of body and good muscular shoulders and loins, but was just slightly deficient in depth of body and breadth of forehead; and from the peculiar forward lay of his small ears, and from his produce, I have since suspected a remote dash of boarhound in him. The bitch was obtained by Bill George from a dealer in Leadenhall Market. Nothing was known of her pedigree, but I am as convinced of its purity as I am doubtful of that of the dog. There was nothing striking about her. She was old, with shoulders a trifle flat. She had a grey muzzle, but withal stood 29 in. at the shoulder, and had a broad round head, good loin, and deep lengthy frame. From crossing these dogs with various strains I was easily able to analyze their produce, and I found in them two distinct types—one due to the dog, very tall, but a little short in the body and high on the leg, while their heads were slightly deficient in breadth; the other due to the bitch, equally tall, but deep, lengthy and muscular, with broad massive heads and muzzles. Some of these latter stood 33 inches at the shoulder, and by the time they were two years old weighed upwards of 190 lbs. They had invariably a fifth toe on each hind leg, which toe was quite distinct from a dew-claw, and formed an integral portion of their feet. By bad management, I was only able to bring a somewhat indifferent specimen with me on my return to England from America—a badly reared animal, who nevertheless stood 32 in. at the shoulder, and weighed 170 lbs.

Fig. 30.—ROUGH ST. BERNARD, TELL.

This dog Lion was the sire of Governor and Harold, by Mr. Lukey's bitch Countess, and so certain was I of the vast size of the breed in him, that I stated beforehand, much to Mr. Lukey's incredulity, that the produce would be dogs standing 33 in. at the shoulder—the result being that both Governor and his brother Harold were fully that hight. In choosing the whelps, Mr. Lukey retained for himself the best marked one, an animal that took after the lighter of the two strains that existed in the sire; for Governor, grand dog and perfect mastiff as he was, compared to most others of the breed, was nevertheless shorter in the body, higher on the leg, and with less muscular development than Harold, while his head, large as it was, barely measured as much around as did his brother's. I, who went by the development of the fifth toe (in this case only a dew-claw), chose Harold, a dog which combined all the best points except color of both strains, and was a very perfect reproduction on a larger scale of his dam Countess. This dog was the finest male specimen of the breed I have met with. His breast at ten months old, standing up, measured 13 in. across, with a girth of 41 in., and he weighed in moderate condition 140 lbs., and at twelve months old 160 lbs., while at 13¼ months old, Governor only weighed in excellent condition 150 lbs. with a girth of 40 in.; and inasmuch as Governor eventually weighed 180 lbs. or even more, the size to which Harold probably attained must have been very great. His head also in size and shape promised to be perfect."

The points of the mastiff are:—A head of large size, between that of the bloodhound and bulldog in shape, having the volume of muscle of the latter, with the flews and muzzle of the former, though, of course, not nearly so deep; the ear being of small size but drooping, like that of the hound. The teeth generally meet, but if anything there is a slight protuberance of the lower jaw, never being uncovered by the upper lip like those of the bulldog; eye small; in shape there is a considerable similarity to the hound, but much heavier in all its lines; loin compact and powerful, and limbs strong; tail very slightly rough, and carried high over the back when excited; voice very deep and sonorous; coat smooth; color red or fawn with black muzzle, or brindled, or black; or black, red, or fawn and white, the latter mixture objected to; hight about 28 to 31 inches.

150 WATCH DOGS, HOUSE DOGS, AND TOY DOGS.

Fig. 31.—SMOOTH ST. BERNARD, MONARQUE.

THE MOUNT ST. BERNARD DOG.

Closely allied to the mastiff, but resembling the Newfoundland in temper and in his disposition to fetch and carry, is the Mount St. Bernard breed, until lately confined to the Alps and the adjacent countries, where he is used to recover persons who are lost in the snow-storms of that inclement region. Wonderful stories are told of the intelligence of these dogs and of the recovery of travellers by their means, which are said to extend almost to the act of pouring spirits down the throats of their patients; but, however, there is no doubt that they have been and still are exceedingly useful, and the breed is kept up at the monastery of Mount St. Bernard. The hight is about 28 to 31 inches; length six feet, including the tail. The coat varies a good deal in length, there being in England two distinct varieties founded upon this point, viz., the rough and the smooth. Mr. Macdona, who has been at great trouble and expense to import both of the best Swiss strains, leans to the rough, but there are many who still adhere to the smooth variety. The smooth dog is red and white, or brindled and white, a broad white collar of white of a peculiar shape distinguishing the true breed. The rough dog is most highly prized when of a deep tawny brindle, still with some white, but not so much as in the smooth kind. Both dogs are remarkably good-tempered, and may be trusted with the care of women or children with great dependence. The absence of dew-claw on the hind leg is considered a defect by some judges, and there is no doubt that many imported specimens of the breed have the double dew-claw. The illustrations of the two varieties mentioned are portraits of dogs owned by Mr. Macdona.

THE THIBET DOG.

This animal, as before remarked, resembles the English mastiff in general appearance, and, being also put to the same use, the two may be said to be nearly allied. According to Mr. Bennet, he is bred on the Himalaya Mountains, on the borders of Thibet, for the purpose of guarding the flocks and the women who attend them.

152 WATCH DOGS, HOUSE DOGS, AND TOY DOGS.

Fig. 32.—POODLE DOG.

THE POODLE.

The engraving given on this page represents the poodle as he is generally to be seen, shaved in part, so as to resemble the lion in having a mane; the tip of his tail having a tuft left on it. He is by many supposed to be the produce of a cross between the water and land spaniels, but there is no good reason to suppose that the breed is not quite as distinct as either of them. For many years it has been known in France and Germany, particularly the former country, and it is there occasionally used for sporting purposes, though, as in England, it is chiefly as a companion that this dog is kept. With more intelligence than falls to the lot of any other dog, he unites great fidelity to his master, and a strong love of approbation, so that he may readily be induced to attempt any trick which is shown him, and the extent to which he may be taught to carry out the secret orders of his instructor is quite marvellous. He fetches and carries very readily, swims well, and has a good nose, but has no particular fondness for hunting game, often preferring a stick or a stone to a hare or pheasant. Two of

THE POODLE DOG. 153

these dogs which were exhibited in London astonished every one by their clever performances, sitting up to table gravely, and playing a game at cards as quickly as a human being, the cards being placed before them, and the one to be played being selected by the dog's foot. Of course this was all done by preconcerted signal, but nevertheless it was remarkably well managed, and showed a degree of intelligence and discipline worthy of a better purpose.

The poodle is characterized by a large wide head, rising sharply at the forehead, long falling ears clothed with thick curly hair, rather small eyes, square muzzle, with a liberal allowance of jowl, and a sedate appearance until roused by any prospect of fun; a well-formed pointer-like body, but covered with thick closely curling hair, hanging down in ringlets below; tail usually cropped more or less, naturally covered with crisp curls; legs straight, and covered all round with hair hanging in short ringlets; feet small and round, and moderately hairy; color white or black, or white and black; hight from 16 to 20 inches.

The *Barbet* is merely a small variety of the poodle, which it resembles in all respects but size.

Fig. 33.—MALTESE DOG, FIDO.

MALTESE DOG.

This beautiful little dog is a Skye terrier in miniature, with, however, a far more silky coat, a considerably shorter back, and a tail stiffly curved over the hip.

Points.—The weight should never exceed 5 or 6 lbs.; head closely resembling that of the Skye, but with more shining and silky hair; coat as long as that dog's, but more transparent and silky; actions lively and playful, and altogether rendering it a pleasing pet. The tail is curved over the back, very small and short, with a brush of silky hair; color white, with an occasional patch of fawn on the ear or paw. The breed was so scarce some time ago, as to induce Sir E. Landseer to paint one as the last of his race; since which several have been imported from Malta, and, though still scarce, they are now to be obtained. A strain bred by Mr. Mandeville has kept possession of the show bench since 1862, when the first class of this kind of toy dog was established at the Agricultural Hall Show, in which Mr. Mandeville's Mick and Fido were first and second. In the following year, at Ashburnham, the same kennel again produced the first and second prize holders, Fido being at the head of his class, and a dog called Prince second. Since then Mr. Mandeville's strain has held undisputed possession of the prize list.

THE LION DOG.

This toy dog appears to be crossed between the poodle and the Maltese dog, being curly like the former, but without his long ears and square visage. He is now very seldom seen anywhere, and is not prized among fanciers of the canine species. Like the poodle he was generally shaved to make him resemble the lion.

THE SHOCK DOG.

This dog also is now almost unknown. But formerly he was very generally kept as a toy dog. He is said to have been a cross between the poodle and small spaniel, both of which varieties he resembled in part.

TOY SPANIELS.

Two breeds are known and recognized under this head, namely, the King Charles and the Blenheim spaniels, the former being slightly the larger of the two, and by most people considered the more handsome. To an ordinary observer the chief points of distinction in the King Charles are, the color, which is black and tan more or less mixed with white, the less the better; and the length of the ears, which is greater than in the Blenheims; these being also lighter in frame, and always yellow or red and white. Both are small delicate dogs, and though they have pretty good noses, and will hunt game readily, yet they so soon tire that they are rarely used for the purpose, and are solely kept for their ornamental properties. They make good watch dogs in-doors, barking at the slightest noise, and thus giving notice of the approach of improper persons   Though they are somewhat timid they are not readily silenced, as their small size allows of their retreating beneath chairs and sofas from which asylum they keep up their sharp and shrill note of defiance   The great objection to these handsome little creatures as pets is that they follow badly out of doors, and as they are always ready to be fondled by a stranger, they are very liable to be stolen.   Hence many people prefer the toy terrier, or the Skye, which is now introduced very extensively

Fig. 34.—KING CHARLES SPANIEL, YOUNG JUMBO.

as a toy dog, and might with propriety be inserted under this chapter.   The King Charles and Blenheim spaniels are often crossed, and then you may have good specimens of each from the same litter, but if true, their colors never vary.

The points of the King Charles spaniel are: extremely short muzzle, which should be slightly turned up; black nose and palate; full prominent eye, which is continually weeping, leaving a gutter of moisture down the cheek; a round bullet-shaped head, with a well-marked "stop" between the eyes; very long, full-haired, and silky ears, which should fall close to the cheeks, and not stand out from them; the body is covered with wavy hair of a silky texture, without curl; and the legs should be feathered to the toes, the length and silkiness of this being a great point; tail well feathered, but not bushy; it is usually cropped; the color should be a rich black and tan, without a white hair; but those marked with an unusual amount of white are not to be despised. They sometimes make their appearance in a litter of which both sire and dam have scarcely a white hair; the weight

Fig. 35.—BLENHEIM SPANIEL.

should never exceed 6, or at the utmost 7 lbs.; and they are valued the more if they are as low as 4½ or 5 lbs. (See portrait.)

The points of the Blenheim vary very little from those of the King Charles, except in color, which is always a white ground with red or yellow spots or patches, with well-marked blaze of white between the eyes. The ears should be colored, and also the whole of the head, with the exception of the nose and a white mark up the forehead, as is shown in the cut, which represents the Blenheim pretty accurately. The palate is black, like that of the King Charles; and there is little difference in shape, though an experienced eye could detect the one from the other even irre spective of color. This dog is generally smaller than the King Charles.

THE PUG.

This curly-tailed and pretty little toy dog was out of fashion in England for some years, but has recently come again into such vogue that a good pug will fetch from 100 to 200 dollars. The British breed, however, which is one of those known to have existed from the earliest times, was never entirely lost, having been carefully preserved in a few families. The Dutch have always had a fondness for the pug dog, and in Holland the breed is common enough, but the same attention has not been paid to it as in England, and yellow masks, low foreheads, and pointed noses are constantly making their appearance in them, from the impure blood creeping out, and showing evidences of the crosses which have taken place. The very beautiful pair of these dogs, which is engraved on the next page, have the following history. During the decade 1840-50, several admirers of pugs attempted to breed them from good foreign strains. Foremost among these was the then Lady Willoughby de Eresby, who, after a great deal of trouble, obtained a dog from Vienna which had belonged to a Hungarian countess, but was of a bad color, being a mixture of the stone-fawn now peculiar to the "Willoughby strain," and black; but the combination of these colors was to a certain extent in the brindled form. From accounts which are to be relied on, this dog was about twelve inches high, and of good shape, both in body and head, but had a face much longer than would now be approved of by pug fanciers. In 1846 he was mated with a fawn bitch imported from Holland, of the desired color, viz., stone-fawn in body, with black mask and trace, but with no indication of brindle. She had a shorter face and heavier jowl than the dog, and was altogether in accordance with the type now recognized as the correct "Willoughby pug." From this pair are descended all the strain named after Lady Willoughby de Eresby, which are marked in color by their peculiar cold stone-fawn, and the excess of black often showing itself, not in brindled stripes, but in entirely or nearly entirely black heads, and large " saddle marks " or wide " traces."

But coincidently with this formation of a new strain was the existence of another, showing a richer and more yellow fawn, and no tendency to excess of black. This strain was possessed by the late Mr. Morrison, of Walham Green; the late Mr. H. Gilbert, of Kensington: Mr. W. Macdonald, now of Winchmore Hill, but at that

Fig 36.—PAIR OF PUG DOGS.

time residing in London; and some other fanciers of less note. According to Mr. Morrison's statement to me (which, however, he did not wish made public during his life), this strain was lineally descended from a stock possessed by Queen Charlotte, one of which is painted with great care in the well-known portrait of George III. at Hampton Court; but I could never get him to reveal the exact source from which it was obtained.

These dogs are not remarkable for sagacity displayed in any shape, but they are very affectionate and playful, and bear the confinement of the house better than many other breeds, racing over the carpets in their play as freely as others do over the turf. For this reason, as well as the sweetness of their skins, and their short and soft coats, they are much liked by the ladies as pets.

Their points are as follows:—General appearance low and thick-set, the legs being short, and the body as close to the ground as possible, but with an elegant outline; weight from 6 to 10 lbs; color fawn, with black mask and vent. The clearer the fawn, and the more distinctly marked the black on the mask, which should extend to the eyes, the better; but there is generally a slightly darker line down the back. Some strains have the hair all over the body tipped with "smut," but on them the mask is sure to shade off too gently, without the clear line which is valued by the fancier; coat short, thick, and silky; head round, forehead high; nose short, but not turned up; and level-mouthed; ears, when cut, cropped quite close, naturally rather short but falling; neck of moderate length, stout, but not throaty; chest wide, deep, and round; tail short, and curled closely to the side, not standing up above the back. It is remarkable that the tail in the dog generally falls over the off side, while in the bitch it lies on the near. The legs are straight, with small bone, but well clothed with muscle; feet like the hare, not cat-footed; no dew-claws on the hind legs. The hight is from 11 to 15 inches.

Fig. 37.—TOY TERRIER BELLE, AND BLACK-AND-TAN QUEEN III.

TOY TERRIERS.

These are of the various breeds described under the head of the terrier, but of smaller size than the average, and with great attention paid to their color and shape. The smooth English terrier, not exceeding 7 lbs. in weight, is much prized; and when he can be obtained of 3¼ or 4 lbs. weight, with perfect symmetry, and a good rich black and tan color without a white hair, he is certainly a very perfect little dog. The black lines (" pencilling ") of the toes, and the richness of the tan on the cheeks and legs, are points much insisted on.

Above is a portrait of Mr. Mapplebeck's wonderfully good toy terrier Belle, winner of the first prize at Birmingham, and at the late Kennel Club show held at the Alexandra Palace, together with his Queen III., also a first prize winner at the latter show in the class for black and tan or Manchester terriers—the latter serving as a contrast to the former in point of size. This little dog is, in fact, the large black and tan terrier reduced in size from 15 lbs. or 16 lbs. to 3 lbs. or 4 lbs., the one being exactly a copy of the larger kind, except in size, and possessed of equal hardihood and spirit. The two bitches are reproduced with fidelity. The great difficulty is to breed such little dwarfs without loss of symmetry or substance, the general result being a reduction of the size of the body and an enlargement proportionally of the head. The pedigree of Belle is unknown.

As the points of this breed are precisely similar to those of the larger variety, it is needless to reproduce them here.

Most of the toy terriers now sold are either crossed with the Italian greyhound or the King Charles spaniel. With the former, the shape is preserved, and there is the greatest possible difficulty in distinguishing this cross from the pure English terrier; indeed, I am much inclined to believe that all our best modern toy terriers are thus bred. They have the beautiful long sharp nose, the narrow forehead, and the small sharp eye, which characterize the pure breed, but they are seldom good at vermin, though some which I have known to be half Italian have been bold enough to attack a good strong rat as well as most dogs. Many of these half-bred Italians are used for rabbit coursing, in which there is a limit to weight, but it is chiefly for toy purposes that large prices are obtained for them. When the cross with the spaniel has been resorted to, the forehead is high, the nose short, and the eye large, full, and often weeping, while the general form is not so symmetrical and compact; the chest being full enough, but the brisket not so deep as in the true terrier, or in the Italian cross.

The *Skye Terrier*, as used for toy purposes, is often crossed with the spaniel to get silkiness of coat. See page 77.

The points are as there described.

Scotch Terriers are seldom used as toys, and are not considered such by the fanciers of the animal.

The *Halifax Blue Tan Terrier* is a toy dog, whether the weight is 16 lbs. or 3 lbs., between which every gradation may be found. The color of the back is a blue, sometimes stained with fawn, all the rest of the body being a rich golden tan. The hair is long and silky, always parting down the middle, and very long at the muzzle, from which it hangs like a beard. The shape resembles that of the Scotch terrier.

The *Italian Greyhound* has been already described on page 52.

CHAPTER VII.

CROSSED BREEDS.

RETRIEVER.—BULL-TERRIER.

Although many of the breeds which have been enumerated in the preceding chapters were most probably the produce originally of crosses between distinct varieties, yet at present they are continued by breeding from a sire and dam of the same kind. But with those which we are now about to consider, there is constantly a necessity for having recourse to the original breeds. For instance, many breeds of the greyhound are known to be crossed with the bull, and the identical animal with which the cross first commenced is well ascertained, as in the case of Sir James Boswell's "Jason," Mr. Etwall's "Eurus," etc.; so also with the foxhound, though here the particular cross is not so well ascertained, but it is admitted to have taken place within the last century. Yet these are not called mongrels, and the breed, instead of being despised as such, is more highly prized than those of the pure strain which formed one side of the parent stock. The term mongrel may more properly be applied to those chance crosses which occur from accident or neglect, the bitch selecting her own mate, and being guided by caprice, without regard to the fitness of the match in reference to the progeny resulting.

THE RETRIEVER.

In speaking of the retriever, it is generally understood that the dog for recovering game on land is meant, the distinct kind known as the water spaniel being already alluded to on page 118. With regard to the propriety of using a separate dog for retrieving in open or covert shooting, there is a great difference of opinion. This part of the subject will be considered under the next division of this book. I now confine myself to a description of the crosses used solely as retrievers, including the ordinary cross between the Newfoundland and setter, and that between the terrier and the water spaniel, which is recommended by Mr. Colquhoun, and which I have found especially serviceable.

The qualities which are required in the regular retriever are: Great delicacy of nose, and power of stopping (which latter is often not possessed by the pointer); cleverness to follow out the windings of the wounded bird, which are frequently most intricate, and puzzle the intelligence as well as the nose to unravel them; love of approbation, to induce the dog to attend to the instructions of the master, and an amount of obedience which will be required to prevent his venturing to break out when game is before him. All these are doubtless found in the retriever, but they are coupled with a large heavy frame, requiring a considerable amount of food to keep it, and space in the vehicle when he is to be conveyed from place to place. Hence, if a smaller dog can be found to do the work equally well, he should be preferred, and as some think he can, both shall be described.

The *Large Black Retriever* is known by his resemblance to the small Newfoundland, and the Irish water spaniel, or setter, between which two he is bred, and the forms of which he partakes of in nearly equal proportions, according to the cross. Hence the modern retriever is distinguished as either the curly-coated or wavy-coated, separate classes being made for them at most of our shows, and sometimes a third depending on color alone.

The *Wavy-coated Retriever* has a head like that of a heavy setter, but with shorter ears, less clothed with hair. The body is altogether larger and heavier, the limbs stronger, the feet less compact than those of the setter, while the gait more or less resembles in its peculiarities that of the Newfoundland. The color is almost always black, with very little white; indeed, most people would reject a retriever of this kind, if accidentally

WAVY-COATED RETRIEVERS. PARIS AND MELODY

of any other color. The coat is slightly wavy, but not very long or curly; and the legs are but little feathered. The hight is usually about 23 or 24 inches, sometimes slightly more or less. This dog can readily be made to set and back; and he will also hunt as well as a setter, but slowly, and lasting for a short time only.

The *Curly-coated Retriever* is distinguished by having the whole body covered with short crisp curls like those of the Irish water spaniel. The head is quite free from these, a well-marked line being apparent just behind the ears. Like the wavy-coated dog he should have a long deep jaw, and with the exception of the coat the two breeds resemble each other closely. The curly-coated dog is black or of a deep liver color, without white.

The *Terrier cross* is either with the beagle or the pointer, the former being that which I have chiefly used with advantage, and the latter being recommended by Mr. Colquhoun in his "Lochs and Moors." He gives a portrait of one used by himself, which he says was excellent in all respects; and, from so good a sportsman, the recommendation is deserving of all credit. This dog was about 22 inches high, with a little of the rough coat of the Scotch terrier, combined with the head and general shape of the pointer. The sort I have used is, I believe, descended from the smooth white English terrier and the true old beagle; the nose and style of hunting proclaiming the hound descent, and the voice and appearance showing the preponderance of the terrier cross. These dogs are small, scarcely ever exceeding 10 lbs. in weight, and with difficulty lifting a hare, so that they are not qualified to retrieve "fur" any great distance. They must, therefore, be followed when either a hare or pheasant is sought to be recovered. They are mute in "questing," and very quiet in their movements, readily keeping at heel, and backing the pointers steadily while they are "down charge," for as long a time as may be required; and when they go to their game they make no noise, as is too often done by the regular retriever. They do not carry so well as the larger dog, but in all other respects they are his equal, or perhaps superior. Owing to their small size they are admissible to the house, and being constant companions are more easily kept under command; besides which, they live on the scraps of the house, while the large retriever must be kept tied up at the keeper's, and costs a considerable sum to pay for his food.

THE BULL-TERRIER.

Many of our smooth terriers are slightly crossed with the bulldog, in order to give courage to bear the bites of the vermin which they are meant to attack. When thus bred, the terrier shows no evidence of pain, even though half a dozen rats are hanging on to his lips, which are extremely tender parts of the body, and where the bite of a mouse even will make a badly bred dog yell with pain. In fact, for all the purposes to which a terrier can be applied, the half or quarter cross with the bull, commonly known as the "bull-terrier" or "half-breed dog," is of more value than either of the purely bred progenitors. Such a dog, however, to be useful, must be more than half terrier, or he will be too heavy and slow, too much under-jawed to hold well with his teeth, and too little under command to obey the orders of his master. Sometimes the result of the second cross, which is only one quarter bull, shows a great deal of the shape peculiar to that side; and it is not until the third or fourth cross that the terrier shape comes out predominant. This is all a matter of chance, and the exact reverse may just as probably happen, although the terrier was quite free from the stain of the bull, which is seldom the case. This may account for the great predominance of that side in most cases, as we shall see in investigating the subject of breeding for the kennel in the next Book. The field fox-terrier, used for bolting the fox when gone to ground, was of this breed. So also is the fighting-dog par excellence, and, indeed, there is scarcely any task to which a dog of his size may be set that he will not execute as well as, or better than, most others. He will learn tricks with the poodle, fetch and carry with the Newfoundland—take water with that dog, though his coat will not suffer him to remain in so long,—hunt with the spaniel, and fight "till all's blue." For thorough gameness, united with obedience, good temper, and intelligence, he surpasses any breed in existence.

The points of the bull-terrier vary in accordance with the degree of each strain in the specimen examined. There should not be either the projection of the under jaw, or the crooked fore legs, or the small and weak hind-quarters; and until these are lost, or

Fig. 38.—BULL TERRIER, TARQUIN.

nearly so, the crossing should be continued on the terrier side. The perfect bull-terrier may, therefore, be defined as the terrier with as much bull as can be combined with the absence of the above points, and showing the full head (not of course equal to that of the bull), the strong jaw, the well-developed chest, powerful shoulders, and thin fine tail of the bull-dog, accompanied by the light neck, active frame, strong loin, and fuller proportions of the hind-quarter of the terrier. A dog of this kind should be capable of a fast pace, and will stand any moderate amount of road work. The hight varies from 10 inches to 16, or even 20. The color most admired is white, either pure or patched with black, blue, red, fawn, or brindle, sometimes black and tan, or self-colored red. The dog whose portrait is given, is Tarquin, bred and owned by Mr. Vero Shaw, of England.

BOOK II.

THE BREEDING, REARING, BREAKING, AND MANAGEMENT OF THE DOG, IN-DOORS AND OUT.

CHAPTER I.

BREEDING.

PRINCIPLES OF BREEDING.—AXIOMS FOR THE BREEDER'S USE.—CROSSING AND CROSSED BREEDS.—IMPORTANCE OF HEALTH IN BOTH SIRE AND DAM.—BEST AGES TO BREED FROM.—IN-AND-IN BREEDING.—BEST TIME OF YEAR.—DURATION OF HEAT.—MANAGEMENT OF THE BITCH IN SEASON.—THE BITCH IN WHELP.—PREPARATIONS FOR WHELPING.—HEALTHY PARTURITION.—DESTRUCTION OR CHOICE OF WHELPS AT BIRTH.

GENERAL PRINCIPLES OF BREEDING.

The principles upon which the breeding of the dog should be conducted are generally in accordance with those necessary for the production of other domestic animals of the class *Mammalia*, remembering always that it is not safe to argue from one class of animals to another, because their habits and modes of propagation vary so much as to interfere with the analogy. Thus as the pigeon, in common with other birds, does not rear her young with the produce of her own body to the same comparative size as most of the individuals of the class *Mammalia*, the mother has not so much more to do with the process than the father, as is the case with the bitch, mare, and cow, etc., where the quantity and quality are to be taken into the calculation. Hence, in selecting a sire and dam for breeding purposes among dogs, the bitch is most to be considered for many reasons, one being that she usually continues the property of the breeder, while the sire can be changed each time she breeds; but the chief argument in her favor is founded upon the supposition that she really impresses her formation upon her progeny more than the dog does. This, however, is a vexed question in natural history as well as in practical breeding, but from my own experience I think this is true of the bitch. Many horses and dogs may be instanced which have got good stock from all sorts of mares and bitches. Yet in opposition to this may be instanced the numbers which have had great opportunities for showing their good qualities, but while they have succeeded with one or two they have failed with the larger proportion of their harems. So with mares and bitches, some have produced, every year of their breeding lives, one or more splendid examples of their respective kinds, altogether independent of the horse or dog which may be the other parent, so long as he is of the proper strain. It is usually supposed that the sire impresses his external formation upon his stock, while the bitch's nervous temperament is handed down; and very probably there is some truth in the hypothesis. Yet it is clearer that not only do the sire and dam, but also the grandsires and grand-dams affect the progeny on both sides, and still further than this up to the sixth and perhaps even the seventh generations, but more especially on the dam's side, through the granddam, great granddam, etc. There is a remarkable fact connected with breeding which should be generally known, viz., that there is a tendency in the produce to a separation between the different strains of which it is composed; so that a puppy composed in four equal proportions of breeds represented by A, B, C, and D, will not represent all in equal proportions, but will resemble one much more than the others. And this is still more clear in relation to the next step backwards, when there are eight progenitors; and the litter which, for argument's sake, we will suppose to be eight in number, may consist of animals each "going back" to one or other of the above eight. This accounts for the fact that a smooth terrier bitch put to a smooth terrier will often "throw" one or more rough puppies, though the breed may be traced as purely smooth for two or three generations, beyond which, however, there must have been a cross of the rough dog. In the same way color and particular marks will be changed or obliterated for one, two, or even three generations, and will then reappear. In most breeds of the dog this is not easily proved, because a record of the various crosses is not kept with any great care; but in the greyhound the breed, with the colors, etc., for twenty generations, is often known, and then the evidence of the truth of these facts is patent to all. Among these dogs there is a well-known strain descended from a greyhound with a peculiar nose, known as the "Parrot-nosed bitch." About the year 1825 she was put to a celebrated dog called "Streamer," and bred a bitch called "Ruby," none of the litter showing this peculiar nose; nor did "Ruby" herself breed any in her first two litters; but in her third, by a dog called "Blackbird," belonging to Mr. Hodgkinson, two puppies showed the nose ("Blackbird" and "Starling"). In the same litter was a most celebrated bitch, known as "Old Linnet," from which are descended a great number of first-rate greyhounds. In these, however, this peculiarity has never appeared, with two exceptions, namely, once in the third generation, and once in the fifth, in a dog called "Lollypop," bred by Mr. Thomas, of Macclesfield, the possessor of the whole strain. One of the bitches of this breed is also remarkable for having always one blue puppy in each litter, though the color is otherwise absent, never having been seen since the time of the above mentioned "Ruby," who was a blue bitch. These facts are very remarkable as showing the tendency to "throw back" for generations, but, as they are well known and fully recognized by all breeders, it is unnecessary to dilate upon them, and the above instances are only introduced as absolutely proving to the uninitiated what would otherwise depend upon dogmatic assertion.

AXIOMS FOR THE BREEDER'S USE.

But it may be asked,—What then are the principles upon which breeding is to be conducted? To this, in many of the details, no answer can be given which can be relied on with certainty. Nevertheless, there are certain broad landmarks established which afford some assistance, and these shall be given, taking care to avoid all rules which are not clearly established by general consent.

1. The male and female each furnish their quota towards the original germ of the offspring; but the female, over and above this, nourishes it until it is born, and consequently may be supposed to have more influence upon its formation than the male.

2. Natural conformation is transmitted by both parents as a general law, and likewise any acquired or accidental variation. It may therefore be said that, on both sides, "like produces like."

3. In proportion to the purity of the breed, will it be transmitted unchanged to the offspring. Thus a greyhound bitch of pure blood put to a mongrel, will produce puppies more nearly resembling her shape than that of the father.

4. Breeding in-and-in is not injurious to the dog, as may be proved both from theory and practice. Indeed it appears, on the contrary, to be very advantageous in many well-marked instances of the greyhound, which have of late years appeared in public.

5. As every dog is a compound animal, made up of a sire and dam, and also their sires and dams, etc.; so, unless there is much breeding in-and-in, it may be said that it is impossible to foretell with absolute certainty what particular result will be elicited.

6. The first impregnation appears to produce some effect upon the next and subsequent ones. It is therefore necessary to take care that the effect of the cross in question is not neutralized by a prior and bad impregnation. This fact has been so fully established by Sir John Sebright and others, that it is needless to go into its proofs.

By these general laws on the subject of breeding, we must be guided in the selection of the dog and bitch from which a litter is to be obtained, always taking care that both are as far as possible remarkable, not only for the bodily shape, but for the qualities of the brain and nervous system, which are desired. Thus, in breeding the pointer, select a good-looking sire and dam by all means, but also ascertain that they were good in the field; that is, that they possessed good noses, worked well, were stout, and if they were also perfectly broken, so much the better. So, again, in breeding hounds, care must be taken that the animals chosen are shaped as a hound should be; but they should also have as many of the good hunting qualities, and as few of the vices of that kind of dog; and if these points are not attended to, the result is not often good.

To secure these several results, the pedigrees of the dog and bitch are carefully scanned by those who are particular in these matters, because then assurance is given that the ancestors, as far as they can be traced, possessed all those qualifications, without which their owners would not in all human probability retain them. Hence a pointer, if proved to be descended from a dog and bitch belonging to Lord Sefton, Lord Lichfield, or any well-known breeder of this dog in the present day, or from Sir H. Goodrich, Mr. Moore or Mr. Edge, so celebrated for their breeds some years ago, would be valued more highly than another without any pedigree at all, though the latter might be superior in shape, and might perform equally well in the field. The importance of pedigree is becoming more fully recognized every year, and experienced breeders generally refuse to have anything to do with either dog or bitch for this particular purpose, unless they can trace the pedigree to ancestors belonging to parties who were known to be themselves careful in their selections. In most cases, this is all that is attempted, especially in pointers, setters, spaniels, etc., but in greyhounds and foxhounds of first-class blood, the genealogy may generally be traced through half a dozen kennels of known and established reputation; and this same attention to breed ought to prevail in all the varieties of the dog whose performances are of importance, and indeed without it the reproduction of a particular shape and make cannot with anything like certainty be depended on. Hence the breeders of the valuable toy dogs, such as King Charles spaniels, Italian greyhounds, etc., are as careful as they need be, having found out by experience that without this attention they are constantly disappointed.

IMPORTANCE OF HEALTH IN BOTH SIRE AND DAM.

Health in both parents should be especially insisted upon, and in the bitch in particular there should be a sufficiently strong constitution, to enable her to sustain the growth of her puppies before birth, and to produce milk enough for them afterwards, though in this last particular she may of course be assisted by a foster-nurse.

BEST AGE TO BREED FROM.

The best age to breed from, in almost all breeds, is soon after the sire and dam have reached maturity. When, however, the produce is desired to be very small, the older both animals are, the more likely this result is, excepting in the last litter which the bitch has, for this being composed of only one or two puppies, they are not smaller than the average, and are sometimes even larger. All bitches should be allowed to reach full maturity before they are permitted to breed, and this period varies according to size, small dogs being adult at one year, whereas large ones are still in their puppyhood at that time, and take fully twice as long to develop their proportions. The mastiff is barely full grown at two years, large hounds at a year and a half, greyhounds at the same time, pointers and setters from a year and a quarter to a year and a half, while terriers and small toy dogs reach maturity at a year old, or even earlier.

IN-AND-IN BREEDING.

The questions relating to in-and-in breeding and crossing are of the greatest importance, each plan being strongly advocated by some people, and by others as strenuously opposed. Like many other practices essentially good, in-breeding has been grossly abused. Owners of a good kennel having become bigoted to their own strain, and, from keeping to it exclusively, having at length reduced their dogs to a state of idiotcy and delicacy of constitution which has rendered them quite useless. Thus I have seen in the course of twenty years a most valuable breed of pointers, by a persistence in avoiding any cross, become so full of excitability that they were perpetually at "a false point," and backing one another at the same time without game near them; and, what is worse, they could not be stirred from their position. This last was from a want of mental capacity, for it is by their reasoning powers that these dogs find out when they have made a mistake, and without a good knowledge-box the pointer and setter are for this reason quite useless. But the breed I allude to, when once they had become stiff, were like Chinese idols, and must be absolutely kicked or whipped up in order to make them start off beating again. Mr. A. Graham, who has had a long experience in in-breeding greyhounds, and was at one time so successful as to obtain the name of the "Emperor of Coursers," has laid down the rule that "once in and twice out" is the proper extent to which breeding in the greyhound should be carried, and probably the same will apply to other breeds. Sometimes a sister may be put to a brother even, when there has been no previous relationship in their sire and dam; but though this has answered well two or three times, it is not to be generally recommended. A father may in preference be put to a daughter, because there is only half the same blood in them, when the sire and dam of the latter are not related; or an uncle to a niece; but the best plan is to obtain a dog which has some considerable portion of the same blood as the bitch, but separated by one or two crosses; that is to say, to put two animals together whose grandfathers or great-grandfathers were brothers, but whose mothers and grandmothers were not related to each other. This relationship will do equally well on the dam's side, and the grandmother may be sister to the grandsire, quite as well as having the two grandsires brothers. The practice of breeding-in to this extent has been extensively adopted of late years, and has answered well with the greyhound, in which breed, as used for public coursing, the names of "Harriet Wilson," "Hour-glass," "Screw," "Sparrowhawk," "Vraye Foy," "Motley," "Miss Hannah," and "Rival" speak volumes in its approbation, all being in-bred and all wonderfully successful. The last-named bitch is a remarkable instance, being by a half-brother out of a half-sister, and yet continuing honest up to her sixth season, when she broke a toe in running the last course but one in a large stake at Ashdown. In her case, too, the blood of the dam was somewhat notorious for a tendency to run cunning; and, indeed, the same might be said of nearly all the strains of which she was composed; nevertheless, throughout her career she was entirely free from this vice, and left off without a stain. She has, however, unfortunately refused to breed; but as I have never known this peculiarity confined to in-bred bitches, I do not allege the fact as arising from her close in-breeding. Thus I have shown that in practice, in-and-in breeding, within certain bounds, is not only not prejudicial, but absolutely advantageous, inasmuch as it does not injure the nervous temperament and mental qualities of the produce; and that the body does not suffer is a well-known fact, easily capable of proof by examining the external forms of the dogs so bred. Theoretically, also, it ought to answer, because we find in nature gregarious wild animals resorting to in-breeding in all cases, the stag adding his daughters to his harem as long as he has strength enough to beat off his younger rivals. In the same way the bull and the stallion fight for supremacy, until at length from age or accident they are beaten off, and a younger and more vigorous animal masters them and their female attendants. Yet this appears to be Nature's mode of insuring a superior stock, and preventing the degeneration which occurs among human beings, when a feeble pair take upon themselves the task of producing a family. It would appear that man is an exception to the general rule, for there is a special revelation prohibiting intermarriages, while we find them constantly going on among brutes, and especially, as above remarked, among gregarious animals. Hence it should not lead us to reason by analogy from one to the other, nor because we find that first cousins among our own race are apt to produce defective children, bodily and mentally, should we conclude that the same evil results will occur when we breed from dogs or horses having the same degree of relationship to their mates. At the same time, when all that can be desired is obtainable without in-breeding, I should be inclined to avoid it; always taking care to resort to it when it is desired to recover a particular strain, which is becoming merged in some other predominant blood. Then by obtaining an animal bred as purely as possible to the desired strain, and putting him or her to your own, it may be expected that the produce will "go back" to this particular ancestry, and will resemble them more than any other.

BEST TIME OF YEAR.

The best time of the year for breeding dogs is from April to September, inasmuch as in the cold of winter the puppies are apt to become chilled, whereby their growth is stopped, and some disease very often developed. Among public greyhounds there is a particular reason for selecting an earlier period of the year, because as their age is reckoned from the 1st of January, and as they are wanted to run as saplings or puppies, which are defined by their age, the earlier they are born, the more chance they have in competition with their fellows of the same year. Hounds and game dogs are wanted to begin work in the autumn, and as they do not come to maturity until after they are a year old, they should be whelped in the spring. This is more especially the case with pointers and setters, which are then old enough to have their education nearly completed at "pairing time," in the spring of the next year, when only their breaking can properly be carried on, as birds then lie like stones, and allow the dog to be reached and properly kept under by his breaker. Toy dogs and all small dogs, which are reared in the house, may be bred almost at any time of the year; but even they are stronger and healthier if born in the summer months, because the puppies may then be supposed to get more air and sun than they could do in the winter, when the warmth of the fire is essential to their well-doing.

DURATION OF HEAT.

The duration of the period of heat in the bitch is about three weeks, during the middle week of which she will generally take the dog; but about the eleventh or twelfth day from the first commencement is, on the average, the best time to bring her to him. During the first three or four days of the middle week the bitch "bleeds" considerably from the vulva, and while this is going on she should not have access to the male, nor will she generally, if left to herself. But as soon as it subsides, no time should be lost, as it often happens that very shortly afterwards she will refuse him altogether, and thus a whole year may be lost. Most bitches are "in heat" twice a year, at equal periods; some every five, or even every four, months; others every seven, eight, nine, ten, eleven, or twelve months; but the far greater proportion of bitches of all breeds are "in season" twice a year pretty regularly. There is, therefore, a necessity for ascertaining the rule in each bitch, as it varies so considerably; for, when it is known, the calculation can better be made as to the probability of the heat returning at the desired time. The period between the first and second "heats" will generally indicate the length of the succeeding ones; but this is not invariable, as the "putting by" of the animal will sometimes throw her out of her regular course.

MANAGEMENT OF THE BITCH IN SEASON.

When bitches are not intended to breed, they are carefully "put by," that is to say, they are secluded from the dog, and during that time they are in great measure deprived of their usual exercise. From this circumstance they are very apt to get out of health, and some injury is thereby done to their offspring as well as themselves. At this time, from their general feverishness, as well as from their deprivation of exercise, they ought to be kept rather lower than usual, and very little meat should be given. Slops and vegetables, mixed with biscuit or oatmeal, form the most suitable diet; but, if the bitch has been accustomed to a great deal of flesh, it will not do to deprive her of it altogether. Bearing in mind then this caution, it is only necessary to remember that she must be lowered in condition, but not so starved as to suffer by the sudden change. After the end of the period, a little cooling medicine will often be required, consisting of a dose of oil or salts.

MANAGEMENT OF THE BITCH IN WHELP.

When it is clearly ascertained that the bitch is in whelp, the exercise should be increased and carried on freely until the sixth week, after which it should be daily given, but with care to avoid strains either in galloping or jumping. A valuable bitch is often led during the last week, but some way or other she should have walking exercise to the last, by which in great measure all necessity for opening medicine will be avoided. During the last few weeks her food should be regulated by her condition, which must be raised if she is too low, or the reverse if she is too fat, the desired medium being such a state as is compatible with high health, and not tending towards exhaustion or inflammation. Excessive fat in a bitch not only interferes with the birth of the pups, but also is very liable to interfere with the secretion of milk, and, if this last does occur, it aggravates the attendant or "milk" fever. To know by the eye and hand how to fix upon this proper standard, it is only necessary to feel the ribs, when they should at once be apparent to the hand, rolling loosely under it, but not evident to the eye so as to count them. It is better to separate the bitch from other dogs during the last week or ten days, as she then becomes restless, and is instinctively and constantly looking for a place to whelp in, whereas, if she is prevented from occupying any desirable corner she is uneasy. At this time the food should be of a very sloppy nature, chiefly composed of broth, or milk and bread, adding oatmeal according to the state of the bowels.

PREPARATION FOR WHELPING.

The best mode of preparing a place for the bitch to whelp in is to nail a piece of old carpet over a smooth boarded floor, to a regular "bench," if in a sporting kennel; or on a door or other flat piece of board raised a few inches from the ground, if for any other breed. When a regular wooden box or kennel, as these are called in ordinary language, is used for the bitch, she may as well continue to occupy it, as she will be more contented than in a fresh place; but it is not so easy to get at her there if anything goes wrong with either mother or whelps, and on that account it is not a desirable place. A board, large or small, according to the size of the bitch, with a raised edge to prevent the puppies rolling off, and supported by bricks a few inches from the ground, is all that is required for the most valuable animal; and if a piece of carpet, as before mentioned, is tacked upon this, and some straw placed upon all, the hight of comfort is afforded to both mother and offspring. The use of the carpet is to allow the puppies to catch their claws in it as they are working at the mother's teats; for without it they slip over the board, and they are restless, and unable to fill themselves well; while at the same time they scratch all the straw away, and are left bare and cold.

HEALTHY PARTURITION.

During whelping, the only management required is in regard to food and quiet, which last should as far as possible be enjoined, as at this time all bitches are watchful and suspicious, and will destroy their young if they are at all interfered with, especially by strangers. While the process of labor is going on no food is required, unless it is delayed in an unnatural manner, when the necessary steps will be found described in the Third Book. After it is completed, some lukewarm gruel, made with half milk and half water, should be given, and repeated at intervals of two or three hours. Nothing cold is to be allowed for the first two or three days, unless it is in the hight of summer, when these precautions are unnecessary, as the ordinary temperature is generally between 60° and 70° of Fahrenheit. If milk is not easily had, broth will do nearly as well, thickening it with oatmeal, which should be well boiled in it. This food is continued until the secretion of milk is fully established, when a more generous diet is gradually to be allowed, consisting of sloppy food, together with an allowance of meat somewhat greater than that to which she has been accustomed. This last is the best rule, for it will be found that no other useful one can be given; those bitches which have been previously accustomed to a flesh diet sinking away if they do not have it at this time, when the demands of the puppies for milk drain the system considerably; and those which have not been used to it being rendered feverish and dyspeptic if they have an inordinate allowance of it. A bitch in good health, and neither over-reduced by starvation nor made too fat by excessive feeding, will rarely give any trouble at this time; but, in either of these conditions, it may happen that the secretion fails to be established. (For the proper remedies see Parturition, in Book III.) From the first day the bitch should be encouraged to leave her puppies twice or thrice daily to empty herself, which some, in their excessive fondness for their new charge, are apt to neglect. When the milk is thoroughly established, they should be regularly exercised for an hour a day, which increases the secretion of milk, and indeed will often bring it on. After the second week, bitches will always be delighted to leave their puppies for an hour or two at a time, and will exercise themselves if allowed to escape from them. The best food for a suckling bitch is strong broth, with a fair proportion of bread and flesh, or bread and milk, according to their habits.

DESTRUCTION OR CHOICE OF WHELPS AT BIRTH.

Sometimes it is desirable to destroy all the whelps as soon as possible after birth, but this ought very seldom to be done, as in all cases it is better to keep one or two sucking for a short time, to prevent milk fever, and from motives of humanity also. If, however, it is decided to destroy all at once, take them away as fast as they are born, leaving only one with the mother to engage her attention, and when all are born, remove the last before she has become used to it, by which plan less cruelty is practised than if she is permitted to attach herself to her offspring. Low diet and a dose or two of mild aperient medicine, with moderate exercise, will be required to guard against fever, but at best it is a bad business, and can only be justified under extraordinary circumstances.

CHAPTER II.

REARING.

MANAGEMENT IN THE NEST.—CHOOSING.—THE FOSTER NURSE.—FEEDING BEFORE WEANING.—CHOICE OF PLACE FOR WHELPING.—REMOVAL OF DEW-CLAWS, ETC.—WEANING. — LODGING. — FEEDING. — EXERCISE.— HOME REARING *v.* WALKING.—FOOD.—GENERAL MANAGEMENT.—CROPPING, BRANDING, AND ROUNDING.

THE MANAGEMENT OF WHELPS IN THE NEST.

Until weaned, the management of dogs does not require much care beyond the feeding of the mother, and the necessity for removing a part when the numbers are too great for her strength to support. For the first fortnight, at least, puppies are entirely dependent upon the milk of their dam or a foster-nurse, unless they are brought up by hand, which is a most troublesome office, and attended also with considerable risk. Sometimes, however, the bitch produces twelve, fourteen, or even sixteen whelps, and these being far beyond her powers to suckle properly, either the weak ones die off, or the whole are impoverished, and rendered small and puny. It is better, therefore, especially when size and strength are objects to the breeder, to destroy a part of the litter, when there are more than five or six in the greyhound, or seven or eight in the hound or other dog of that size. In toy dogs a small size is sometimes a desideratum, and with them, if the strength of the dam is equal to the drain, which it seldom is, almost any number may be kept on her. For the first three or four days, the bitch will be able to suckle her whole litter; but if there are more puppies than she has good teats, that is, teats with milk in them, the weak ones are starved, unless the strong ones are kept away in order to allow them access, so as to fill themselves in their turn. To manage this, a covered basket, lined with wool if the weather is at all cold, should be provided; and in this one-third or one-half of the puppies should be kept, close to the mother, to prevent either from being uneasy, with the lid fastened down or she will take them out in her mouth. Every two or three hours a fresh lot should be exchanged for those in the basket, first letting them fill themselves, when they will go to sleep and remain contented for the time fixed above, thus allowing each lot in its turn to fill itself regularly. At the end of ten days, by introducing a little sweetened cow's milk on the end of the finger into their mouths, and dipping their noses in a saucer containing it, they learn to lap. After this there will be little difficulty in rearing even a dozen; but they will not, however carefully they may be fed, be as large as if only a small number were left on her. Therefore greyhound breeders limit their litters to five, six, or at most seven; destroying the remainder, or rearing them with a foster-nurse.

CHOICE OF WHELPS.

In choosing the whelps in the nest which are to be kept, most people select on different principles, each having some peculiar crotchet to guide himself. Some take the heaviest, some the last born; others the longest of the litter; while others again are entirely guided by color. In toy dogs, and those whose appearance is an important element, color ought to be allowed all the weight it deserves, and among certain toy dogs, the value is often affected a hundred per cent, by a slight variation in the markings. So also among pointers and setters, a dog with a good deal of white should be preferred, on the score of greater utility in the field, to another self-colored puppy which might otherwise be superior in all respects. Hounds and greyhounds are however chosen for shape and make, and though this is not the same at birth as in after life, still there are certain indications which are not to be despised. Among these the shoulders are more visible than any others, and if on lifting up a puppy by the tail, he puts his forelegs back beyond his ears, it may be surmised that there will be no fault in his shape in reference to his fore quarter, supposing that his legs are well formed and his feet of the proper shape, which last point can hardly be ascertained at this time. The width of the hips, and shape of the chest, with the formation of the loin, may also be conjectured, and the length of the neck is in like measure shadowed forth, though not with the same certainty as the shoulders and ribs. A very fat puppy will look pudgy to an inexperienced eye, so that it is necessary to take this into consideration in making the selection; but fat is a sign of strength, both actual and constitutional, when it is remarkably permanent in one or two among a litter, for it can only be obtained either by depriving the others of their share of milk by main force, or through such constitutional vigor as to thrive better on the same share of aliment. The navel should be examined to ascertain if there is any rupture, and this alone is a reason for deferring the choice until nearly the end of the first week, up to which time there is no means of judging as to this defect. Indeed, if possible, it is always better to rear nearly all until after weaning, either on the dam herself or on a foster-nurse, as at that time the future shape is very manifest, and the consequences of weaning are shown, either in a wasting away of the whole body, or in a recovery from its effects in a short time. Sometimes, however, there are not conveniences for either, and then recourse must be had to an early choice on the principles indicated above.

THE FOSTER-NURSE.

The foster nurse need not be of the same breed as the puppies which she is to suckle; a smooth-skinned bitch is superior for the purpose to one with a rough coat, which is apt to harbor fleas, and in other ways conduces to the increase of dirt. For all large breeds the bull-terrier (which is most commonly kept among the class who alone are likely to sell the services of a nurse) answers as well as any other, and her milk is generally plentiful and good. For small breeds any little house dog will suffice, taking care that the skin is healthy, and that the constitution is not impaired by confinement or gross feeding. Greyhound puppies are very commonly reared by bull-bitches without any disadvantage, clearly proving the propriety of the plan. It may generally be reckoned, in fixing the number which a bitch can suckle with advantage, that, of greyhound or pointer puppies, for every seven pounds in her own weight the bitch can nurse one; so that an average bull-terrier will rear three, her weight being about twenty one pounds, and smaller dogs in proportion. When the substitution is to be made, the plan is to proceed as follows:—Get a warm basket, put in it some of the litter in which the bitch and her whelps have been lying, then take away all her own progeny, and put all in the basket, together with the whelps to be fostered, mixing them so that the skins of the fresh ones shall be in contact with the bitch's own pups, and also with the litter. Let them remain in this way for three hours, during which time the bitch should be taken out for an hour's walk, when her teats will have become painfully distended with milk. Then put all the pups in her nest, and, carefully watching her, let her go back to them. In ninety-nine cases out of a hundred, she will at once allow them all to suck quietly, and if she licks all alike, she may be left with them safely enough; but if she passes the fresh ones over, pushing them one side, she should be muzzled for twelve hours, leaving all with her, and keeping the muzzle on excepting while she is fed, or watched until she is observed to lick all alike. On the next day, all but one of her own puppies may be withdrawn, with an interval of one hour or two between each two, taking care that she does not see what is done. After two days the last may also be taken away, and then she acts to her foster-puppies in every way the same as to her own. Some people squeeze a little of the bitch's milk out of her teats, and rub this over the puppies, but I have never seen any advantage in the plan, and, as I have never had any difficulty in getting puppies adopted, I do not recommend any other than that I have described. In most cases the foster-bitch is strange to those about her, having been brought from her own home, and in that case a muzzle is often required for the safety of the servants watching her as well as for the whelps; but if she seems quiet and good tempered, it may be dispensed with.

FEEDING BEFORE WEANING.

The food of whelps before weaning should be confined at first to cow's milk, or, if this is very rich, reduced with a little water. It is better to boil it, and sweeten it with a little fine sugar, as for the human palate. As much of this as the whelps will take may be given them three times a day, or every four hours, if they are a large litter. In the fourth week get a sheep's head, boil it in a quart of water until the meat comes completely to pieces, then carefully take away every particle of bone, and break up the meat into fragments no larger than a small horse-bean; mix all with the broth, thicken this to the consistence of cream with fine wheat flour, boil for a quarter of an hour, then cool and give alternately with the milk. At this time the milk may also be thickened with flour; and as the puppies grow, and the milk of the bitch decreases in quantity, the amount of milk and thickened broth must be increased each day, as well as more frequently given. Some art, founded on experience, is required not to satiate the puppies; but, by carefully increasing the quantity whenever the pups have finished it greedily the last time or two, they will not be overdone. In no case should the pan containing the food be left in the intervals with the puppies, if they have not cleared it out, as they only become disgusted with it, and the next time refuse to feed. A sheep's head will serve a litter of large-sized puppies two days up to weaning, more or less, according to numbers and age.

CHOICE OF PLACE FOR WHELPING.

The whelping-place, up to the third week, may be confined to a square yard or two, floored with board as already described.

After the third week, when the puppies begin to run about, access should be given them to a larger run, and an inclined plane should be arranged for them to get up and down from their boarded stage. If the weather is cold, the best place for a bitch to whelp is in a saddle-room warmed by a stove, or an empty stall, with a two-foot board placed across the bottom, opposite the stall-post, so as to prevent the puppies getting among the horses. In either case there is 'an amount of artificial heat, which conduces to the growth of the puppies, and allows them to be reared sufficiently strong to bear any cold afterwards with impunity. If the weather is not cold, an ordinary horse-box is the best place which can be chosen, fixing the boarded stage at a distance from the door, and either sanding or slightly littering the brick floor, according to the weather; but the latter is to be preferred, excepting in a very hot summer. In these boxes puppies take a vast amount of exercise, which they require for health, and to give that appetite without which sufficient food for growth is not taken.

REMOVAL OF DEW-CLAWS, ETC.

Before weaning, any cropping which is intended, whether of the dew-claw or tail, should be practised, but the ears should be left alone until the third or fourth month, as they are not sufficiently developed before. If, however, the operator does not understand his business thoroughly, it is better to leave the latter organs alone, until a later period, as otherwise the proper quantity may not be cropped or rounded, as the case may be. Indeed, ever the most skillful hand will hardly ever manage either the one or the other well before the fifth month; and in hounds it is usual to defer it until they are nearly full grown, as they often lose a considerable quantity of blood, which interferes with their growth. But the tail and dew-claws may always be best done, and with least pain, while with the dam; besides which, her tongue serves to heal the wound better than that of the young puppy, who has hardly learned to use it. Regular dog-fanciers bite off the tail, but a pair of scissors answers equally well; and the same may be said of the dew-claw. If, however, the nail only is to be removed, which always ought to be done, the teeth serve the purpose of a pair of nippers, and by their aid it may be drawn out, leaving the claw itself attached, but rendered less liable to injury, from having lost the part likely to catch hold of any projecting body.

WEANING.

When weaning is to be commenced, which is usually about the fifth or sixth week, it is better to remove the puppies altogether, than to let the bitch go on suckling them at long intervals. By this time their claws and teeth have become so sharp and so long, that they punish the bitch terribly, and therefore she does not let them fill their bellies. Her milk generally accumulates in her teats, and becomes stale, in which state it is not fit for the whelps, and by many is supposed to encourage worms. The puppies have always learned to lap, and will eat meat, or take broth or thickened milk, as previously described; besides which, when they have no chance of sucking presented to them, they take other food better, whereas, if they are allowed to suck away at empty teats, they only fill themselves with wind, and then lose their appetites for food of any kind. But, having determined to wean them, there are several important particulars which must be attended to, or the result will be a failure, at all events for some time. That is to say, the puppies will fall away in flesh, and will cease to grow at the same rate as before. In almost all cases, what is called the " milk-fat " disappears after weaning, but still it is desirable to keep some flesh on their bones, and this can only be done by attending to the following directions, which apply to dogs of all kinds, but are seldom rigidly carried out, except with the greyhound, whose size and strength are so important as to call for every care to procure them in a high degree. In hounds, as well as pointers and setters, a check in the growth is of just as much consequence; but as they are not tested together as to their speed and stoutness so closely as greyhounds are, the slight defects produced in puppyhood are not detected, and, as a consequence, the same attention is not paid. Nevertheless, as most of these points require only care, and cost little beyond it, they ought to be carried out almost as strictly in the kennels of the foxhound and pointer as in those devoted to the longtails. These chief and cardinal elements of success are,—1st, a warm, clean, and dry lodging; 2ndly, suitable food; 3rdly, regularity in feeding; and, 4thly, a provision for sufficient exercise.

NECESSITY FOR WARM AND DRY LODGING.

All puppies require a dry lodging, and in the winter season it should also be a warm one. Greyhound whelps, up to their third or fourth month, are sometimes reared in an artificial temperature, either by means of a stove, or by using the heat of a stable, the temperature chosen being 60° of Fahrenheit. Beyond this age, it can never be necessary to adopt artificial heat in rearing puppies, because for public coursing they are required to be whelped after the last day of the year, and four months from that time takes us on to May, when the weather is seldom cold enough to require a stove; then during the summer months they are gradually hardened to the vicissitudes of the weather, and as they become older their growth is established, and they are no longer in danger of its being checked. It is true that some few breeders always keep their kennels at 60°; but on the whole, as we shall hereafter find, the plan is not a good one, and need not be considered here. But far beyond the warmth, dryness is essential to success. Dogs will bear almost any amount of cold if unaccompanied by damp, provided they have plenty of straw to lie in; but a damp kennel, even if warm, is sure to lead to rickets or rheumatism, if the puppies escape inflammation of some one or more of the internal organs. Take care, therefore, to give a dry bedstead of boards, lined with the same material towards the wall (the cold of which strikes inwardly and gives cold), and raised somewhat from the floor, which will otherwise keep it damp. Puppies soon learn to lie on this, and avoid the cold stones or bricks, except in the heats of summer, when these do no harm. The stone or brick floor should be so made as to avoid absorption of the urine, etc., which can only be effected by employing glazed tiles or bricks that are not porous, or by covering the whole with a layer of hydraulic cement, or with asphalt, which answers nearly as well. Care should be taken that there are no interstices between the boards, if the kennel is made of them; and in every way, while ventilation is provided, cold draughts must be prevented. Cleanliness must also be attended to rigidly by sweeping out the floor daily, and washing it down at short intervals, and by changing the litter once a week at the least. In the summer time, straw is not desirable, as it harbors fleas, and, if the boarded floor is not considered sufficient, a thick layer of pine sawdust will be the best material, as it is soft enough, without harboring vermin of any kind; the only objection to it being that the puppies are apt to wet it often, after which it becomes offensive.

FEEDING.

The feeding of puppies is all important, and, unless they have plenty of food sufficiently nourishing to allow of a proper growth, it is impossible that they should become what they might be if fed with the best materials for the purpose. From the time of weaning to the end of the third month, when a decision must be arrived at, as to their subsequent management, very little deviation is required from the plans described on page 191; that is, the puppies should be fed every four hours upon the thickened broth made from sheep's head, and thickened milk alternately. After that time, however, their food must be given them rather stronger and of a somewhat different nature, as we shall find in its proper place. This food will be required for any kind of dog, but a single puppy may very well be reared upon thickened milk, with the scraps of the house in addition, including bones, which it will greedily pick, and any odds and ends which are left on the plates.

Regularity of feeding in puppies, as in adult animals, is of the utmost importance; and it will always be found that if two puppies are equally well reared in other respects, and one fed at regular hours, while the other is only supplied at the caprice of servants, the former will excel the latter in size and health, as well as in the symmetrical development of the body. It is also very necessary to avoid leaving any part of one meal in the pans or feeding-troughs until the next, as nothing disgusts the dog mo.e than seeing food left in this way. The moment the puppies fill themselves, take away the surplus; and, indeed, it is better still to anticipate them by stopping them before they have quite done. All this requires considerable tact and experience, and there are very few servants who are able and willing to carry out these directions fully.

EXERCISE.

Exercise is necessary at all ages, but the fully developed dog may be confined for some little time without permanent injury, the formation of his feet and the texture of his bones and muscles being then finally settled. On the other hand, the puppy will grow according to the demand made upon his mechanism, and if the muscles are left idle they do not enlarge; while the feet remain thin and weak, with the tendons and ligaments relaxed, so that they spread out like a human hand. Growing puppies should be provided with an area sufficiently large for them to play in, according to their size, and under cover up to the end of the third month; after which, if they have a sheltered sleeping-place to run into, they will generally avoid heavy rain. Young puppies play sufficiently in a loose box or similar enclosure; but, after the time specified above, they must either have their entire liberty, or be allowed the run of a larger space, the alternative being bad feet, defective development, and weak joints.

HOME REARING *VERSUS* WALKING.

When one or two puppies only are to be reared, they may be readily brought up at home, excepting in towns or other confined situations, where due liberty and a proper amount of sun and air can not be obtained. But where a larger number are to be reared, as in the case of hounds, greyhounds, pointers, and setters, etc., there is a difficulty attending upon numbers, as a dozen or two of puppies about the house are not conducive to the neatness and beauty of the garden; besides which, the collection together in masses of young dogs is prejudicial to their health. To avoid this evil, therefore, it is customary to send puppies out at three or four months of age to be kept by cottagers, butchers, small farmers, etc., at a weekly sum for each, which is called "walking" them. Young greyhounds may be reared in a large enclosure, which should be not less than thirty or forty feet long, with a lodging-house at one end; but hounds do not take exercise enough in a confined space, and should invariably be sent out. It is only, therefore, in reference to the rearing of greyhounds that the two plans can be compared, or perhaps also with pointers and setters, if they are taken out to exercise after they are four or five months old.

The two plans have been extensively tried with the longtails, and in my own opinion the preference should be given to the home rearing if properly carried out, because it has all the advantages of the "walk" without those disadvantages attending upon it, in the shape of bad habits acquired in chasing poultry, rabbits, and often hares, during which the puppy learns to run cunning. One of the first symptoms of this vice is the waiting to cut off a corner, which is soon learned if there is the necessity for it, and even in mutual play the puppy will often develop it. Hence I have seen a "walked" greyhound, with his very first hare, show as much waiting as any old worn-out runner, evidently acquired in his farm yard education, or possibly from having been tempted after a hare or two by the sheep-dog belonging to the farm. Moreover, the home-reared puppy, being confined in a limited space during the greater part of his time, is inclined to gallop when first let out, and takes in this way more exercise than those brought up on the other plan; so that, after considering both methods, I have come to the conclusion that the home rearing is preferable on the whole, though there is no doubt that good dogs may be reared in either way.

The best plan is to fence off a long slip of grass; or, if a small walled enclosure can be procured, fence off about a yard or two all round, by which last plan an excellent gallop is secured, without the possibility of cutting corners, and with a very slight loss of ground. An admirable plan is to build four large sleeping rooms in a square block, and then all round this let there be a run two yards wide, which may be separated into four divisions, or thrown into one at will. If the latter, the puppies will exercise themselves well round and round the building, which is a practice they are very fond of; and, even if two or more lots are wanted to occupy the compartments, the whole can be thrown open to each lot in turn. When this plan is adopted, the run should be paved, so that the expense is much greater than in the other mode, in which the natural soil is allowable, because the puppies are not kept on it long enough to stain it.

THE FOOD OF PUPPIES AT HOME OR "AT WALK," AND ITS PROPER PREPARATION.

Whether at home or out, puppies require the same kind of food, and the more regularly this is given as to quantity and quality, as well as the times of feeding them, the more healthy they will be, and the faster they will grow. Many people consider milk to be by far the best article of food for growing puppies, and undoubtedly it is a good one, but it is not superior to a mixed diet of meal and animal food in proper proportions, and occasionally varied by the addition of green vegetables. Indeed, after three months, or at most four, puppies may be fed like grown dogs as to the quality of their food, requiring it however to be given them more frequently the younger they are. Up to six months they require it three times a day, at equal intervals, and after that age twice; for although there is a difference of opinion as to the propriety of feeding the adult once or twice a day, there is none about the puppy demanding a supply morning and evening. In all cases, they should be encouraged to empty themselves (by allowing a run, if they are confined to kennel) just before feeding, and for an hour or two afterwards they are best at rest. If milk is given, it may be thickened by boiling in it oatmeal or wheat-flour, or both together, or biscuits may be scalded and added to it; but no flesh is needed in addition, bones only being required to amuse the dog and to clean his teeth by gnawing them. With these any dog may be reared very well, but the plan is an expensive one, if the milk has any thing like the ordinary value attached to it, and if it has to be purchased, the cost is generally quite prohibitory of its use.

Besides milk, various other articles are employed in feeding dogs. Of these, Indian meal is by far the best in proportion to its price (being quite equal to anything but the very best wheat-flour, which is perhaps slightly more nourishing), and, being so much cheaper, is, on that account, to be preferred. It requires to be mixed with oatmeal, in about equal proportions, or less of the latter if the bowels are at all relaxed. Oatmeal is considerably dearer, though the grain itself is cheaper; but the quantity of meal obtained, owing to the amount of chaff, is so small, that when this is got rid of the meal is necessarily sold at a higher price, according to the season. But a much larger bulk of thick stuff, commonly called "puddings," is produced by oatmeal than can be obtained from any other meal in proportion to weight, the absorption of water being greater, and also varying in different qualities of oatmeal itself; so that, after all, this meal is not so expensive as it looks to be, when comparing an equal weight of it with barley or Indian meal. The real coarse Scotch oatmeal yields the greatest bulk of puddings, and is to be preferred on that account; besides which, it appears to agree best with dogs, and altogether is a very superior article; but in any case it ought to be nearly a year old. It may therefore be considered that me 1 or oatmeal is the best meal, unless the price of wheat-flour can be afforded, when the best red wheat should be coarsely ground and not bolted, and in this state made into biscuits or dumplings, or used to thicken the broth.

If corn meal is employed, it must be mixed with the water or broth while cold, and then boiled for at least an hour, stirring it occasionally to prevent burning. If it is intended to mix oatmeal with the corn meal, the former may be first mixed with cold water to a paste, and then stirred in after boiling the latter for three quarters of an hour; then boil another quarter, reckoning from the time that the contents of the copper came to the boiling point a second time.

Wheat-flour should be boiled from fifteen to twenty minutes, and may be mixed with the oatmeal in the same way as the corn meal.

Oatmeal pudding, and porridge, or stirabout, are made as follows: the first name being given to it when so thick as to bear the weight of the body after it is cold, and, the last two to a somewhat thinner composition. In any case the meal is stirred up with cold water to a thick paste, and, when quite smooth, some of the broth should be ladled out and added to it, still stirring it steadily. Then return the whole to the boiler, and stir until it thickens, ladle out into coolers, and let it "set," when it can be cut with a spade and is quite solid. The directions as to the length of time for the boiling of oatmeal vary a good deal, some preferring at least half an hour's boil, while others are content with ten or fifteen minutes, but for most purposes from a quarter to half an hour is the proper time, remembering that this is to be reckoned from the moment that the water boils.

The animal food used should be carefully selected to avoid infectious diseases, and the flesh of those creatures which have been loaded with drugs should also be avoided. Horseflesh, if death has been caused by accident, is as good as anything, and in many cases of rapid disease the flesh is little the worse, but though in foxhound kennels there is little choice, yet for greyhounds those horses which have been much drugged for lingering diseases, and those also which are much emaciated, are likely to do more harm than good. Slipped calves and lambs, as well as beef and mutton, the result of death from natural causes, make an excellent change, but are seldom better than bad horseflesh. Still, as variety is essential to success in rearing, they should not be rejected. Whatever this kind of food is composed of, it should be boiled, with the exception of paunches, which may be given raw, but even they are better boiled, and I think an occasional meal of well-kept horseflesh is rather a good change. The flesh with the bones should be boiled for hours, until the meat is thoroughly done; then take it out and let it hang until cold; cut or strip it from the bones and mix with the puddings or stirabout according to the quantity required. The broth should always be used, as there are important elements of nutrition dissolved in it, which are absent in the boiled flesh. It is therefore necessary to make the puddings or stirabout with it, or to soak in it the biscuit, when this is the food selected. The bones should be given for the dogs to gnaw, together with any others from the house which can be obtained, but taking care to remove all fragments small enough for them to swallow whole. Bones should be given on grass or clean flags

The comparative value of the various articles of diet enumerated according to the authority of Liebig, is as follows:

The proportions in		Materials used for making muscle, bone. etc.	Materials used in respiration, or in forming fat.
		Parts.	Parts.
Cow's milk	are	as 10	to 30
Fat mutton	"	10	27 to 45
Lean mutton	"	10	19
Lean beef	"	10	17
Lean horseflesh	"	10	15
Hare and rabbit	"	10	2 to 5
Wheat-flour	"	10	46
Oatmeal	"	10	50
Barley meal	"	10	57
Potatoes	"	10	86 to 115
Rice	"	10	153

From this high authority it appears that barley-meal is superior both to wheat-flour and oatmal in fat-making materials, but it is greatly inferior in muscle-making power, and hence, in dogs where fat is not required, it is of inferior value. Science and practical experiment here go hand in hand, as they always do when the former is based upon true premises. In cow's milk, which is the natural food of the young of the Mammalia, the proportion is 30 to 10, and this seems to be about what is required in mixing the animal and vegetable food. Now by adding equal weights of wheatmeal and lean horseflesh, we obtain exactly the same proportions within the merest trifle; thus—

    Wheat-flour............................ 10   46
    Horseflesh............................. 10   15
                                            20   61

being equal to 10 of muscle-making to $30\frac{1}{2}$ of fat-making matter; and this is practically the proportion of animal food to meal which best suits the dog's stomach and general system. The reader is not to suppose that a dog is to be fed on equal parts of cooked meat and pudding, but of raw meat and dry meal, which when both are boiled would, by the loss of juice in the flesh and the absorption of water in the meal, become converted into about two quantities by weight of pudding to one of cooked meat. Even this proportion of flesh is a large one for growing dogs which have not much exercise, but those which are "at walk" or which have their liberty in any situation will bear it. Most people prefer a much smaller proportion of meat, especially for hounds, pointers, setters, and spaniels, which depend on their nose, this organ being supposed to be rendered less delicate by high feeding. From long experience in this matter, however, I am satisfied that, while the health is maintained in a perfect state, there is no occasion to fear the loss of nose, and that such may be avoided with the above diet I am confident from actual practice. At the same time it must not be forgotten that all dogs so fed require a great supply of green vegetables, which should be given once or twice a week during the summer, without which they become heated, and throw out an eruption as a proof of it, the nose also being hot and dry.

Green cabbage, turnip tops, turnips, nettle-tops, or carrots, as well as potatoes, may all be given with advantage boiled and mixed with the meal and broth, in which way they are much relished.

Scraps, bought at the provision stores, and consisting of the refuse of the fat melted to make tallow, are a very common article for flavoring the meal of sporting dogs of all kinds. Beyond this they have little value, but they certainly afford some degree of nourishment, and are not altogether to be despised. They are boiled in water first until soft, and then mixed with the meal to form the stirabout or pudding. With oatmeal they form a good food enough for pointers and setters, as they are not so heating as flesh.

The quantity by weight which is required by the growing puppy daily of such food as the above, is from a twelfth to one-twentieth of the weight of its body, varying with the rapidity of growth, and a good deal with the breed also. Thus a 12 lb. dog will take from five-eighths of a pound to a pound, and a 36 lb. dog from two pounds to three pounds. When they arrive at full growth, more than the smaller of these weights is very seldom wanted, and it may be taken as the average weight of food of this kind for all dogs in tolerably active exercise.

GENERAL TREATMENT.

During the whole time of growth, the only general management required is, first, a habit of obedience, the dog being taught his kennel name, to follow at heel, and to lead. Some breeds require more than this; as, for instance, the pointer and setter, which will be mentioned under the head of breaking. Secondly, secure cleanliness in all respects, the kennel being kept scrupulously clean by washing the floor, and at least once a year lime-washing the walls, while the skins are freed from any vermin which may be found by the means described in the Third Book. In the summer a straw bed is seldom required, but in the winter it must be given for the sake of warmth, and changed once or twice a week.

Physic is not needed as a regular practice, if feeding is conducted on the above plan, and the exercise is sufficient; but if the puppies are dull, a dose of castor oil occasionally will do good.

CHOICE OF PUPPIES AFTER WEANING THEM.

Puppies of all kinds vary in form so much between the weaning time and the period of full growth, that there is great difficulty in making a choice which shall be proved by subsequent events to be on reliable grounds. All young animals grow by fits and starts, the proportions varying with the stage of development in which any part is at the time of examination. Thus at the fourth month a puppy may look too long, but during the next month he may have grown so much in the legs that he no longer looks so. Again, another may be all legs and wings in the middle of his growth, but he may finally grow down to a strong, low, and muscular dog. So also with the fore and hind quarters, they may grow alternately, and one month the fore quarter may be low, and the next the hind. None but an experienced eye therefore can pretend to foresee, after the period of weaning, what will be the final shape; but either soon after that time, or a day or two after birth, a pretty good guess may be given, subject to the continuation of health, and to proper rearing in all respects. Bad feet can soon be detected, but the limbs grow into a good shape after most extraordinary deviations from the line of beauty, particularly in the greyhound, which is often apparently deformed in his joints when half grown. The most unwieldy-looking animals often "fine" down into the best shapes, and should not be carelessly rejected without the fiat being pronounced by a breeder of experience.

CROPPING, BRANDING, AND ROUNDING.

If terriers are to be cropped, the beginning or end of the fourth month is the best time for this; and, before sending out to walk,

CROPPING, BRANDING, AND ROUNDING.

hounds are branded with the initials of the master or of the hunt, a hot iron shaped like the letter itself being used. Both cropping and rounding require practice to perform them well, a large sharp pair of scissors being used, and care being necessary to hold the two layers of skin in the ear in their natural position, to prevent the one rolling on the other, and thus leaving one larger than the other Foxhounds have so much work in covert that rounding is imperatively called for to prevent the ears from being torn, and it always has been adopted as a universal practice, different huntsmen varying in the quantity removed. Some people after cutting one ear lay the piece removed on the other, and so mark exactly the amount which is to be removed from it; but this is a clumsy expedient, and, if the eye is not good enough to direct the hand without this measurement, the operation will seldom be effected to the satisfaction of the owner of the dog. It is usual to round foxhound puppies after they come in from their walks; but it would be far better to perform the operation before their return, as it only makes them more sulky and unhappy than they otherwise would be, and is a poor introduction to their new masters. The men could easily go around to the different walks during the summer, and it would insure a supervision which is often required.

CHAPTER III.

KENNELS AND KENNEL MANAGEMENT.

GREYHOUND KENNELS.—FOXHOUND KENNELS.—POINTER KENNELS.—KEN-
NELS FOR SINGLE DOGS.—HOUSE DOGS.

Between the kennels intended for the various kinds of dogs, and the methods of management therein, some considerable difference exists, though the same principles are adopted throughout. Thus, packs of foxhounds are often kept to the number of 80 or even 100 couples, and these must be managed rather differently from the three or four brace of greyhounds or pointers, which usually constitute the extent of each of these kinds in one man's possession, or at all events in the building. Besides this, foxhounds are much more exposed to the weather than greyhounds, which are usually clothed out of doors, and otherwise protected by dog-carts, etc. The former therefore must be hardened to the duties they have to perform, while the latter may be brought out in more vigorous health, and with their speed very highly developed, but at the same time in so delicate a condition as to be liable to take cold if allowed to remain in the rain for any length of time. Hence it will be necessary to describe the kennels for greyhounds, hounds, pointers, etc., separately.

GREYHOUND KENNELS.

Every kennel intended for greyhounds should be thoroughly protected from the weather, and should have the yard covered in as well as the lodging-house. The plan for the kennel intended to rear puppies in is also best adapted for their future keeping, and this it will be desirable to describe more fully here.

The central square, comprised between the four angles $a\ b\ c\ d$, is divided into four lodging-houses, having a ventilating shaft in the middle, with which they all communicate. These are filled with benches separated by low partitions as shown in the diagram, and raised about a foot from the ground. Each opens into a yard, with a door of communication so arranged as to be left partly open without allowing the slightest draught to blow upon the beds. These yards, *ab, bc, cd, da*, are all roofed in, and bounded on the outer side by pickets guarded by coarse wire net, to prevent the teeth of the inmates gnawing them. They are separated by narrow partitions, which slide up to allow of the dogs having the whole

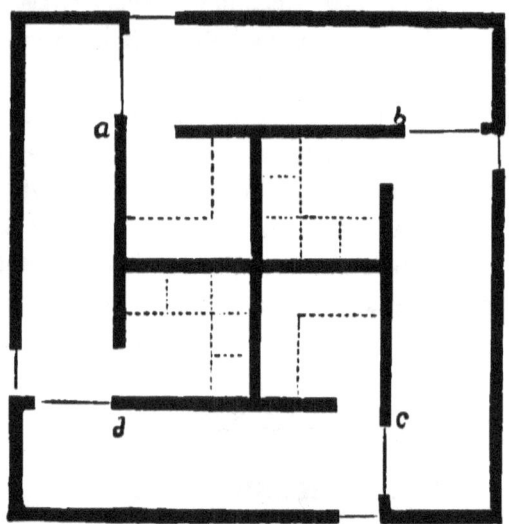

Fig. 39.—PLAN OF KENNEL.

run; or they may be left down, and the upper part open, so as to encourage the puppies to fence, by the necessity for jumping over them, in pursuing one another. The floors should be of glazed tiles, bricks, or cement, the last being the most clean and free from absorption, which ought always to be entirely prevented. Each sleeping-place and yard should have a trapped drain, so as to carry off any wet directly it falls, and the former should be built exteriorly of brick cemented at least a foot from the ground, with board partitions between. A window should be in each, which is capable of being opened, and the ventilation should be secured in some satisfactory manner. This always ensures a down-current as well as an up-current, so that there is little or no necessity for having the door open except for cleanliness, but in very windy weather the ventilation on the side of the wind should be closed, or the down-draught will be enough to chill the greyhounds. As these kennels are to be paved with a non-porous material, the soil is not of much consequence, but the situation should be dry and healthy, and the shade of a large tree is to be obtained if possible.

The kennel management of the greyhound consists in little more

Fig. 40.—ELEVATION OF KENNEL.

than the adoption of cleanliness, which should be of the most scrupulous kind, together with regular feeding. Water is by some people constantly left for them to get at, but others object to it for dogs in training, and they then only give it with the food. My own opinion is decidedly in favor of the constant supply, as it is impossible to prevent these animals from getting to it when at exercise; and I am sure that, when they are kept from it in-doors, they take too much while they are out. On the contrary, if it is regularly supplied to them, they take very little, and are quite careless about it at all times.

FOXHOUND AND HARRIER KENNELS, ETC.

Unlike the greyhound kennel in many respects, that which we are now considering must be adopted for from thirty to a hundred couples of hounds, and the accommodation should therefore be more extensive, while a less degree of protection from the weather is desirable, because these hounds must be constantly exposed to long-continued wind and wet, and should therefore be hardened to them.

The kennel should be placed upon some high and dry situation; the building should face the south, and there should be no large trees near it.

Nothing is more prejudicial to hounds than damp lodging-rooms, a sure cause of rheumatism and mange, to which dogs are peculiarly liable. I have seen them affected by rheumatism in various ways, and totally incapacitated from working. Sometimes they are attacked in the loins, but more often in the shoulders, both proceeding either from a damp situation, damp lodging-room, or damp straw, often combined with the abuse of mercury in the shape of physic. In building kennels, therefore, the earth should be removed from the lodging-room floor to the depth of a foot at least, and in its place broken stones, sifted gravel, or cinders, should be substituted, with a layer of fine coal-ashes, upon which the brick floor is to be laid, in cement or hot coal-ash mortar, taking care to use bricks which are not porous, or to cover them with a layer of cement, which last is an admirable plan. Outside and close to the walls, an air-drain about three feet deep should be constructed with a draining pipe of two inch-bore at the bottom, and filled with broken stones to within six inches of the surface. This drain is to be carried quite round the building, and should fall into the main drain. For a roof to the building, I prefer shingles to tiles as affording more warmth in winter and coolness in summer; but as slate or tiles are more agreeable to the eye, a thin layer of paper placed under the tiles will answer the purpose.

Over the center of the lodging-rooms should be a sleeping-apart-ment for the feeder, which being raised above the level of the other roof, will break the monotony of its appearance. At the rear of the kennel there should be the boiling-house, feeding-court, straw-house, and separate lodgings for bitches. In front of the kennels, and extending round to the back door of the feeding-house, there should be a good large green yard enclosed by a wall or pickets. I prefer the former, although more expensive, because hounds, being able to see through the latter, will be excited by passing objects; and young hounds, for whose service the green yard is more particularly intended, are inclined to become noisy, barking and running round the fence when any strange dog makes his appearance.

In the boiling-house two cast-iron boilers will be required, one for the meal, the other for flesh. Pure water must be conducted in some way to the kennels, both for cleanliness and for the preparation of food, and this should be placed at the service of the kennel-man at all parts, so that there may be no excuse on the score of trouble in carrying it. There must also be coolers fixed in proportion to the number of hounds, each couple requiring from half a foot to a foot superficial, according as it is intended to make the puddings daily or every other day. Stone or iron feeding and water-troughs are the best; the latter should be fixed high enough to keep them clean.

To each lodging-room there should be two doors; one at the back with a small sliding panel, and high up, through which the huntsman may observe the hounds without their seeing him; and another in the front with a large opening cut at the bottom, high enough and wide enough for a hound to pass through easily, and which should always be left open at night to allow free egress to the court. In addition, there must also be another between each of the rooms, so as to throw two into one in the summer for the purpose of making them more airy. The benches should be of pine or oak spars, and if they are made to turn up according to the following plan several advantages result. This plan is described by a recent authority as follows:

KENNEL BENCHES.

"My benches are made of inch pine, cut into widths of three inches, and nailed half an inch apart to two transverse pieces, to which hinges are fixed to connect the bench with a board six inches wide, fastened firmly to the wall about a foot from the ground. In front is a piece of board about three inches in width, to keep the straw from drawing off with the hounds. To prevent the hounds from creeping under, I nail two long laths the length of the bench across in front of the legs, which are hung with

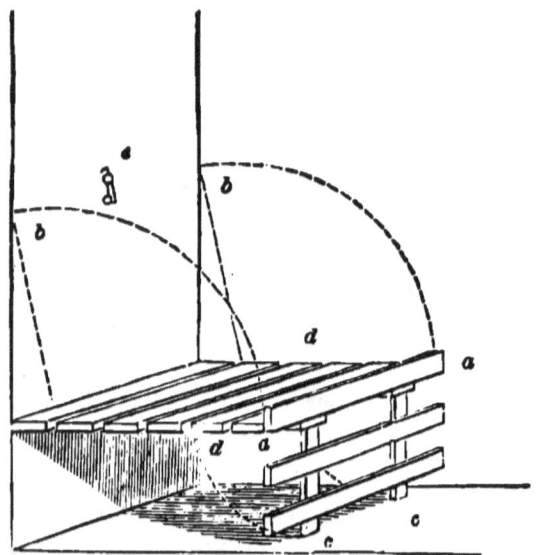

Fig 41.—BENCH FOR A KENNEL.—*a a* folds to *b b*, *c c* folds to *d d*, *e*, hook to fasten bench back.

hinges in front of the bench, so that when the bench is hooked back they fall down and hang flat. By having the six-inch board between the hinges and the wall, it prevents the former from being strained when the bench is hooked back with straw upon it."

In some establishments there is a separate kennel for the young hounds, with a grass yard attached, for their own use, and it is certainly very advantageous; but with a little management the buildings above recommended will be sufficient, and with a saving of considerable expense. The hounds during the hunting season will not require it at all, as they should be walked out several times a day into a paddock or field, and should not be allowed to lie about anywhere but on their benches.

In the rear of the kennels there should be a covered passage into which the doors of the middle kennel can open, and leading to the feeding-house, which stands under the same roof as the boiling-house, only separated from it by a partition. This passage

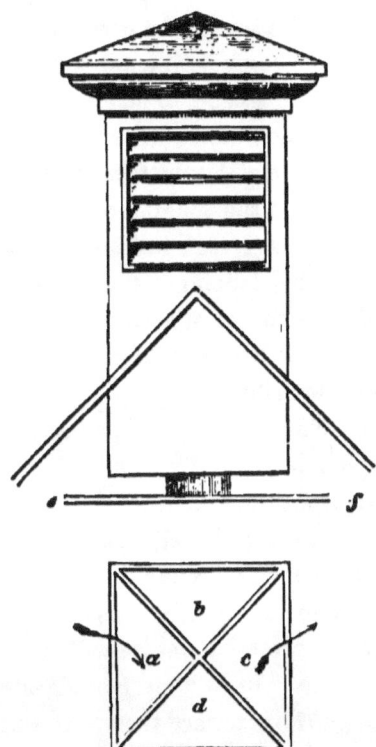

Fig. 42.—VENTILATING SHAFT.—a, b, c, d, the four divisions of shaft; e, f, board for distributing down current.

should be so constructed as to make a foot-bath for the hounds as they pass through after hunting, the bricks being gradually sloped from each end to the center, where it should be a foot deep, with a plugged drain in the lowest part, to let the hot liquor or water off into a drain. On each side of this passage there should be a paved court with a small lodging-house at each end; one for lame hounds, and the other for those which are sick.

The ventilation of the rooms composing the lodgings of the hounds must be carefully attended to, and for this purpose the shaft shown at fig. 42 is especially well adapted. It resembles in external appearance that usually placed above well-constructed stables, etc.; but there is this important internal alteration, that the square is divided perpendicularly into four triangular tubes, one of which is sure to be presented to the wind from whatever quarter of the compass it is blowing, while the opposite one allows the foul air to escape, to make room for that descending through the first-named tube. When this is once constructed, it only remains to lead a metal tube from each of these four compartments to every one of the lodging-rooms, which will thus be as effectually ventilated as if each had an apparatus to itself. To carry this out well, the lodging-rooms should be in a block, and then there will be a corner of each meeting in a common center, above which the ventilator should be placed with the arrangement of tubes above described.

The kennel management of hounds is a much more difficult and important affair than is generally supposed, as upon its proper performance, in great measure, depends the obedience of the pack in the field. Sometimes it is entirely committed to the care of the feeder, but every huntsman who knows his business will take as much pains with his hounds in kennel as out, and though he will not, of course, prepare the food, yet he will take care to superintend it, and will always "draw" his hounds himself, for no one else can possibly know how to feed them. During the season, this duty must of necessity devolve on the feeder or kennel-man on the hunting days, but the huntsman should always carry it out himself whenever he can. Hounds can not be too fond of their huntsman, and though "cupboard love" is not to be encouraged in man, yet it is at the bottom of most of that which is exhibited by the dog, however much it may appear to take a higher range when once it has been properly developed.

The regular daily kennel discipline is as follows: With the four lodging-rooms described there should always be two dry and clean in the early morning, having been washed the day before. Into these the general pack should be turned, as soon as the doors are opened, or, if the morning is not wet, directly after a short airing in the paddock. The feeder then sweeps out the room in which they have slept, and afterwards mops it clean, drying the floor as much as possible, so that by ten or eleven o'clock it is fit for the hounds to re-enter. The men then get their breakfast, and directly afterwards the hounds are taken out to exercise, or the hunting hounds to their regular day's work. If the former, they are brought back to kennel at eleven o'clock, fed, and returned to their regular lodging-room, or in some kennels they are still kept in a separate room during the day and night, always taking care that they are not turned into a room while the floor is damp, and that strict cleanliness is practised nevertheless. The hour of feeding is generally fixed for eleven o'clock, but for the day before hunting it should be an hour or two later, varying with the distance they have to travel. Water should be constantly provided, taking care that the troughs are raised above the hight at which dogs can pass their urine into it, which they will otherwise be constantly doing. As before remarked, iron troughs are the best. After feeding, the hounds should remain quiet for the rest of the day. Only stir them in removing them from their day-room to their night-room, if two are allowed, which, I think, is an excellent practice.

The food of hounds is composed of meal flavored with broth, to which more or less flesh is added, or with scraps as a substitute when flesh cannot be obtained. The relative value of the various meals is described at page 201, but I may here remark that old oatmeal is the recognized food of hounds, though corn meal is an excellent substitute. After boiling the flesh until the meat readily leaves the bones, take all out with a pitchfork, and put it to cool, skim all the fat off the broth, and fill up with water to the proper quantity; next mix the meal carefully with cold water, and then pour this into the hot broth, keeping it constantly stirred until it thickens; after which it is to be boiled very gently until it has been on the fire for half an hour, continuing the stirring to prevent its burning. Lastly, draw the fire, and ladle out the stuff into the coolers, where it remains until it has set, when it acquires the name with the solidity of "puddings." There should always be two qualities made, one better than the other for the more delicate hounds, which must be apportioned by the huntsman properly among them. This may be reduced with cold broth, when wanted, to any degree of thinness; and the meat, being cut or torn up, is mixed with it.

In feeding the hounds, the huntsman, having the troughs supplied with the different qualities of food, orders the door to be thrown open which communicates with the lodging-room; then, having the hounds under proper control, they all wait until each is called by name, the huntsman pronouncing each name in a decided tone, and generally summoning two or three couple at a time, one after the other. When these have had what he considers sufficient, they are dismissed and others called in their turn; the gross feeders being kept to the last, when the best and most nourishing part has been eaten. By thus accustoming hounds in kennel to wait their proper turn, and to come when called, a control is obtained out of doors which could never be accomplished in any other way. Once a week, on a non-hunting day in the winter, and every three or four days in the summer, some green food, or potatoes or turnips, should be boiled with the puddings. They serve to cool the hounds very considerably. If this is attended to, very little physic is required, except from accidental causes.

A regular dressing and physicing is practised in some kennels, the former to keep the skin free from vermin and eruptions, and the latter with the same view, but also to cool the blood. This is by no means necessary, if great care is taken with regard to cleanliness, feeding, and exercise; and in the royal kennels neither one nor the other is practised, excepting when disease actually appears, and not as a preventive measure. When it is considered desirable to adopt either or both, directions for their use will be found given in the next Book.

POINTERS AND SETTERS.

These dogs do not require a covered yard, and may be treated in all respects like hounds, the only difference being in regard to numbers. More than three or four brace should not be kept together if it can be avoided, as they are apt to quarrel when not thoroughly exercised or worked, and then a whole lot will fall upon one and tear him almost to pieces. The rules of cleanliness, feeding, etc., are the same as for hounds.

SINGLE DOGS KENNELLED OUT OF DOORS.

Where a single dog is kept chained to what is called a kennel, care should be taken to pave the ground on which he lies, unless he can be moved every month, or still more frequently, as in course of time his urine stains the ground so much as to produce disease. It should always be borne in mind that the dog requires more exercise than he can take when chained, and he should therefore be set at liberty for an hour or two daily, or at all events every other day.

HOUSE DOGS.

The great bane of dogs at liberty to run through the house is that they are constantly receiving bits from their kitchen, as well as from their parlor, friends. The dog's stomach is peculiarly unfitted for this increasing demand upon it, and, if the practice is adopted, it is sure to end in disease before many years are passed. The rule should be strictly enforced, to avoid feeding more than once or twice daily, at regular hours, and then the quantity and quality should be proportioned to the size of the dog and to the amount of exercise which he takes. About one-twentieth to one-twelfth of the weight of the dog is the proper amount of food, and all beyond this is improper in most cases, though of course there are some exceptions. Dogs are very cleanly animals, and often refuse to dirty a carpet or even a clean floor. They should therefore be turned out at proper times to relieve themselves. To neglect to do this is cruel, as well as injurious to the health. I have known dogs retain their excretions for days together, rather than expose themselves to the anger which they think they should incur, and I believe some high-couraged animals would almost die before they would make a mess. Long-haired dogs, when confined to the house, are apt to smell disagreeably if they have much flesh, and they should therefore be chiefly fed upon oatmeal porridge, with very little flavoring of broth or meat mixed with it.

CHAPTER IV.

BREAKING AND ENTERING

THE ENTERING OF THE GREYHOUND AND DEERHOUND.—OF FOXHOUNDS AND HARRIERS.—BREAKING THE POINTER AND SETTER.—THE RETRIEVER (LAND AND WATER).—THE SPANIEL.—THE VERMIN DOG.

With the exception of the greyhound, sporting dogs require some considerable education for the sport in which they are to be engaged. Unlike the hound and the dogs intended for the gun, greyhounds have only their instinctive desires to be developed, and as no restraint is at any time placed upon these, except that depending upon mechanical means which they cannot get rid of, nature has uncontrolled sway. Hence their entering is a very easy process; nevertheless, there are some precautions to be taken which it is necessary to describe. The deerhound, as well as the greyhound, is held in slips, a single one being used for him, and a double slip, or pair of slips as it is called, for the two greyhounds which form the complement for coursing the hare—a greater number being considered unfair, and therefore unsportsmanlike. These slips are so made that by pulling a string the neck-strap is loosed, and the two dogs are let go exactly at the same moment. They are always used in public coursing, but in private the greyhounds are sometimes suffered to run loose, waiting for the moment when the hare is put up by the beaters or by the spaniels, which are occasionally employed. Hounds also are coupled under certain circumstances, but they are never slipped at the moment when game is on foot, and they must therefore be made steady from "riot."

THE ENTERING OF THE GREYHOUND AND DEERHOUND.

Whether for public or private coursing, the greyhound should not be suffered to course a hare until he is nearly at maturity; but as the bitches come to their growth before the dogs, they may be entered earlier than the latter. About the tenth month is the best time for forward bitches, and the twelfth or fourteenth for dogs. If therefore a greyhound is to be allowed to see a hare or two at this age, he or she must be bred early in the year, in order to have a brace late in the spring, so as to be ready for the next season. Some people invariably prefer keeping them on to the autumn, and for private coursing there is no reason whatever for beginning so early; but public coursers begin to run their dogs in puppy stakes in the month of October, prior to which there is so little time after the summer is passed, that they prefer beginning in the spring if their dogs are old enough, and if they are not they will not be fit to bring out in October.

Before being entered the dogs must be taught to lead quietly, as they cannot be brought on to the ground loose; if not previously accustomed to it, they knock about and tear themselves dreadfully, and moreover will not go quietly in slips. As soon therefore as the ground is soft, after they are six or eight months old, they should have a neck-strap put on, and should be led about for a short time daily, until they follow quietly. Some puppies are very violent, and fight against the strap for a long time, but by a little tact they soon give in, and follow their leader without resistance. The coursing-field is the best school for this purpose, as the puppies have something to engage their attention, and until they will bear their straps without pulling against them, their education in this respect is not complete. A dog pulling in slips will do himself so much harm as often to cause the loss of a course, and therefore every precaution should be taken to avoid this fault. The leader should never pull against the puppy steadily, but the moment he finds him beginning to hang forward, give him a severe check with the strap, and repeat it as often as necessary. It is a very common defect, but never ought to occur with proper management; though when once established the habit is very difficult to break. Two or three days' leading on the coursing-field will serve to make any puppies handy to lead if properly managed, and they may then be put in slips with perfect safety.

The condition of the puppy at the time of entering, is too often neglected. It should be known that a fat over-fed puppy without previous exercise may be seriously injured even by a short course, which, moreover, can never be assured under any circumstances, as the hare will sometimes run in a different direction to that which is expected.

A sapling, as the young greyhound is called to the end of the first season after he is whelped, should never be trained like an old one, as the work is too severe, and his frame is not calculated to bear it, but he may be reduced in flesh by light feeding, and allowed to gallop at liberty for two or three hours a day. With these precautions, he will be fit to encounter any hare in a short course, which is all that should ever be permitted.

Whether an old assistant or a young one shall be put down with a sapling is a subject which admits of some discussion. If the former, the young dog has small chance of getting to work at all, and if the latter, he may have so little assistance as to be greatly distressed. Few people like to put down an honest old dog with a sapling, and a cunning one soon teaches the tricks which he himself displays. Sometimes young dogs have great difficulty in killing, and want the encouragement afforded by blood; in such cases a good killer may be desirable, but with no other object could I ever put down an old dog with a sapling. Before they are going to run in a stake, an old dog of known speed should be put in slips with the puppy, in order to arrive at a knowledge of the powers of the latter; but this is with a view to a trial, and not as part of the entering of the greyhound. When a sapling has run enough hares to know his work, and has killed a hare, or been present at the death of one, he may be put by as properly entered; and the number required will average about five or six—more or less according to the capability of the particular animal, which will generally depend upon his breed.

The deerhound is entered at his game on the same principles as the greyhound. It is always better to slip him with an older companion, but beyond this precaution everything must be left to his natural sagacity. As his nose is to be brought into play, and as he may possibly cross the scent of hares or other game, he must be made steady from all "riot," and, if possible, should be taken up, in couples, to the death of a deer once or twice and "blooded," so as to make him understand the nature of the scent. His instinctive fondness for it will, however, generally serve him without this, but the precaution is a good one, and may save some trouble and risk. He will not do much in aid of his older companion in hunting the animal he is slipped at, but when "at bay" he is soon encouraged by example to go in and afford his help, and this is the time when a second deerhound is chiefly wanted.

THE ENTERING OF FOXHOUNDS AND HARRIERS.

The first thing to be done with hound puppies, when they come into kennel, is to get them used to their new masters and to their names, which ought to have been given them "at walk." For some little time the puppy often refuses to be reconciled to its confinement in his new home, and sulks by himself in a corner, refusing to eat and to follow his feeder or huntsman. This, however, soon goes off; but until it does there is no use in attempting to do anything with the dog. When the puppies are quite at home, they may be taken out by the feeder, at first in couples, and then by degrees removing these and allowing them to run free. For some time it will be prudent to take only six or seven couples at a time, as when any "riot" makes its appearance there is enough to do even with this number, and more would be quite unmanageable. Indeed the huntsman will do well to take out only a couple or two at a time into the paddock with him, until they are thoroughly accustomed to his voice, and have found out that he must be obeyed. As soon as they are tractable on the road, they may be walked among sheep and deer, where they should at first all be in couples, and then only one or two should be loosed at a time; but before long, the whole pack should be accustomed to resist the temptation, until which time they are unfit to be entered. It is also highly necessary that foxhounds should in the same way be broken from hare and rabbit; but too much must not be attempted with them until they are entered to fox, as their spirit and dash would be discouraged, if the whip or scold were always being used without the counter-cheer in favor of some kind of game.

All hounds require daily exercise, without which they cannot be preserved in health, nor can their high spirits be controlled, for, if they are not exercised, they will always be requiring the whip. If, however, the huntsman takes them out daily in the morning on the road, which hardens their feet, and in the evening in the paddock, they are so orderly that anything may be done with them. For this purpose the men should be mounted in the morning, but in the evening they may be on foot.

Cub-hunting, which is the name given to the process by which young hounds are entered, begins in August as soon as the wheat is cut, and the time will therefore vary with the season and the country. In some places it may be carried on at any time, but this month is early enough. It is better to take out the old hounds once or twice, until they have recovered their summer idleness, as a good example is everything to a young hound. When the young entry are to be brought out, it is very desirable to find as quickly as possible, and some cautious huntsmen go so far as to keep them coupled until the old hounds have found their fox; but if they have been made steady from "riot" there is no occasion for this. If, however, they have never been rated for "riot," there is no great harm in their hunting hare or anything else at first, until they know what they ought to do; after which they must be rigidly kept to their game. But cub-hunting is not solely intended to break in and "enter" the hound. It has also for its object to disperse the foxes from the large woodlands which form their chief holds in all countries. Independently of the above object cub-hunting is practised in August, September, and October, first, in order to give the young hounds blood, which they can obtain easily from a litter of fat cubs; secondly, to break them from "riot," while they are encouraged to hunt their own game; and, thirdly, to endeavor to break them of sundry faults, such as skirting, etc.; or, if apparently incurable, to draft them at once.

These objects are generally attained by the end of October, when the regular season begins.

Harriers and beagles are entered to hare on the same principle, the scent of the fox and deer, as well as that of the rabbit, being "riot" to them, and strictly prohibited. Otterhounds also have exactly the same kind of entry, although the element they work in is of a different character.

THE BREAKING OF THE POINTER AND SETTER.

The following observations on the breaking of these dogs are believed to embody the general practice of good breakers: As the method is the same for each kind, whenever the word pointer is used, it is to be understood as applying equally to the setter.

It is scarcely necessary for me to remark that no single life would suffice to bring the art of breaking dogs to all the perfection of which it is capable, when the various improvements of succeeding generations are handed down from one to the other; and therefore I neither pretend to be the inventor of any method here detailed, nor do I claim any peculiarity as my own. All the plans of teaching the young dog that will be found described by me are practised by most good breakers; so that there will be nothing to be met with in my remarks but what is well known to them. Nevertheless, they are not generally known; and there are many good shots who are now entirely dependent upon dog-dealers for the supply of their kennels, and who yet would infinitely prefer to break their own dogs, if they only knew how to set about it. Others, again, cannot afford the large sum which a highly accomplished brace of pointers or setters are worth in the market; and these gentlemen would far rather obtain two or three good puppies and break them with their own hands, with expenditure of little more than time, than put up with the wretchedly broken animals which are offered for sale by the dozen at the commencement of every shooting season. To make the utmost of any dog requires great experience and tact, and therefore the ordinary sportsman, however ardent he may be, can scarcely expect his dogs to attain this amount of perfection; but by attending to the following instructions, which will be given in plain language, he may fairly hope to turn out a brace of dogs far above the average of those belonging to his neighbors. One advantage he will assuredly have when he begins the actual war against the birds in September; namely, that his dogs will cheerfully work for him, and will be obedient to his orders; but at the same time he must not expect that they will behave as well then as they did when he considered their education complete in the previous April or May. No one who values "the bag" above the performance of his dogs will take a young pointer into the field at all, until he has been shot over for some time by a man who makes it his business to break dogs, and who is not himself over-excited by the sport. It is astonishing what a difference is seen in the behavior of the young dog when he begins to see game falling to the gun. He may go out with all the steadiness which he had acquired by two months' drilling in the spring; but more frequently he will have forgotten all about it, unless he is well hunted in the week previous to the opening of the campaign. But no sooner has he found his birds or backed his fellow-pointer, and this good behavior has been followed by the report of the gun, heard now almost for the first time, and by the fall of a bird or two within a short distance, than he becomes wild with excitement, and, trying to rival the gun in destructiveness, he runs in to his birds, or plays some other trick almost equally worthy of punishment. For this there is no remedy but patience and plenty of hard work, as we shall presently find. I only mention it here, in order that my readers may not undertake the task without knowing all the disagreeable as well as agreeable things attending upon it.

Assuming, therefore, that a gentleman has determined to break a brace of pointers for his own use, without assistance from a keeper, let us now consider how he should set about it.

In the first place, let him procure his puppies of a breed in which he can have confidence. He will do well to secure a brace and a half, to guard against accidents or defects in growth. Let these be well reared up to the end of January, or, in fact, until the birds are paired and will lie well, whatever that time may be. They should be fed as has been previously directed. A few bones should be given daily, but little flesh, as the nose is certainly injuriously affected by this kind of food. Without attention to his health, so as to give the dog every chance of finding his game, it is useless to attempt to break him. The puppies should either be reared at full liberty at a good walk, or they should have an airy yard. They should also be walked out daily, taking care to make them know their names at a very early age, and teaching them instant obedience to every order, without breaking their spirit. Here great patience and tact are required; but, when the owner walks them out himself two or three times a week and makes them fond of him, a little severity has no injurious effect. In crossing fields the puppies should never be allowed to "break fence," even if the gates are open, and should be called back the moment they attempt to do so. These points are of great importance, and by attending to them, half the difficulty of breaking is gotten over; for, if the puppy is early taught obedience, you have only to let him know what he is required to do, and he does it as a matter of course. So also the master should accustom his puppies from the earliest age to place a restraint upon their appetites when ordered to do so; and if he will provide himself with pieces of biscuit and will place them within reach of the dog, while he prevents his taking them by the voice only, he will greatly further the object he has in view. Many breakers carry this practice so far as to place a dainty morsel on the ground before the dog when hungry, and use the word "Toho" to restrain him; but this, though perhaps afterward useful when inclined to run in upon game, is by no means an unmixed good, as the desire for game in a well-bred dog is much greater than the appetite for food, unless the stomach has long been deprived of it.

Besides these lessons prior to breaking, it will be well to teach the dog to come to heel, and too keep there, also to run forward at the word of command; to lie down when ordered, and to remain down. All these several orders should be accompanied by the appropriate words afterwards used in the field, viz.

WORDS OF COMMAND USED TO THE POINTER AND SETTER.

1. To avoid breaking fence—"Ware fence."
2. To come back from chasing cats, poultry, hares, etc.—"Ware chase."
3. To come to heel, and remain there—"To heel," or "Heel."
4. To gallop forward—"Hold up."
5. To lie down—"Down," or "Down charge."
6. To abstain from taking food placed near, equally applied to running in to birds—"Toho."

When these orders are cheerfully and instantly complied with by the puppy, it will be time to take him into the field, but not until then. Many breakers during this period accustom their dogs to the report of the gun, by firing a pistol occasionally while they are a short distance off, and in a way so as not to alarm them. This is all very well, and may prevent all danger of a dog becoming "shy of the gun;" but with a well-bred puppy, properly reared, and not confined so much as to make him shy in other respects, such a fault will seldom occur. Nevertheless, as it does sometimes show itself, from some cause or other, the above precaution, as it costs little trouble or expense, is not to be objected to. It is also advantageous to accustom the dog to drop when the pistol is discharged, and, if he is of high courage, he may be drilled to this so effectually that he never forgets it. By the aid of a "check cord," wherever the dog be, when the pistol is discharged, he is suddenly brought up and made to drop with the command "Down charge;" and in process of time he associates one with the other, so that whenever he hears a gun he drops in an instant. Timid dogs may however be made shy in this way, and unless the puppy is evidently of high courage, it is a dangerous expedient to resort to; as, instead of making the dog, it may mar him forever.

Next comes the teaching to "range," which is about the most difficult part of breaking. Many sportsmen who have shot all their lives are not aware of the extent to which this may be, and indeed ought to be, carried; and are quite content if their dogs "potter" about where they like, and find game anyhow. But the real lover of the dog, who understands his capabilities, knows that for perfect ranging the whole field ought to be beaten systematically, and in such a way as to reach all parts in succession—the dog being always as near to the gun as is consistent with the nature of the ground, the walking powers of the man, and the degree of wildness of the game. All these varying points of detail in the management of the dog while beating his ground will, however, be considered more in detail hereafter; so that at present, taking it for granted that what I have assumed is the real desideratum, we will proceed to inquire how this mode of ranging is best taught. It must be understood that what we want is,—first, that the puppy should hunt freely, which soon comes if he is well bred; secondly, that he should range only where he is ordered, and that he should always be on the look-out for his master's hand or whistle to direct him. This also is greatly dependent on breed, some dogs being naturally wilful, while others from their birth are dependent upon their master, and readily do what they are desired. Thirdly, great pains must be taken to keep the puppy from depending upon any other dog and following him in his line, and also from "pottering," or dwelling on "the foot-scent," which, again, is a great deal owing to defective blood. Now, then, how are these points to be attained? By a reference to the annexed diagram, the principle upon which two dogs should beat their ground is laid down; the dotted line representing the beat of one, and the plain line that of the other dog. But, with a raw puppy, it is useless to expect him to go off to the right while his fellow proceeds to the left, as they afterwards must do if they perform their duty properly. But, taking an old dog into a field with the puppy, the former is started off with the ordinary words "Hold up" in either line laid down, which, being properly broken, he proceeds to follow out, accompanied by the puppy, who does not at all understand what he is about. Presently the old dog "finds," and very probably the young one goes on and puts up the birds, to the intense disgust of his elder companion, but to his own great delight, as shown by his appreciation of the scent, and by chasing his game until out of sight. At the present stage of breaking, the puppy should by no means be checked for

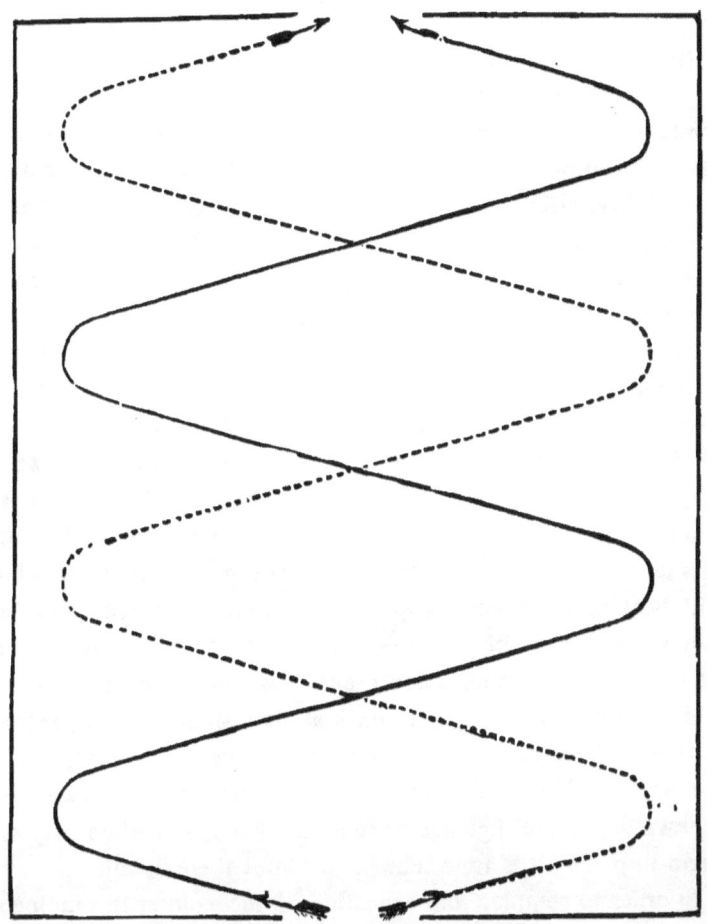

Fig. 43.—PLAN OF QUARTERING GROUND.

this, as he knows no better, and the great object is to give him zest for the work, not to make him dislike it; so that, even if he runs in to half a dozen pairs of birds, it will do him no harm, however jealous it may make the old dog. As soon, however, as the young one seems decidedly inclined to go to work by himself, take up the old dog, and hunt the young one until he is thoroughly tired or until he begins to point. At first, when he comes upon a scent, he will stop in a hesitating way, then draw rapidly up and flush his birds, chasing them as before; but gradually, as he tires, he gains steadiness, and, after a time, he assumes the firm attitude of the true pointer or setter, though this is seldom shown in perfection for the first two or three days. Let it be clearly understood, that the present lesson is solely with a view to teach the range; steadiness in the point, being at first quite subordinate to this quality, although, in well-bred dogs, it may often be taught at the same time. Hundreds of puppies are irretrievably spoiled by attempting, to begin with teaching them to stand, when, by undue hardship and severity, their relish for hunting or beating the ground is destroyed; and they are never made to do this part of the work well, although their noses are good enough when they come upon game, and they stand for a week if allowed to do so. Keep to the one object until the puppy will beat his ground as shown in the diagram, at first single-handed, and then crossing it with another dog. It seldom answers to use two together until steadiness at "the point" is attained, as there are few old dogs which will beat their ground properly, together, when they find that they are worked with a young one which is constantly flushing his birds or committing some other *faux pas*. For these reasons it is better to work the young ones at first singly, that is, as soon as they will work; and then—after they range freely and work to the hand and whistle, turning to the right or left, forwards or backwards, at the slightest wave of the hand, and when they also begin to point—it is time enough to "hunt them double."

In order to complete the education of the pointer in ranging or beating his ground, it is not only necessary that he should "quarter" it, as it is called, but that he should do it with every advantage of the wind, and also without losing time by dwelling on a false scent, and, above all, avoiding such careless work as to put up game without standing to a point at all. I have before explained the principle upon which a field is to be "quartered," and described the way in which the dog is to be set to do his work, by the hand and voice, aided by the whistle. As a general rule, pointers find their game by the scent being blown to them from the body, constituting what is called a "body-scent," and not from that left by the foot on the ground, which is called a "foot-scent." Hence it is desirable in all cases to give the dog the wind, that is to say, to beat up towards the "wind's eye;" and, therefore, the breaker will put his dogs to work in that direction, and then, though they do not always beat directly towards the wind, yet they have it blowing from the game towards them in each of their crossings. (See diagram on page 228.) But suppose, as sometimes happens, that the sportsman can not well do this, as when birds are likely to be on the edge of a manor, with the wind blowing on to it from that over which he has no right of shooting; here, if he gave his dog the wind in the usual way, he would drive all the birds off his own beat; and, to avoid this, he begins at the edge of it, and makes his pointers (if they are well enough broken) leave him, and go up the other side to the far end of the field (if not too long), and then beat towards him in the usual way. It is true that the necessity for this kind of beating does not often occur; but sometimes a considerable number of shots are lost for want of teaching it, and the perfect dog should understand it thoroughly. When, therefore, the puppy has learned to range in the ordinary way, and will work to the hand well, as before described, give him a lesson in this kind of beating; and, if any difficulty occurs, send a boy to lead him until he is far enough away, and then let the biped loose his charge, first catching the dog's eye yourself, so as to make him aware that you are the person he is to range to. In a few lessons, he soon begins to find out the object of this departure from the usual plan, and by a little perseverance he will, of his own accord, when he finds he has not got the wind, work so as to make a circuit, and get it for himself. Nevertheless, a good dog, who has a master as good as himself, should always wait for orders, and there is always some excuse for very clever ones becoming headstrong when they are constantly misdirected. Let me again repeat what I have observed on the importance of teaching, at first, the correct mode of quartering the ground, and of persevering (without regard to standing or pointing) in the lessons on this subject alone, until the puppy is tolerably perfect in them. At the same time, it is true that some little attention may be paid to the " point ;" but this of far less consequence at the early stage which we are now considering. Indeed, in most well-bred dogs, it comes naturally; but none beat to the hand without an education in that particular department.

But at this stage it will frequently be necessary to correct various faults which are apt to show themselves in young dogs, such as (1) " hunting too low," leading to " pottering or dwelling on the foot-

Fig. 44.—" PUZZLE PEG."

scent ;" (2) hunting too wide from the breaker; and (3) " blinking," or leaving the game as soon as found, which last is a fault depending on undue previous severity. With regard to the first of them, there is, unfortunately, no certain remedy for it; and the puppy which shows it to any great extent after a week or ten days' breaking will seldom be good for much, in spite of all the skill and training which an experienced breaker can apply. The method of cure most commonly adopted is that called hunting with a " puzzle-peg," which is shown in the annexed cut. It consists of a piece of strong wood, such as ash or oak, attached to the neck by a leather collar, and to the jaw by a string tied just behind the tusks or canine teeth, so as to constitute a firm projection in continuation of the lower jaw; and, as it extends from six to nine inches beyond it, the dog cannot put his nose nearer to the ground than that amount of projection will allow of. The young dog should be well accustomed to it in kennel and in the field, before he is hunted in it; for when it is put on for the first time it inevitably "cows" him so much as to stop all disposition to range; but by putting it on him for an hour or two daily while he is at liberty and not expected to hunt, he soon becomes tolerably reconciled to it, and will set off on his range when ordered or allowed. With it on, a foot-scent can seldom be made out, unless pretty strong; but, at all events, the dog does not stoop to make it out in that spaniel-like style which occasions its adoption. Nevertheless, when it is left off, the old tendency to stoop most frequently reappears, more or less, and the sportsman finds that all his care has been thrown away. Still I have known it to cure this fault, and if it fails I have no other suggestion to offer but sixpennyworth of cord or "a hole in the water." If used at all, it must be kept on for many days together, that is to say, while at work, and when left off it should be occasionally reapplied if the dog shows the slightest tendency to put his nose down, or dwell on the scent where birds have been rising or have "gone away." I may here remark that "false pointing" is altogether different from this low hunting, though often coupled with it; but this we shall come to after describing the nature of, and mode of teaching, that part of the pointer's education. There is a wonderful faculty in some breeds of discovering a body-scent at long distances, while they have no perception of the foot-scent, and this is the quality which ought to be most highly prized in the pointer or setter, unless he is also wanted to retrieve in which latter case, such a nose will be found to be defective. Bu. of this also we shall come to a closer understanding in a fu ture part of this volume. In addition to the use of the "puzzle-peg,"—which should only be resorted to in extreme cases, and even then, as I before remarked, it is of doubtful utility,—the voice should be used to cheer the dog when he dwells on the scent too long, or carries his nose too low. "Hold up!" may be cried in a cheering way, and the dog encouraged with the hand waved forward as well. Colonel Hutchinson recommends the previous inculcation of the perception of hight,—in fact, to make the dog understand that you mean, when you use the word "Up," that he should raise his head. But this is a refinement in dog-breaking which possibly may be carried out, yet which, I confess, I think practically inoperative. Few of us would like to teach our hacks to lift their knees, by giving them to understand the nature of hight, and then telling them to lift them. We should certainly find it much more simple to select hacks with good action, or to breed them even, rather than to convert our colt-breakers into circus-men. If there is no other method of attaining the object, by all means adopt it; but, when a far easier one is at hand, I should certainly select it in preference. Nevertheless, it may serve to prove the teachableness of the dog; and, knowing the extent to which his education may be carried by patience and preseverance, I have no doubt that Colonel Hutchinson's plan is capable of execution, if the time and trouble necessary for it are properly remunerated. But we must now proceed to the second fault, which consists in ranging too far from the breaker. This may readily be cured, either by compelling attention to the hand and voice, with the aid of the whip in bad cases; or by attaching to the dog's collar a long cord, which is then suffered to trail on the ground, or is held in the hand of the breaker, when the dog is very wild. Twenty, thirty, or at most forty, yards of a small box-cord will suffice for this purpose, and will soon tire down the strongest and most unruly dog. Indeed, an application of it for a short time will make many dogs give in entirely; but some high-couraged ones, and setters especially, will persevere with it on until they are fairly exhausted. This "check-cord," as it is called, is also necessary in some dogs, to perfect their education in other respects, and, indeed, is chiefly wanted at a later period of breaking, not being often required at this stage.

Having described the mode of teaching pointers and setters to beat their ground, I have now to consider the best modes of teaching them (1) to point, set, or stand (which are different names for the same act), (2) to back, (3) to down charge, (4) to retrieve, if considered desirable, and (5) how to remedy certain faults, such as blinking, etc.

Pointing, setting, or standing can be readily taught. It will, of course, be discovered in practice that, in teaching the range, most dogs begin to point, and nineteen out of twenty, if well-bred, become steady enough without the gun, before they are perfect in the proper mode of beating their ground. For these, then, it is unnecessary to describe any other means of teaching their trade; but there are some few exceptions, in which, even after a fortnight's work, the dog is still deficient in this essential, and, though he beats his ground in ever so perfect a manner and finds his birds well enough, yet he invariably runs them up, sometimes with great zest and impudent disregard of his breaker, and at others with evident fear of the consequences. Here, then, something more must be done, and it is effected by taking the young dog out with a steady companion and hunting them together; then, keeping the old dog within forty yards, let him, if possible, be the one to find, and take care to walk up to him before the young one comes up, which he is sure to do as soon as he catches his eye on the point. Now use your voice in a severe but low tone to stop him; and, as he has been accustomed to halt with the word "Toho!" he will at once do so, generally standing in a cautious attitude, at a distance varying with his fear of his breaker and the amount of courage which he possesses. If the birds lie close, let him draw up and get the scent. The excitement will then be so great, that, if the dog is under sufficient command to be held in check by the "Toho!" he will be sure to assume the rigid condition, characteristic of his breed. Now go quietly up to him, pat him, and encourage him, but in such a tone as to prevent his running in,—still using the "Toho! good dog, toho!"—and keeping him for a few minutes where he is, so long as he can scent his birds, which he shows by champing and frothing at the mouth. After the lapse of this time, walk quietly forward, keeping your eye on him, and still restraining him with the "Toho," put up the birds, and then, if possible, make him drop with the words "Down charge!" the meaning of which he has already been taught. But, if he is very wild and of high courage, do not attempt this at first, as it is better to proceed step by step, and to teach each lesson thoroughly before another is commenced. In this way, by perseverance and hard work (which last is the keystone of the breaker's arch), any dog, whether of the special breeds used for the purpose or not, may be made to point when he finds game; but none but the pointer and setter become rigid or cataleptic, a peculiarity which is confined to them. In very high-couraged dogs, a check-cord, thirty or forty yards in length, is sometimes suffered to trail on the ground, or is held by the breaker, so as to assist the voice in stopping the dog when he is wanted to make his stand; but the cases where this is wanted are so rare as scarcely to require any allusion to it, if the breaker is sufficiently industrious to give work enough to his charge. This part of the education is generally accomplished in a couple of lessons, without trouble, and, indeed, the young dog often points steadily enough at the first or second scenting of game.

Backing.—When a dog has acquired the merely instinctive property already described, he is said to be "steady before," and may be used alone or single-handed without any further education; but when he is to be hunted with other dogs he requires to be made "steady behind," that is to say, he must be taught to "back" another dog as the latter stands. In very high-bred dogs, this property, like the former, is developed very early; but the more hardy and courageous the breed, the longer they generally are in acquiring it, and therefore the young breaker should not be discouraged if he finds that his puppies give him some trouble after they have learned to stand perfectly steady. Backing is usually taught in the same way as described for standing, that is to say, by hunting with an old steady dog, taking care that he is one whose find is to be depended on, and then stopping the young one with the voice and hand, or with the aid of a check-cord if necessary. The great art consists here in managing to get between the two dogs at the moment when the old one stands, and thus to be able to face the puppy as he rushes up to share the scent with his rival, which he at first considers his companion to be. Jealousy is a natural feeling in all dogs from their desire to obtain approbation; but it must be eradicated in the pointer and setter, or they never become steady together, and which ever finds first, the other tries to run up and take the point from him. To avoid this failing, leave the dog which first finds, alone, and walk up to the one which you have stopped, pat and encourage him with the word "Toho!" in a low but pleased tone; let him not on any account creep forward a step, but keep him exactly where he is for some minutes, if the birds lie well. Then walk forward to the old dog, but take no notice of him, and, with your eye still on the puppy, put up the birds, having stopped him with voice and hand if he moves a limb. Supposing the old dog has pointed falsely, the young one is materially injured, inasmuch as he has lost confidence in him, and next time he is with more difficulty restrained from running in to judge for himself; hence the necessity for a good nose in the old dog, who ought to be very steady and perfect in all respects. It will thus be seen that very little art is required in carrying out this part of the education, which really demands only hard walking, patience, and perseverance to complete it in the most satisfactory manner. It should be pursued day after day, until the young dog not only finds game for himself and stands quite steadily, but also backs his fellows at any distance, and without drawing towards them a single step after he sees them at point. When this desirable consummation is effected to such an extent that the puppy will back even a strange dog, and has already learned to beat his ground properly, as explained in my previous remarks, he is steady and well broken as he can be without the gun, and may be thrown by, until a fortnight before the shooting season, when he ought to be taken out again for two or three days, as in the interval he will generally have lost some of his steadiness. Still he will only require work to restore it, as he knows what he ought to do; and with patience, joined if necessary with a little punishment, he soon re-acquires all that he has forgotten. Many masters now fancy that all is done towards "making the pointer;" but, on the contrary, they find that

POINTER, DAISY

after birds are killed the puppy which was previously steady becomes wild and ungovernable, and spoils the day's shooting by all sorts of bad behavior. Hence it is that breakers so often are blamed without cause; but when it is found by experience that such conduct is the rule, and not the exception, young dogs are left by their owners to be shot over by a keeper for a few days, or even longer, before they are taken into the field. Another reason for this wildness may be assigned; namely, the dogs are often hunted in the commencement of the season by almost perfect strangers, two or three guns together; whereas, if their breaker had the management, they would be under much more control, and especially if he went out quietly by himself. Here again is another reason for gentlemen breaking their own dogs, or, at all events, finishing their education by giving their dogs and themselves a few lessons together.

Down charge, as already described, ought to be taught from a very early period, the dog being made to drop at the word or elevation of the hand of his master, without the slightest hesitation. It is not, therefore, necessary to dwell upon this part of his education, further than to remark that after each point, or, indeed, directly after birds rise under any circumstances, the dog should be made to drop by the voice, using the order "Down charge!" or by raising the hand, if the eye of the dog can be caught. When this practice is made habitual, there is little trouble in carrying out the order until the gun is added; but then it will be found that great patience and forbearance are required to prevent the dog from running to his birds as they drop; for, if this is allowed, it is sure to make him unsteady in every case, as soon as his eye catches sight of game, whether after the point or not. It is now that the advantage of having made the dog drop to the gun is manifested, for the first thing he thinks of, when the gun is fired, is the necessity for dropping, and if this is encouraged all goes on well. Too often the shooter himself produces unsteadiness, by disregarding his dog at the moment when he ought to attend to him most particularly, and by running in himself to take care of his "bag," considering that more important than the steadiness of his dog. It is true that a runner is sometimes lost by the delay of a few seconds while the discharged barrel is reloaded; but in the long run, the shooter who keeps his dog down until he has loaded, will bag the most game.

The faults which chiefly require correction at this stage are: blinking, shying the gun, pottering at the hedges, hunting too wide, and chasing fur. The vice of blinking has been caused by over-severity in punishment for chasing poultry, etc., and takes a great deal of time to remove. Indeed, until the dog sees game killed, he seldom loses the fear which has produced it. It is therefore frequently useless to continue the breaking, in the spring, although such a dog sometimes becomes very useful by careful management in the shooting season. Generally speaking, it is occasioned by undue severity, either applied for chasing cats or poultry, or for chasing game when first hunted. The former kind of castigation, should be cautiously applied, as the puppy is very apt to associate the punishment given for the chasing of game with that due to the destruction of poultry or cats; and as he has been compelled to leave the latter by the use of the whip, and has been afterwards kept "at heel," so he thinks he must do so now, and in fear he comes there, and consequently "blinks his birds." This defect is only to be remedied by instilling confidence, and by avoiding punishment; but it is often one which gives great trouble before it is got over. It is not so bad as the obstinately refusing to work at all, but is only next to it. Both occur in dogs which are deficient in courage, and both require the most delicate and encouraging treatment to remove them. Let such dogs run "riot," and commit any fault they like, without fear for a time; then afterwards, that is, when they begin to be quite bold, and are full of zest for game, begin very cautiously to steady them, and something may yet be done. In very bad cases, all attempts at breaking must be given up at "pairing time," and the gun must be relied on as a last resource, the killing of game having sometimes a wonderful effect in giving courage to a dog which has been depressed by undue correction. Punishment is not to be condemned altogether, for in some breeds and individuals without the whip, nothing could be done; but it should be very cautiously applied, and the temper of each dog should be well studied in every case before it is adopted. Kindness will effect wonders, especially where united with firmness, and with a persevering determination to compel obedience somehow; but, if that "how" can be effected without the whip, so much the better; still, if it cannot, the rod must not be spared, and, if used at all, it should be used efficaciously.

Shyness of the gun will generally also pass off in time; but, as it seldom occurs, except in very timid and nervous dogs, they do not often become very useful even when they have lost it. The best plan is to lead a shy dog quietly behind the shooters, and not to give him an opportunity of running off, which he generally does on the first discharge. When game falls, lead him up and let him mouth it; and thus, in course of time, he connects cause with effect, and loses that fear of the report, which he finds is followed by a result that gives him the pleasure of scenting fresh blood.

Pottering at the hedges in partridge-shooting, is the result of using dogs to find rabbits, or of allowing them to look for them, which they always are ready to do, especially if permitted to chase or even to retrieve hares. There is no remedy for it, and a potterer of this kind is utterly worthless and irreclaimable.

Hunting too wide for close partridge-shooting may be easily remedied by constantly keeping in the dog by the whistle and hand; and, if he has been properly taught to range at command, little trouble is required in making him change from the wide beat, necessary in countries where game is scarce, to the confined and limited range of sixty yards, which is best where it is thick on the ground

Chasing fur, and also running in to dead birds, are often most unmanageable vices; but either can be generally cured by patience and severe treatment, aided, if necessary, by the check cord, or in very bad cases by the spike-collar in addition. When these are used, it is only necessary to work the dog with them on, the cord either trailing loosely on the ground or held in an assistant's hand. Then, the moment the dog runs in, check him severely, and, if he is not very bold, the plain collar will suffice, as it may be made by a sharp jerk to throw him back, to his great annoyance. Pointer Daisy, page 237, took first prize in her class, New York Bench Show of 1877.

BREAKING TO RETRIEVE.

Retrieving, in my opinion, should be invariably committed to a dog, specially kept for that purpose; but, as this is not the universal practice, it will be necessary to say a few words on this subject. When pointers or setters are broken to retrieve, in addition to those qualities peculiar to them, they should always be so much under command as to wait "down charge," until they are ordered on by the words "seek dead," when they at once go up to the place where they saw their game drop, and, taking up the scent, foot it until they find it. Some breeds have no nose for a foot-scent, and, if ordered to "seek dead," will beat for the body-scent as they would for a single bird; and, when they come upon the lost bird, they "peg" it with a steady point in the same way. This does not injure the dog nearly as much as working out a runner by the foot-scent; but a retrieving pointer of this kind, is of little use for any but a badly wounded bird, which has not run far. Few pointers and setters will carry game far, nor indeed is it worth while to spend much time in teaching them to do so; and when they are set to retrieve, it is better to follow them, and help them in their search, so as to avoid all necessity for developing the "fetch and carry" quality, which in the genuine retriever is so valuable. But it is chiefly for wounded hares or running pheasants that such a retriever is required; and as the former spoil a pointer or setter, and are sure to make him unsteady if he is allowed to hunt them, it is desirable to keep clear of the position altogether, while pheasants are so rarely killed to these dogs that their retrieval by them need not be considered.

The regular land retriever requires much more careful education, inasmuch as he is wanted to abstain from hunting, and from his own especial duties, except when ordered to commence. The breed generally used is the cross of the Newfoundland with the setter or water-spaniel, but, as I have explained in another place, other breeds are equally useful. In educating these dogs, they should be taken at a very early age, as it is almost impossible to insure perfect obedience at a later period. The disposition to "fetch and carry," which is the essence of retrieving, is very early developed in these dogs, and without it there is little chance of making a puppy perfect, in his vocation. Young dogs of this breed will be seen carrying sticks about, and watching for their master to throw them, that they may fetch them to him. This fondness for the amusement should be encouraged to a certain extent, almost daily, but not so far as to tire and disgust the dog, and care should always be taken that he does not tear or bite the object which he has in charge. On no account should it be dragged from his mouth, but he should be ordered to drop it on the ground at the feet of his master, or to release it, directly it is laid hold of. The consequence of pulling anything out of the young retriever's mouth is that he becomes "hard bitten," as it is called; and, when he retrieves a wounded bird, he makes his teeth meet, and mangles it so much, that it is utterly useless. A dog which is not naturally inclined to retrieve, may be made so by encouraging him to pull at a handkerchief or a stick; but such animals very seldom turn out well in this line, and it is far better to put them to some other task. As soon as the puppy has learned to bring everything to his master when ordered, he may be taught to seek for trifling articles in long grass or other covert, such as bushes, etc. When he succeeds in this, get some young rabbits which are hardly old enough to run, and hide one at a time at a little distance, after trailing it through the grass so as to imitate the natural progress of the animal when wounded. After putting the young retriever on the scent at the commencement of the "run," let him puzzle it out, until he finds the rabbit, and then make him bring it to his master without injuring it in the least. Encouragement should be given for success, and during the search, the dog should have the notice of his master, by the words:

"Seek! seek! seek dead!" etc. A perseverance in this kind of practice will soon make the dog very bright, in tracing out the concealed rabbits, and in process of time he may be intrusted with the task of retrieving a wounded partridge or pheasant in actual shooting. But it is always a long time before the retriever becomes perfect, practice being all important to him.

Many shooters use a slip for the retriever, the keeper leading him in it, until he is wanted, which is a good plan when a keeper is always in attendance. In any case, however, these dogs should be made to drop "down charge," as the gun may be used while they are at work, and if they are not broken to drop, they become excited, and often flush other game before it is reloaded.

The breaking of the water-spaniel or retriever is also a complicated task, and, as he has to hunt in the water and on the banks, his duties are twofold. These dogs are used in the punt as well as on the edge of the water, but when the education is finished in the river, the pupil will generally do what is wanted from the punt. As in the land retriever, so in this variety, the first thing to be done is to get the puppy to "fetch and carry" well; after which he may be introduced to "flappers" in July and August, when the water is warm, and he does not feel the unpleasantness and ill effects, attendant on a cold winter's day with a wet coat. The young birds are also slow and awkward, in swimming and diving, so that every encouragement is afforded to the dog, and he may readily be induced to continue the sport, to which he is naturally inclined, for hours together. The chief difficulty at first is in breaking the water-spaniel from rats, which infest the banks of most streams, and which are apt to engage the attention of most dogs. The dog should be taught to beat to the hand, and, whenever a flapper is shot and falls in the water, then he must be encouraged, to bring it to land without delay. No art must be neglected to induce him to do this, and, every other plan failing, the breaker must himself enter the water; for, if the dog is once allowed to leave a duck behind him, he is much harder to break afterward. Indeed, perseverance in the breaker is necessary at all times, to insure the same quality in the pupil.

The object in teaching the spaniel the range to hand is, because without this there will often be difficulty in showing him where a bird lies in the water—the eye of the dog being so little above its level, and the bird very often so much immersed, that when there is the slightest ruffle, he can scarcely see it a yard from his nose. As in all other cases, the water-retriever must be strictly "down charge," and he must be thoroughly steady and quiet at heel, or he will be sure to disturb the water-fowl when the shooter is in ambush waiting for them. The slightest whine is fatal, and the dog should, therefore, be taught to be as quiet as a mouse until ordered to move.

THE ENTERING AND BREAKING OF THE COVERT SPANIEL.

The breaking of all spaniels should be commenced as early as possible, as they are naturally impetuous, and require considerable restraint to keep them near enough to the shooter, while they are at work. After teaching them the ordinary rules of obedience, such as to "come to heel," to "hold up," to drop "down charge," etc., which may all be done with the pistol and check-cord, aided if necessary by the spiked-collar, the next thing is to enter them to the game, which they are intended to hunt. These dogs are better taken out, first into small coverts or hedgerows (provided there are not too many rabbits in the latter), as they are more under command here than in large woodlands. The dog should not be allowed to hunt by himself nor for himself, but should be taught that he must keep within shot. For this purpose spaniels must learn not to press their game until the shooter is within range, which is one of the most difficult things to teach them. When they are to be kept exclusively for "feather," they must be stopped and rated as soon as it is discovered that they are speaking to "fur." This requires a long time, and therefore few spaniels are worth much until they have had one or two seasons' practice, from which circumstance it should not occasion surprise that a thoroughly broken Clumber spaniel fetches from $150 to $250. When they are too riotous and hunt too freely, these methods of sobering them are adopted:—1st, put on a collar, and slip one of the fore legs into it, which compels the dog to run on three legs; 2ndly, buckle a small strap, or tie a piece of tape, tightly round the hind leg above the hock, by which that limb is rendered useless, and the dog has to go upon three also; and, 3dly, put on a collar loaded with shot. If either of the legs is fastened up, it must be occasionally changed, especially if the strap is adopted, as it cramps the muscles after a certain time, and, if persisted in too long, renders the dog lame for days afterwards. In hunting fence-rows, the young dog should at first be kept on the same side as the shooter, so that his movements may be watched; but, as soon as he can be trusted, he should be sent through to the other side, and made to drive his game towards the gun—always taking care that the dog does not get out of shot. In first introducing a young dog to a large covert, he must be put down with a couple of old dogs which are very steady; and, at the same time, he should have a shot-collar, or one of his legs tied up. Without this precaution, he will be sure to range too wide, and, if he gets on the scent of a hare, he will probably follow her all over the covert, to the entire destruction of the day's sport. With the above precautions, he is prevented from doing this, and by imitating his fellows, he soon learns to keep within the proper distance. In working spaniels in covert, stillness is desirable, as game will never come within distance of the shooter, if they hear a noise proceeding from him; hence the constant encouragement to the dogs, which some sportsmen indulge in, is by no means necessary. If the spaniel is properly broken, he can hear his master as he passes through the underwood, and will take care to drive the game towards him, while, if he is slack and idle, the voice does him little good, and prevents the only chance of getting a shot, which might otherwise occur.

THE ENTERING AND BREAKING OF VERMIN DOGS.

Terriers are entered to vermin with great facility, and require very little breaking, unless they are intended to be used with ferrets. Then they must be broken to let these animals alone, as they are apt to make their appearance occasionally in passing from one hole to another. It is only necessary to let the ferret and the terrier be together in a yard or stable for a few times, cautioning the latter not to touch the former, and the young dog soon learns to distinguish his friends from his foes. Some terriers are not hardy enough to brave the bites which they are liable to in ratting, etc., and, indeed, the true terrier without any cross of the bull-dog is a great coward, so that he is quite useless for the purpose. In such a case, he must be encouraged by letting him kill young rats at first, and as he gains confidence, he will perhaps also increase in courage. If, however, the terrier is well bred, he will rarely require anything more than practice.

CHAPTER V.

THE USE OF THE DOG IN SHOOTING.

GROUSE AND PARTRIDGE (QUAIL) SHOOTING.—SNIPE AND WOODCOCK SHOOTING.—WILD-FOWL SHOOTING.—SHOAL-WATER FOWL.—DEEP-WATER FOWL.—HARE HUNTING.—DEER HUNTING.

The dogs used in aid of the gun are: the pointer, the setter, in grouse and quail shooting; the spaniel, the beagle, and terrier in covert or timber shooting; either of the above in snipe and woodcock shooting; the water spaniel or retriever in wild fowl shooting; and the hound or dachshund in deer shooting.

GROUSE AND PARTRIDGE (QUAIL) SHOOTING.

North America is exceeded by no other country in the world in the number and varieties of its game birds, and among these the grouse of different species and the true partridge—the so-called quail—furnish more recreation to the sportsmen and more food for domestic uses, than any other of our birds. Curiously the partridge, so-called in common parlance, is not the true one, but belongs to the grouse family, of which we have ten species, the ruffed grouse, (*Tetrao umbellus*), the prairie hen, (*Tetrao cupido*), the spruce grouse (*Tetrao Canadensis*) of the East and West, and the dusky grouse (*Tetrao obscurus*) of the Pacific Coast, being the most commonly known of these birds. The true partridge, of which we have at least seven species, are commonly called quail. The best known species is the Virginia partridge, (*Ortyx Virginianus*), whose cry, at the brooding season, so nearly like "bob-white," with a slowly drawn lengthening of the first syllable and a quick sharply accented rising inflection of the latter one—is so well known to every rural dweller.

The Ruffed Grouse is scattered all over the country east of the Mississippi, where woods now exist, or have previously existed. It is found in cultivated fields, patches of woods, and in the deep forests. Under the influence of moderate protection at the breeding season, it is sufficiently plentiful to afford recompense for the time occupied in pursuing it. It is too well known to need any description, indeed it is so well known and so constantly and persistently hunted, that were it not an exceedingly shy and wary bird, strong of wing, and direct and swift in its flight, it would soon be exterminated. It is a difficult bird to shoot on the wing, especially in woods and thickets, and it requires a practised hand and a quick eye to bring it to bag, except when started by a snapping cur, often trained to "tree" these birds, it takes refuge upon the nearest tree, and giving sole attention to the dog is easily shot by a sharp-eyed hunter, who can distinguish its speckled brown plumage from the similarly colored bark against which it crouches. In the open, it is more easily shot over a setter or a pointer, and in open woods with a good dog, its chase is by no means so unsuccessful as to discourage the sportsman. It must be hit hard, to kill; and will frequently carry off a load of shot to a considerable distance before it drops. As it rises before the dog it flies off with a loud, sharp whirr, which greatly confuses a novice until he becomes accustomed to it.

The Pinnated Grouse, or Prairie hen, is abundant from Texas through all the prairie country northward to Canada, but it has been driven out of the Middle States where it was formerly abundant, in the openings among the timber. Thirty years' slaughter have been sufficient to exterminate this game bird from the Atlantic Coast to the Mississippi River, except in a few localities where now it is gradually disappearing; when it was formerly so abundant as to feed in the farm yards and appear in the streets of villages. This confiding habit has perhaps led to its general destruction. The attitude of this bird is not so graceful as that of the ruffed grouse, but its walk is bold and erect. When startled it runs with swiftness until taking wing, or squats until it is flushed.

In August and September they lie well to a dog, and can be shot with ease. Later they gather in flocks, and become wild, rising out of gun shot and flying away for a long distance; but if followed and again started they scatter, and, lying close, may be flushed singly and bagged. In the fall they frequent the corn fields and pick up the scattered corn, but are difficult to shoot in such places, from the noise made in passing through the rustling leaves which startles them before the hunter can get within shot. Sport under such circumstances is weary and unprofitable work.

The Dusky Grouse, is the finest of the whole family, exceeding all others in size, and being equal to any in delicacy of flesh. The male has been found to weigh 3¼ lbs., while 3 lbs. is a common weight. In color it is generally greyish brown, mottled with reddish brown and black; the throat is white, crossed with black; the breast and belly are lead color; the tail feathers are black with the terminal cross band of grey usual in the grouse family.

The young birds when half grown in August are easily killed, and are much sought for on account of the tenderness and delicacy of their flesh. The mature birds have the same habit which the related species of the east possess of taking refuge in the nearest tree, and remaining crouched against the trunk on a limb. They lie very close to dogs, and are easily killed when found away from the thick pine forest in which they usually harbor.

The Virginia Partridge or Quail, is known by its right name in Pennsylvania and further South, although the residents there make up for this accuracy by wrongly calling the grouse a pheasant. As a quail, it is wrongly known in New England and the Northern States. No more familiar sound is heard in the spring, when the bird is mating or brooding, than the cheery "bob-white" which at morning, noon, and night, is sung by the male and answered by the female. The nest is made on the ground, of grass, and is sheltered by some tall tuft. The young birds run as soon as hatched, and the brood roost together at night upon the ground, in a circle with their heads outwards. If disturbed they take flight, each in a direct line, and thus spread in separate courses. The note of alarm is a low twittering sound, not unlike that made by young chickens; the note of recall, after a scattering, is loud and frequent, with a tone of tenderness and anxiety expressed in it. At the hunting season in September and October, the grain fields furnish a harbor for feeding places, and beveys of four or five, up to thirty, afford sport to the sportsman. The pointer or setter is used to find the game and its direct, steady flight, makes it an easy mark for a fair shot. The partridge abound from Canada to Texas and Florida, and are numerous in the great Western States. Their flesh is white, tender and delicious, and a supper of broiled "quail" is a sufficient reward to the sportman with appetite sharpened by healthful exercise over the stubble fields.

Quail shooting is the most frequent and convenient sport both for the country dweller, and those who are condemned by the pursuits of business to inhabit the cities, from which they can only occasionally steal away to the field. When in pursuit of quail, as the main object, all other kinds of game are taken as they come. Grouse and hares may be picked up occasionally, and the expectation of finding these add to the zest of the sport. The sportsman is therefore required to be constantly on the lookout, and ready to take what it may happen to be. It is not wise to be too early afield after quail. The dew should be off the ground, and the birds should have left their roosting places, else they may lay up for the day out of reach, or they will not lie to the dog. From eight to nine, depending upon the weather somewhat, is early enough. In beating the ground, the first thing, is to drive the whole range up to the wind, so as to give the dogs a chance to scent and to get the best shots, as quail prefer to fly with the wind rather than against it. When birds are flushed and marked down, they should be approached so as to let the dogs face the wind.

The best ground for quail, early in the morning, is grain stubbles and cornfields, and meadows adjacent to dry boggy swamps, and rank places where briers, low bushes, and cranberries grow. The boundaries of fields, especially where coarse weeds and brush is growing, and on the bushy borders of woods, are likely places to find bevys. After these have been beaten, the middles of the fields may be tried. When the dog stands still, with stern outstretched and rigid, his frame quivering with excitement, the game is close before him. When he wavers, wags his tale wistfully, and looks back, the game is gone, or is at some distance. If he crouches low, and evinces a desire to crawl on the ground, he has a running bevy before him. In the first case, it will be necessary to take such a direction in coming up as will command a good shot when the birds rise, and will drive them to ground which you propose to beat by and by.

This, of course, has been previously laid out in the mind in planning the day's sport. When the birds rise, if a single one leads, he is the old cock, and should be killed by all means, if possible. When he is bagged, the rest of the bevy will alight sooner. When the old pair has been shot, the rest may be counted as already in bag, for, deprived of their leaders, the young birds are bewildered.

If all the bevy rise at once, do not shoot into the body of it, but select the outer bird on your own hand, the right if you are at the right, and the left if your companion has the right. When the outer bird has been dropped, the next should be covered and shot as quickly as possible. At least twelve or fifteen yards should be given before the gun is fired, otherwise the birds will be torn by the shot. As they light, they should be marked down carefully; if they are going down hill, and before the wind, they will go some distance, beyond where they were last seen. If they enter a wood or a field of standing corn, they will rarely go through to the other side, but on alighting will run a few yards, and then squat. If the birds are seen to drop, they may be marked with certainty, otherwise the nature of the ground, the wind, and their flight, must be considered before one can be certain of their whereabouts. After quail have dropped and squatted, they sometimes give no scent, and the best dog may fail to point them. This habit of withholding scent, is supposed to be voluntary and instinctive; or it may be a physiological peculiarity, consequent upon their state of alarm, and involuntary; this is obviously, however, a matter which cannot easily be investigated. But the fact should be known and noted, because it is useless to follow birds to their hiding places immediately, and the time would be

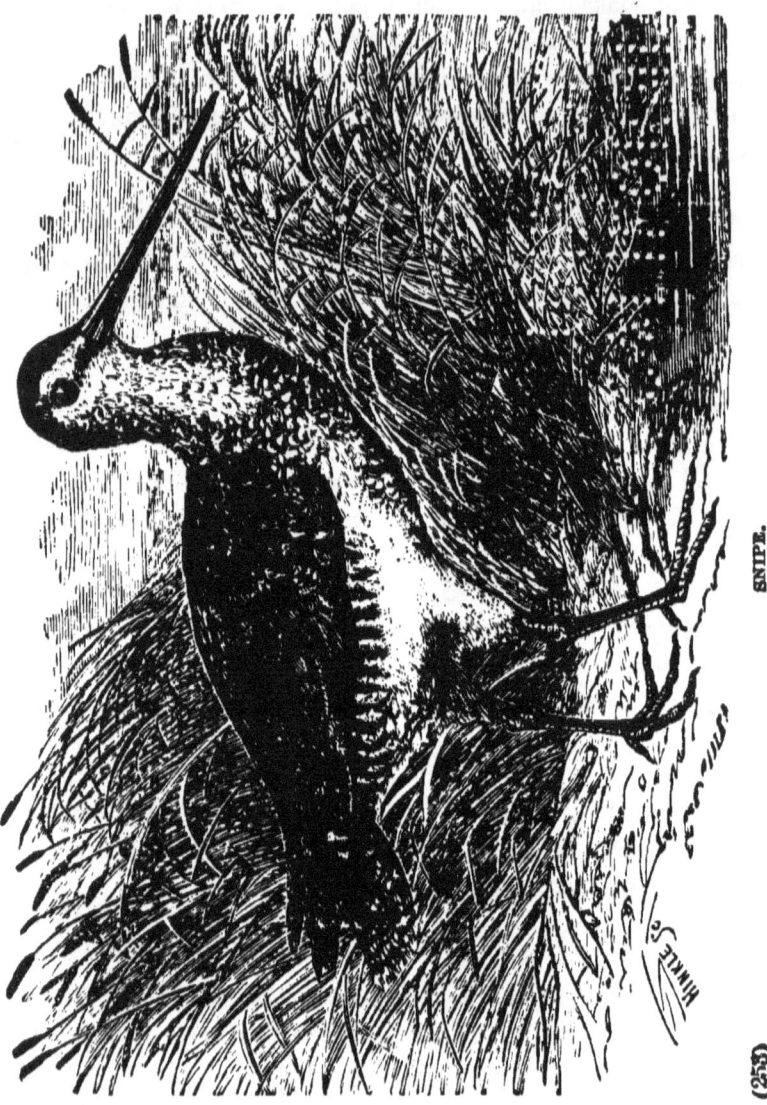

SNIPE.

thrown away in doing so. To secure sport, therefore, in the afternoon, the best way is to continue beating the stubbles, feeding grounds, and edges of woods and dry swamps, and to secure what birds are found, until the scattered birds shall begin to call; then to follow up those which have been flushed in the morning and marked down, into the precise spots or as near as may be, and beat up for them with patience, turning and returning until every bird has been accounted for.

The quail is a difficult bird to shoot in a covert; it flies rapidly, as fast in a thick cover as in the open, carries shot a long distance, and falls suddenly in the midst of its flight. It is necessary for the sportsman to keep close up to his dogs when in covert, and not to lag behind on any account whatever, lest he have only his labor and an empty bag for his pains.

When ruffed grouse have been flushed while hunting quail, it is not difficult to bag them if the precaution is taken to shoot fully three feet ahead of him if he be sailing down on the wind with the wings set; otherwise, when he rises within range, he hangs at first, and if one is cool and shoots quickly, it is not so hard a matter to drop him.

SNIPE AND WOODCOCK SHOOTING.

The first game shooting after the winter is over, is that of the English or Wilson's snipe As soon as the frost is out of the ground, snipe may be hunted in low wet places and meadow swamps. Here they may be found resting for a time before going further north to their breeding places. When first arrived, they are wild and shift constantly from place to place; sometimes they fly in knots of 10 or 20 birds, and rise high, soaring and departing out of sight. No other sport depends more upon the state of the weather than this; nor is any other more uncertain, on account of the errratic and capricious nature of these birds. The most promising conditions for sport are the clearing of a violent

N. E. storm into soft, warm weather, the partial drying up of the early spring floods, and the blowing of a warm, south-westerly breeze. Rough weather disturbs the conditions, and shooting then will be a matter of great uncertainty. At times, snipe will lie in uplands, fallow fields, grassy meadows, and even in woodlands; while in the marshes one may find plenty of borings and droppings, but not a bird. Sometimes one cannot choose, and having come to shoot, must do the best he can. Then, even in rough squally weather, birds may be found about springs and muddy pools, surrounded by brakes and briers, or tall alders, or high bunches of marsh grass or reeds. Thus the sportsman who is after snipe, to succeed in his aims, must know the character of his game and the ins and outs of its curious disposition.

A dark day, a drizzly day, or a windy, is not favorable to sport, unless the wind is from the south or west and not too high. A mild, soft, hazy, sunshiny day, with a gentle south breeze, is just the day for snipe. It may be hot, and if the air is damp, and the breeze gentle, the birds will lie the closer for it, and on such a day their flight is lazy and they will drop often within a few yards of the dog that has flushed them. Then there are no easier birds to kill; all that has to be done is to let them get away a fair distance, so as to allow for the shot to spread, then cover the bird well before the trigger is touched, all the time taking things coolly and deliberately.

Snipe nearly always rise against and go away up-wind, as closely as possible; consequently the mode of beating for this game is different from that used for any other. It is generally the practice to beat down-wind, and the ground is to be entered from the windward instead of from the leeward as for all other game. If this is not possible, the ground must be beaten diagonally, and all the most likely spots, approached by a circuit so as to come on the windward side of it. If the dog points, the sportsman must make a circuit around so as to get the bird, down-wind of him, and for this reason it is very necessary to have a steady dog.

For young sportsmen, a pointer is recommended, but for old and practised sportsmen, a setter is preferred. When the birds are plentiful, a dog is not necessary, as they lie to a man alone, as well as to a man with a dog; but if the ground to be beaten is wide, and the birds few, the help of a dog is needed. A dog must be stanch as well as steady, and should be immovable on his point; he must not crawl in or approach the bird, but must remain stiff, even though the shooter may have to make a circuit and come round facing him. He must be trained to obey the hand. He must follow at heel when called in, without attempting to beat until ordered. This is a great point in snipe-shooting, for a bird will lie close to a man after having been marked down, when it would flush wide of a dog; and when marked down, a snipe can always be found because it never runs more than a few feet from the spot where it alighted. By going down-wind on the game, the sportsman forces the bird to go away to the right or left hand, as it tries to fly up-wind and thus afford a side shot. The moment to deliver the shot is when the snipe poises itself after first rising, and before it gets under way. It is then almost motionless for an instant, and if it rises 15 yards from the gun—and it seldom rises nearer—this is the time to shoot. As the snipe flies quickly, it is necessary to aim the gun a foot ahead of him at 20 yards, and at 40 yards three feet space should be allowed.

In the fall of the year their is less uncertainty in the habits of the birds, and they are neither so wild nor unsteady as in the spring.

WOODCOCK SHOOTING.

Custom or law has authorized the beginning of cock shooting on the 1st day of July in most of our States, but it is too early, both on account of the heat of the weather and the condition of the birds. At this period many broods of woodcock are but recently hatched, so that the killing of the hen bird, is the destruction of the young brood. This may perhaps account for the fact that these birds are rapidly diminishing in numbers, and in many places have been exterminated.

Woodcock return year after year to the same wood to breed, and if owners of grounds could or would prevent shooting birds too early in the season, their care would be for their own benefit, as well as for that of the public.

Early morning and late afternoon are the times to be preferred for summer shooting, though, as this bird feeds and lies upon the same ground all day long, it may be pursued at any time.

The only difficulty in shooting woodcock is in the thickness of the covert in which they lie. In the summer the old birds rise heavily and often drop close to the gun in the effort to cover their young broods; the young ones rise stupidly, and can be found again within a score or two yards. In shooting in a thick covert, one of the guns should be placed in an open spot where the bird can be seen, as it rises, because the one whose point is made can scarcely get a sight of the bird, at times unless he is very quick. Under these circumstances it is best for the shooter to flush his birds and not suffer the dog to do it; in no case should he permit his dog to go out of sight.

The choice of ground, depends upon the season and various other circumstances. In some places the birds lie in open meadows among rushes, bogs, and water-plants, where there is no brush. They are rarely found in woods. In other places they will be found in brakes of alders where there is a muddy bottom, or in grassy meadows where slow running brooks and swales exist, with patches of willow and tall weeds about them. In the valleys of the mountain ranges they haunt the sides of low meadows at the foot of hills, and spots where streams emerge into the lowlands upon beds of black oozy vegetable matter, covered with water plants. A favorite feeding ground is in open woods, upon rich, black alluvial soil, covered with short bunchy grass with soft spots intermingled, and where there is no undergrowth; also in thick, red maple swamps on flat lands adjacent to river banks which are overflowed. In dry, hot weather, the cool, shady, moist ground is most attractive to them.

When woodcock are not to be found in one favorable place, they may often be found in others which might be supposed to be unat-

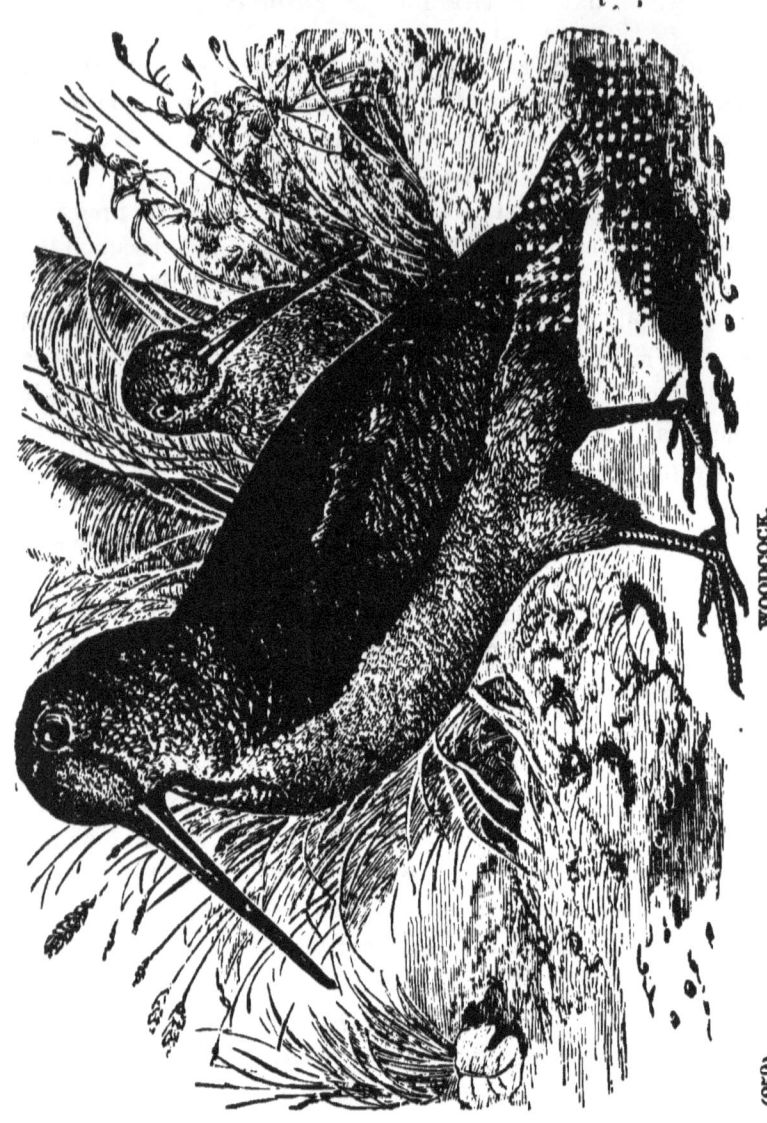

WOODCOCK.

tractive, so that not only must the sportsman be patient and persevering, but he must also be observing, and make use of his well earned experience. Later in the season cock are to be found not only in such places as have been indicated, but upon damp, springy hill sides, where chestnuts are mixed with laurels and low evergreens. Indeed as the season lengthens out to November, such hill sides supply these birds, with the most of their favorite food, which they find hidden under fallen leaves. They are always apt to be found where their food is most abundant. After this month the annual migration occurs, and the birds silently steal away singly, and in the night, to their winter quarters.

The difference in the size of the male and female woodcock is decidedly marked; so much is this the case that warm controversies have occurred between experienced sportsmen upon this subject; some maintaining that there are two distinct species of the bird in this country. It was finally settled that the greater size of the female had misled many observant sportsmen. Woodcock make annual migrations in the spring and autumn, arriving in the Middle States from the latter part of February or first week of March, according as the season may be open or severe, and departing in the months of November and December. In the autumn migration, the birds that have recently arrived, are called "Flight" birds, and are distinguished by the feathers on the breast being brighter in color than of those that have been lying in the feeding ground for some time; the latter's breast color being decidedly duller in hue. Many young cock are lost during the early freshets. Sometimes the weather is dry and mild in the early part of spring, and the woodcock hatching her brood is overtaken by rainy weather, when the young are drowned, or, if unhatched, the eggs are destroyed. Consequently, the sportsmen always desire a continued dry spring, as it is especially favorable to the increase of all species of game. The woodcock often feeds in the night, and persons but slightly acquainted with their habits are astonished at discovering in the morning, the amount of borings, covering the soft ground in a favorite feeding place. In very dry weather woodcock gather in the low wet swamps, while after a rain of a day or two's duration, they scatter through the woods, and may be found on hill sides, and, in fact, on much the same ground as in the fall. They are a most devoted and fearless bird. While on the nest a person may stand quietly within a very short distance of one, and if no unusual motion or noise is made, the hen-bird will gaze without fear upon the intruder.

WILD-FOWL SHOOTING.

The shooting of water-fowl is a sport attended with too much labor, fatigue and exposure to render it very attractive to any but experienced and eager sportsmen, who have perhaps become sated with the commoner recreations of grouse, snipe, quail, or woodcock shooting. Familiarity with this sport is only arrived at through many hardships, if not risks, and exposures in all sorts of weather. Consequently, there are few persons besides those who hunt for a living, who have acquired the necessary knowledge of the habits and natural history of the birds, and the proper methods of circumventing the instinctive wariness of water-fowl, and taking advantage of their peculiar ways, to shoot them successfully. Yet when a taste for the sport has been once acquired, or the first experience of it has been agreeable, there is no other that becomes more fascinating.

Water-fowl may be divided into two classes, those which are found in shoal water, and those which inhabit the deep waters of the sounds and inlets of the sea-coast. The mallard and the different teals are examples of the former, and the canvas-back is the type of the latter. The shoal water birds rarely go under water when feeding, although they will dive and swim long distances under water, when wounded or alarmed. This class of birds includes the mallard, the blue and green winged teal, the summer or wood duck, the pintail, the grey duck, shoveler, widgeon, and the black or dusky duck, together with the wild goose. The deep water varieties include the canvas-back, the broad bill, tufted duck, and the buffle head.

The methods of hunting wild fowl in general use require the exercise of considerable ingenuity and knowledge of the habits of the different species, their feeding places, and favorite food. Their extreme wariness and the necessity of finding the game without the help of dogs, retrieving being the only help afforded by them, add much to the labor and excitement of the sport. The ground, or rather the water, where the fowl abound, is generally inland rivers and ponds, bordered by reedy marshes and the tidal flats of estuaries. There is scarcely a river or marsh in the country East or West, or North or South, where ducks of some variety or other are not found at some season of the year, and sometimes in fabulous numbers. The opening of the spring and the fall are the sporting seasons. The birds are taken either by means of decoys, or by awaiting their passage over a place of ambush in which the hunter is concealed. A boat is generally used, else the labor of wading through the marshes and picking roundabout paths to avoid deep sloughs is intolerable.

Sometimes two persons hunt in company, yet at a distance from each other, one driving the birds towards the other, and the latter driving them back again. In this way many heavy bags are procured. Blinds or screens are provided, behind which the hunter keeps himself concealed until the moment when the game are within range of his gun. These blinds are made in various ways. Full information for their construction is given in the volume by J. W. Long, entitled "American Wild-fowl Shooting."

Decoys are employed to allure the passing flocks or stragglers to alight, being placed in such positions as are habitually chosen by the fowl. These decoys are mostly selected for the deep-water varities, which can not be so well approached as those which haunt the ponds, rivers, and marshes, from the banks of which, screened from observation behind his blind, the hunter can easily reach the approaching game. Decoys of various kinds are used. Those made of pine, and thoroughly coated with priming of raw oil, are to be preferred, as they are light and durable. The main thing in the decoy is to have it as natural as possible in form and color, and so built up and weighted that it will sit steadily in the water without rolling or losing an upright position. A finishing coat of varnish will spoil the best made decoy, on account of its glaring and glistening in the sun. A dead surface is the best. The weight needed to steady the decoy should be made of a strip of sheet lead, placed in a groove at the bottom, and formed like the keel of a boat. Where smooth water only is to be met with, flat-bottomed decoys can be used. These may be carved out of a piece of soft pine plank, but for rough water use, two pieces are needed; one for the top and another for the bottom, which are hollowed out, then put together and painted. Decoys are provided with a line suited to the depth of the water, and a weight of not less than four ounces, made of a quarter length of a pound bar of lead of the kind used for bullets. The line is wound around the body of the duck, towards the tail, from which it unwinds easily as the weight is thrown out, when the decoys are set. A long string is usually tied to one of the decoys by which it may be shaken so as to ripple the water, and cause the whole flock of them to move. A "duck call" being used at the same time when birds are passing will almost surely attract their notice. The decoys are best placed, so that the sun shines on the side towards which the ducks are expected.

A Water Retriever, or a dog that will take to water readily and is furnished with a coat of a nature that resists water, is used in duck shooting. Whatever kind is selected, whether a well-bred curly-coated retreiver, a water spaniel, or a Chesapeake Bay dog, he must be well trained for his work, and not averse to taking to the water however cold it may be. The only native dog of the right kind we have, is known as the Chesapeake Bay dog. Though a descendent of the curly-coated Irish retriever without doubt, he has been educated to his work by breeding and training for some years. There is no better hunting ground in America for wild fowl, than the Chesapeake Bay and its inlets and the sounds along the North Carolina Coast, and here this useful dog has his home and vocation. The dog used for this sport is trained first to know his name; then to instantly drop, wherever he may be, at a word or a signal of the hand, and to lie quietly until ordered or signalled to rise. He should be taught to remain quiet after the discharge of the gun, until ordered to work. This is the most important part of his education, and if not well trained in this, he may easily spoil good sport and lose game by rushing out and spoiling the effect of a second shot. Dead birds need not be gathered until the shooting slackens or good opportunity occurs; otherwise, the dog may alarm the game and prevent birds alighting by his frequent appearance. It is best, however, to secure the cripples as soon as possible, and this a well trained dog will do of his own motion and without waiting for orders; while he will leave dead ducks until ordered to retrieve them. A dog when taught to fetch should never be permitted to drop the game at his master's feet, lest by doing this, when at work, some wounded birds may flutter away and be lost or give much trouble to recapture them. He should be made to deliver only to the hand. Water-Fowl retrievers naturally grip their birds tightly and should be taught to hold them tenderly yet safely. The season for training is the summer when the water is warm; some dogs will refuse to enter water that is very cold after having experienced the discomforts of it in training. When being trained, he should be taught to search for the object he is ordered to retrieve, and to do this, the trainer should secretly throw the object to a distance and then bid the dog search and find it, or motion him with a wave of the arm in the direction he should go. Short and easy lessons will be found the most useful. When punishing a dog for a fault, the castigation should never be so severe as to overbear in his mind the memory of the offence for which it was given. Punishment ought to be administered gently but firmly and instantly. Never delay punishment until it is necessarily disconnected with the fault, and do not be chary of praise for good conduct.

A ducking expedition can hardly be worth much, without the necessity for camping out for a longer or shorter interval. The sportsman should therefore not only know how to make camp, but also be provided with the means for making and furnishing it. In the spring when bark of nearly all kinds peels very easily, a comfortable camp is soon made. Two forked poles set up for the front, a cross bar resting upon these, form the opening and a support for the roof; two saplings reaching from the forks to the ground giving slope for the roof, and a few poles resting on these, and fastened with some withes, finish the frame. Slabs of bark laid upon the top form the roof, and the ends are closed up in the same way; the front is left open. In place of bark, pine or hemlock brush, or coarse grass, will furnish substitutes. Otherwise a pair of gum blankets, or when one has plenty of means, a Δ tent complete, can be provided. Cooking apparatus and comfortable furniture and folding boats or canoes are supplied by the dealers in sporting commodities. A genuine sportsman will always be independent of these appliances, an ax and a box of matches serving to supply all his wants in the way of furnishing camp and cooking materials. As to supplies for camping, it is hardly necessary to mention these, further than to caution the young sportsman never to forget to provide salt, pepper, and sugar; everything else will follow. These are most frequently forgotten, to the great disappointment of those of the party who never trouble themselves about the arrangements.

The camp should never be set in a hollow; a round knoll being safe in case of a sudden heavy rain which might overflow a hollow and make matters very uncomfortable. A shelter for the camp should be chosen where there are no tall trees. Low brush will protect the camp from heavy winds without such danger as would exist among heavy trees in case of sudden gusts. The camp should always face southward.

The color of the dress is an important consideration. This should always be of a neutral tint, matching the surroundings. The light brown waterproof hunting suits made for this special purpose, offer very little contrast with the color of the ground or with faded weeds, grass, leaves, and trunks of trees and brush. Ducks are more suspicious of dark colors than of light, and next to the yellowish-brown clothing, a light grey will be found desirable. A waterproof coat and rubber boots covering the thighs are indispensable.

As to the supply of ammunition that "goes without saying," and as no one would make a secondary matter of this, it may be safely left for each one to please his fancy in this respect.

A pocket compass is indispensable to avoid trouble, for in thick marshes upon cloudy days the direction of the camp is otherwise difficult to find. A man used to the woods is not easily lost; there are many signs which guide him in his course, but so many accidents may occur that it is prudent to have a compass on all occasions. A "pocket pistol" charged with the best quality of any good spirit may be needed in case of sickness. As a safeguard against chills, there should likewise be a supply of quinine on hand. Little hunting should be done before breakfast, and the coffee should be made hot and strong. The drinking of impure water is to be carefully avoided. Lastly, woollen flannel underclothing will be found a great protection in warding off ague.

SHOAL-WATER FOWL.

The species of fowl which frequent shoal water have been already mentioned; but a short description of the principal varieties may be of interest.

The Mallard.—This is a handsome bird, 24 inches in length to the end of the tail when full grown; the extent of the wings is 36 inches, and the weight is about 3 pounds. The male is marked as follows: The bill, greenish-yellow; iris, dark brown; feet, orange-red; head and neck, deep green, with a ring of white about the middle of the neck; fore part of the chest, chestnut brown; fore part of back, yellowish-brown and grey; the rest of the back, brownish-black; the rump, black, with purplish and green shading; the wings are greyish brown, with a "beauty spot" of purple and green, edged with black and white on ten or more of the secondaries; breasts, sides, and belly, pale grey, shaded with dark waves.

The female has the bill black and orange; the iris and feet as in the male; the upper parts generally pale brown, spotted with dusky brown; the head striped or narrowly streaked; the wings and beauty spots nearly as in the male; the under parts dull olive, spotted with brown; length, 22 inches; weight, about 2½ lbs. Mallards breed mostly in the far north and begin to come south in August, staying for a month or more in the Northwestern States and Canada, where vast numbers are sometimes taken. On one occasion 1,365 ducks were killed in 17 days' shooting by one man, with a single barrel, muzzle-loading gun. The rivers and lakes of the Northwestern States furnish unlimited sport in the spring when the birds are on the way to their breeding places, and in the fall when they are returning south. During the winter the open overflowed timber lands of the Southern and Southwestern States are fairly alive with these birds. A great number of them are shot at this season in the large corn fields of the more southern of the Western States, where they stay to feed upon the scattered corn. While shooting ducks in the corn fields, the sportsman will pick up occasionally a few quail or prairie chickens, and should be accompanied by a good dog.

The Blue-Winged Teal.—This is a small, but richly flavored bird, considered to be inferior to none except the canvas-back and the red-head. They are the first to move southward in the fall, and are found in vast numbers in suitable grounds in the western country, where they find acceptable food, such as wild rice, oats, and pond weeds. They congregate about small, muddy streams, where pond lilies and wild rice abound, and also in shallow sloughs. Gravelly streams or ponds are rarely frequented by them. This bird weighs less than one pound, and is about 16 inches in length. The head of the male is black on the upper part, with a half-moon shaped patch of white in front of each eye; the neck is purplish blue; the back brownish black, with green gloss; the lower parts pale reddish orange; the breast purplish red, and spotted with black. The wings are marked with rich lustrous blue. The female's head is pale buff, striped with dark lines. The upper parts are dark brown, the lower parts are dusky brown and grey.

The Green Winged Teal is smaller than the previous variety, and among other differences in color has the wings and back of the neck marked with deep bright green. This bird remains later in the season than the blue teal, but while it remains it associates with the latter, feeding and flying promiscuously with them.

The Pintail Duck is a bird of about 2 pounds weight, and measures full-grown 29 inches from bill to end of tail. The female is smaller and lighter than the male. In color this duck is greenish brown on the head, throat, and upper part of the neck; part of the neck is barred with brownish black and a yellowish white. The spots on the wings are coppery red with green reflections. On each side of the neck is a white band, and the upper parts in general are whitish.

The Sprigtail is the most handsomely formed of the whole duck tribe, and abounds in all parts of the country except in the New England States. Its food consists of the small acorns of the pin oak, the seeds of smartweed, cockle-burr, wild oats, and corn, and beech-nuts. This species is found in immense numbers at the opening of spring, occupying the overflowed fields and prairies, and feeding upon the drifting masses of grass seeds, corn, and waste grain. They soon become fat and in fine condition, and offer the best of sport, flying closely and irregularly, and are thus easily killed; several often dropping at one shot. Decoys are not used for hunting them. When wounded, and on land, they are difficult to retrieve without a good dog, as they can run rapidly and are apt to crouch and hide very closely, and so escape observation.

The Wood Duck is the most beautifully feathered of all the wild fowl, and are common to all parts of the Union except the sea-coast. Their nesting places are in stumps and hollow trees, whence they derive their name. They never dive for food, and are generally found about old musk-rat houses, logs, and banks, on the edges of patches of reeds. In the middle of the day they may nearly always be found in these spots sunning themselves and trimming their feathers. They are in season in August and September.

The American Widgeon is abundant in the waters of some of the

Southern States, more particularly Missouri and Tennessee, and on the Chesapeake Bay, where they feed on the roots of wild celery, which they rarely find by diving for them, but most frequently procure by robbing the canvas-backs of the fruits of their subaqueous labors. They are distinguished from others of their tribe by their length of wing. They are easily brought down, as they fly clustered together, and several may be killed at a shot.

Spoonbills, seldom furnish sport themselves alone, but associating with mallards are often taken with them. They are easily decoyed and are killed by a slight blow; it is not unusual for a flock of 6 or 8 to fall before the discharge of both barrels. They are easily approached from the shore, and their habit of springing up directly in the air several feet before flying off on a course, gives an opportunity for using the second barrel with effect.

The Dusky or Black Duck, weighs 3 pounds. The general color is blackish brown. It is frequently found in the West with the mallard, having the same food and general habits. In the East it is very numerous, and is eagerly pursued by sportsmen. It is very wary and must be approached with caution.

DEEP-WATER FOWL.

The Canvas-Back Duck.—This species is the finest flavored of all wild fowl. Its food in those localities where it is taken in perfection, consists of the roots of the wild celery, which give to its flesh the peculiar flavor for which it is so attractive. Its habits of frequenting open water entail much labor and sometimes exposure and risk to the sportsman; and the uninitiated gunner is foiled in his attempts, time after time, to secure the gamy and highly prized bird, disappointment however only whetting desire and adding to his eagerness. To approach these wary fowl, or to induce them to approach the hunter is the secret of the sportsman's art, and by the help of various stratagems the game is generally brought to bag by the experienced. The system pursued on the

Chesapeake Bay and the North Carolina Sounds, and known as "toling," is the most successful. It is as follows: A small dog, an ordinary poodle, or one very much similar to that, white or brown in color, and called the toler breed, is kept for the purpose. It is trained to run up and down on the shore in the sight of the ducks, directed by the motion of his owner's hand. The curiosity of the ducks is excited, and they approach the shore to discover the nature of the object which has attracted their attention. They raise their heads, look intently, and then start in a body for the shore. When within 40 yards or less, they stop and swim back and forth for a moment before they return. The dog lies low when the ducks are approaching, and at the time when they present their sides is the opportunity to rake the flock. Many ducks then often fall before one gun. To prevent the dogs from disturbing the ducks while they are toling, they are not allowed to go in for the game, but the retrievers known as the Chesapeake Bay dogs are used for this purpose.

When the ducks become bedded, that is, gather in large bodies in one place in open water, for feeding or resting, boats covered with brush and weeds, and propelled silently by paddles, are used by hunters to approach within shooting distance. The sportsman rests upon his knees, in the boat, bending forward to conceal himself, when ducks are approaching. The arrangement of decoys, and taking up the dead ducks, are matters of experience about which no suggestions are needed. Canvas-backs do not drop as mallards do, when alighting on the water, but sweep over the decoys, and circle round again; to alight, if their suspicions are not aroused. The novice may lose his game by haste in firing as they first approach, when by reserving his fire until they come the second time, his chances are greatly improved. The moment of bunching or crossing of the flock as it prepares to alight is the time for the hunter to rise slowly and deliberately so as to create no alarm. A second shot may often be made by taking things coolly, as the ducks, seeing the decoys quiet, are reassured, and often do not leave at the first shot. The big bags are made on rainy days when the ducks are restless and are easily decoyed. Wounded ducks must be shot again at once before the shooter is discovered, otherwise a long and weary chase may be needed before they are secured, as they are expert divers and can swim under water for very long distances. Retrievers cannot be used for picking up crippled canvas-backs, as catching one in this way is out of the question. Canvas backs are found in the spring along the back waters of the Mississippi, in great numbers, when the winter has been severe in the East, as they then make their way up from Galveston Bay and from the mouths and bayous of the river.

The Red-headed Duck is distinguished by the color of its head, which, with more than half the neck, is of a brown-red, glossed with bright red above. Its weight is about $2\frac{1}{4}$ pounds. Its habits are similar to those of the canvas-back, and it subsists upon the same kind of food, chiefly roots of grasses and other aquatic plants. They are found in large flocks, always fly together, but feed along with canvas-backs, and some kinds of shoal-water fowl. They cluster well together and decoy easily. Sometimes they are taken plentifully, foolishly returning to the decoys after a shot, and rising so close together that several are dropped at one discharge, as they rise against the wind, or huddle up before rising. This duck is second only to the canvas-back, as a delicate article of food.

The Scaup-Duck or Blue-Bill, furnishes more sport than many of the more valuable ducks. They settle down to decoys so readily, return so quickly, and pack so closely together, the hunter can hardly fail of being satisfied either with his sport or his bag. They approach shore so carelessly, that with decoys well placed, they may be shot from a blind, built in the bushes, if care is taken to avoid sudden or needless movements.

Ring-necked and Ruffle-headed Ducks, are small, and although furnishing some good sport, are not often hunted. They are found in nearly every part of the country, in both fresh and salt water. The former is a vegetable feeder and its flesh is well flavored; the latter subsists on fish, snails, and other animal foods, and the flesh is ill flavored although it is always fat. It is neglected by the pot hunter as too insignificant for his professional attention.

AMERICAN HARE.

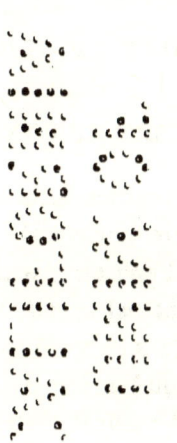

HARE HUNTING.

We have no rabbits in America, although the animals called rabbits—but really hares—are sufficiently plentiful to afford good sport with dogs, in the fall and early winter. It may be of interest to note here that the principal specific differences between hares and rabbits, are that the former breed twice a year only, and make their forms upon the ground under the shelter of bushes or tufts of grass, weeds, or brake, while the latter breed once a month and are burrowing animals, making their hiding-places underground and in company on the sides of dry banks, the places being called "warrens."

The larger hare, which changes its color in the winter, is abundant in the Eastern States, Northern New York, Canada, and the wooded portions of the North-western States. The writer has had excellent sport in the wooded regions of the northern peninsula of Michigan and the adjoining part of Wisconsin, in the early fall, when a few sharp frosts have caused the woods previously dressed in their gorgeous habits of crimson and gold, to drop their foliage and admit the light of day without interference. The most useful dog in such a case, is a setter trained for this especial work, taught to beat the ground properly, point his game, to range low and to retrieve well.

The Small Hare, which does not change color in the winter, affords good sport in the fall, in the cultivated country further south, in open woods, stubble fields, and meadows. For hare shooting alone, a pair of small beagles are to be preferred. The pace of these little hounds is comparatively slow, but they will follow up their game tirelessly through all their doublings and twistings, and will always bring them back to the starting point. Here, covered by a stump, a tree, or a bush, the sportsman stands still, waiting for the return of the game, and listening, meanwhile, to the small music of these melodious little animals during the few minutes the circuit is making. The cry of the hounds will inform the hunter of the direction in which to look for the game, and unless he remains perfectly motionless, without doing more than breathing quietly, and even scarcely winking, he will find the wary and suspicious animal to dart away suddenly, or to steal off unobserved within a few paces under cover of the smallest possible shelter. Sometimes a spoken word, an ejaculation, or a whistle will arrest the fugitive, and give time for an effective shot, almost at point-blank range. With a number of guns in a well furnished covert, and a few couple of beagles, lively sport can be had. The ground best adapted for this sport, and where plenty of game is to be found, is in ranges of scrub oaks, pine barrens, and low bushy thickets, such as occur in many places on Long Island, Southern New Jersey, Eastern Pennsylvania, and the "old fields" of Delaware, Maryland, and Virginia.

DEER HUNTING.

The finest of all American hunting consists, perhaps without exception, in taking deer, either on the run followed by hounds, by stalking or still hunting, or by hunting the game with packs of well trained hounds regularly maintained and followed by fleet high bred hunters, mounted by the keenest sportsmen. The first method is that which is mostly followed in the West and Northern States. It is in this way that a welcome addition to the larder of the enterprising settler or backwoodsman is procured, while his instinctive love of hunting is gratified. This kind of sport is considered slow by those who have once enjoyed the hunt *par excellence* in the open fields or free woods of the South, in which horse and hound are pitted against each other in conflict with the game. But it is by no means to be despised, and the hunter who is not able to join the mounted hunt with a regular pack, may well feel satisfied when he bears to his camp the well-earned game, secured after many miles of exciting tramp or patient eager waiting.

The American deer is found more or less abundantly wherever there are large tracts of woodland, from the central and northern part of New York and Maine, to Texas. The mountains of Central

SHOOTING DEER AT A SALT-LICK.

New York, the great forests of Pennsylvania and of Western Virginia, with the mountain region of the Carolinas and Alabama, and the hummocks of Florida in the East, and the extensive wooded regions of Michigan, Wisconsin, Minnesota, and Canada in the West, furnish the great field for deer hunting of this kind. There the frequent deer paths intersect the woods and fresh scent can always be found upon which to start the dogs. The dogs used are generally cross-bred hounds or deerhounds of impure blood, although the pure, but rarer dachshund, is now being employed in this sport. Speed is not so much a requisite as stanchness and excellent scent; the tireless, unerring following up of the trail, with plenty of tongue to signify the whereabouts of the game, being the chief requisites for this sport. Some hunters who desire great activity are fond of objecting to this as dull plodding amusement; this may be when a party of "tender feet" are stationed at run ways to spend hour after hour and while away the day in the vain hope of seeing game, or even hearing the music of the hounds. But when a lone hunter, or a well-mated party, join in the sport, with a couple of good dogs, and shift their places, as the baying of the dogs gives notice of the course the game is taking, and when the hunter, now following the course over logs and rocks, through brush and swamps, cutting off the game as it sweeps around, and with true woodcraft, meets it at a turn, without giving sight or scent of his presence, and with unerring aim speeds his deadly bullet through the head or heart of his prey—then the most thorough sportsman may find sufficient pleasure and excitement in which to forget the sometimes too vigorous and enduring exercise. Deerhounds well trained for this sport will bring the game around to their starting point, where a a cover of brush may be provided to screen the hunter from observation until the deer is brought within easy distance for a safe shot.

Deer Stalking.—Perhaps the true woodsman will choose to still hunt his game. In this sport there are required: a wonderful acuteness to distinguish "sign" to follow the trail; excessive stealth, yet swiftness of tread, to cover the ground quickly; a rare keenness of vision and of hearing, to detect and discover the game; an accurate sight, and rapid yet steady shooting from the shoulder, and, lastly, the capability of dressing the game and packing it to camp or out of the woods.

Deer Licks.—A safe and sure method of hunting deer is to make what are known as deer licks. The well known appetite of the deer for salt furnishes an opportunity for this sport. A stump or fallen log is chosen near where deer paths cross or are abundant, and in a somewhat open place, such as a windfall, where fallen trees and roots furnish a good blind, to screen the hunter. The blind is chosen on the windward side of the lick, so as to prevent the game from scenting the hunter. The deer frequent the licks in the early morning and about sun-down. At these times the hunter is at his stand prepared for work, and he is generally rewarded by a successful shot for his patient waiting. The engraving on page 277 represents the usual manner of hunting by means of a "lick."

BUFFALO HUNTER'S CAMP.

GAME IN THE FAR WEST.

While Buffalo have almost wholly disappeared from the regions traversed by the great public thoroughfares, and other kinds of game have perceptibly diminished in some quarters, there is no immediate danger of their becoming extinct, as has been argued by some writers. There will be some hunting for several more years to come in many localities in the yet unoccupied regions of Western Colorado, Arizona, Wyoming, Utah, Idaho, Montana, and Dakota. You can leave New York, and in about a week's time reach the hunting centers where one who has a passion for the rod or gun can be fully gratified. Within ten years' time, buffalo were seen in droves from the cars of the passing railway trains in Kansas, Nebraska, and Colorado. Now they have disappeared from Middle and Southern Kansas, and the present range of what is known as the "southern herd" of buffalo, lies in the region of country south of the Arkansas River and extends to the Texas line. Here large numbers of buffalo have been killed during the past six or eight years. Between the scant herbage of the plains, and the merciless destruction of Remington, Winchester, and Sharpe's rifles, the animals have mostly disappeared from this region. The range is reached by going out on the Atchison, Topeka, and Santa Fé road as far as Lakin, and then striking due south. There are a few buffalo left in North Park, Colorado, and the country west of it. They are, however, very wary and difficult to find. A party of us rode over 130 miles in a fruitless eff rt to discover this drove. There are likewise a few buffalo in Northern Nebraska in the Niobrara region. The great northern herd, however, has pushed far northward beyond the Yellowstone country. During November, 1881, we found large numbers of Buffalo between the Little Missouri River and the Yellowstone. The drove was estimated at fully eighty thousand. At Glendive, Montana, we met hunters killing them for their hides. A few years ago, passengers on the Kansas Pacific Road constantly saw Antelope from the windows. Now, however, they are rarely seen except in the western portion of Kansas and along the Colorado boundary. They are likewise diminishing in Colorado and Nebraska. In Wyoming, however, and Northern Colorado, there were more antelope after 1878 than there had been for several seasons, and the hunting has since been good. I know no better locality for hunting antelope than North Park. We found countless numbers here during Nov. 1878, and so tame, that they would occasionally run through our camp before sunrise. After the genuine sportsman has shot one or two of these beautiful creatures, he desists from their further destruction unless it be for food. There are parties, however, calling themselves sportsmen, who shoot down antelope right and left for the mere brutal gratification of being able to tell on their return home of their achievements, and to add to the number of their horns and other trophies. Day after day I have marked the trail of these spurious sportsmen by the carcasses of animals, unnecessarily and inhumanly slaughtered. There is naturally much feeling in Wyoming and Colorado against these butchers, and the frontiersman is often so incensed as to threaten summary vengeance.

Deer and elk are to be found during the summer months in the snowy ranges of Colorado, and likewise on the southern borders of North Park. In October and November they begin to come out of the snow-covered mountains, among the foot-hills, and on the plains, where they are found in considerable numbers. One day, not long ago, while we were riding on the Utah Northern Road, the engineer was compelled to slack up the train for fear of running over a band of deer which were crossing the track in their descent from the mountain regions to the plains.

During the winter months, the best country for hunting elk, deer, or antelope, is in Northern Wyoming, due north from Rawlins, in the Sweet Water and Wind River regions. Here appears to be a kind of winter rendezvous for wild game, and if a hunting party secures the right kind of a guide, they can have their fill of enjoyment in this country. If you can afford the time and expenditure, one of the most adventurous of western trips is to proceed to Bismarck, then to the Yellow Stone River, visit the Parks, and then, pushing down through Wyoming, reach the Union Pacific at Rawlins, Laramie, or some adjacent point.

BOOK III.

THE DISEASES OF THE DOG AND THEIR TREATMENT.

CHAPTER I.

PECULIARITIES IN THE ANATOMY AND PHYSIOLOGY OF THE DOG.

THE SKELETON, INCLUDING THE TEETH.— THE MUSCULAR SYSTEM.—THE BRAIN AND NERVOUS SYSTEM.—THE DIGESTIVE SYSTEM.—THE HEART AND LUNGS.—THE SKIN.

THE SKELETON, INCLUDING THE TEETH.

In the skeleton of the dog and in that of the horse, as well as of all other animals remarkable for their speed, there is a peculiar characteristic of the chest which deserves to be noticed. A narrow-chested horse or dog may have better wind than another with a round barrel, because he is able to alter the cubic contents of his chest more rapidly, and thus inspire and expire a larger volume of air. A medium transverse diameter is therefore to be desired, and is practically found to be advantageous, in allowing a better action of the shoulder blades rolling upon the surface on each side. These facts ought to be taken into consideration in selecting the best kind of frame for the purposes of speed and endurance.

Large size of bone contributes to the strength of the limbs, and foxhounds especially, which have continual blows and strains in their scrambling over or through fences of all kinds, require big limbs and joints. When, however, extreme speed is desired, as in the greyhound, there may be an excess of bone, which then acts as an incumbrance, and impedes the activity. Still, even in this dog, the bones and joints must be strong enough to resist the shocks of the course, without which we constantly find them liable to fracture or dislocation. If, however, a dog is brought up at liberty, and from his earliest years is encouraged in his play, the bones, though small, are strong, and the joints are united by firm ligaments which will seldom give way.

The dog has no collar-bone, so that his fore quarter is only attached to the body by muscular tissue. This is effected chiefly by a broad sling of muscle, which is attached above to the edge of the shoulder-blade, and below to the ribs near their lower ends. It is also moved backwards by muscles attached to the spine, and forwards by others connected in front to the neck and head, so that at the will of the animal it plays freely in all directions.

The teeth are 42 in number, arranged as follows:

$$\text{Incisors } \frac{3-3}{3-3} \quad \text{Canines } \frac{1-1}{1-1} \quad \text{Molars } \frac{6-6}{7-7}$$

TEETH OF THE DOG AT VARIOUS AGES.

The incisors are somewhat remarkable in shape, having three lobules at their edges resembling a *fleur-de-lis* (Figs. 43–44). Next to these come the canine teeth or tusks, and then the molars, which vary in form considerably. In the upper jaw, in front, are three sharp and cutting teeth, which Cuvier calls false molars; then a tooth with two cutting lobes; and lastly two flat teeth, or true molars. In the under jaw, the first four molars on each side are false, or cutters; then an intermediate one, with the posterior part flat; and lastly two tubercular teeth, or true molars. As the incisors are worn away and the dog becomes old, the lobules on the edges wear away and are flattened (see Figs. 45 and 46). The teeth are developed in two sets; the first, called milk-teeth, showing themselves through the gums about a fortnight or three weeks after birth, and lasting until the fifth or sixth month, when they are displaced by the permanent set, the growth of which is accompanied by a degree of feverishness, which is often mistaken for distemper. The dog's teeth should be beautifully white, if he is healthy and well reared, and until the third year there should be no deposit of tartar upon them, but after that time they are always coated with this substance at the roots, more or less, according to the feeding and state of health.

TEETH OF THE DOG. 289

The fore feet are generally provided with five toes, and the hind with four, all furnished with strong nails that are not retractile. The inner toe on the fore feet is more or less rudimental, and is called the dew-claw; while there is also sometimes present in the hind foot a claw in the same situation still more rudimental, inas-

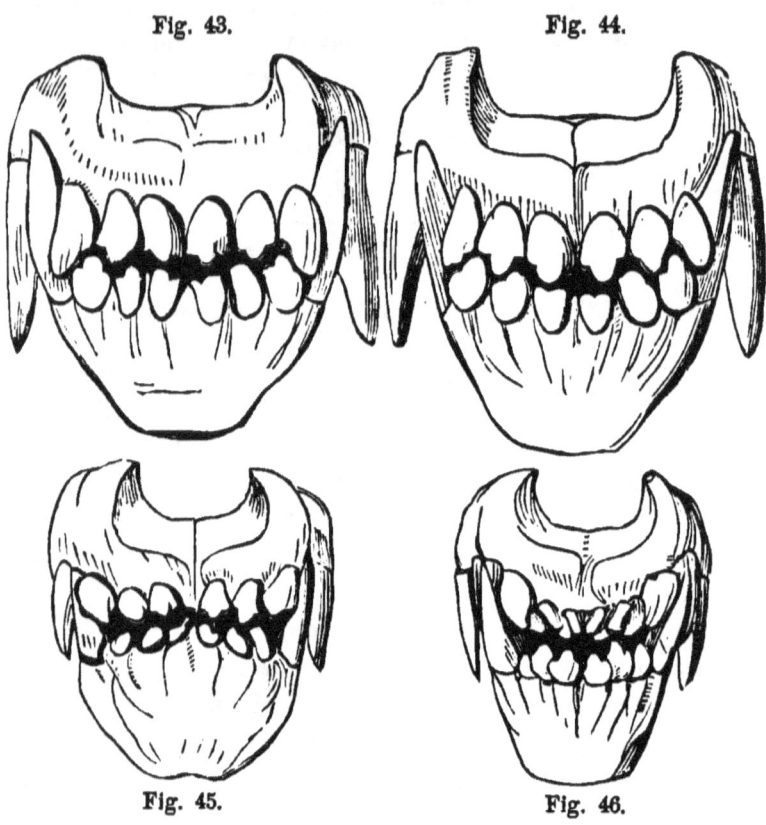

Fig. 43. Fig. 44.

Fig. 45. Fig. 46.

much as there is often no bony connexion with the metatarsal bone. This also is called the dew-claw, when present.

THE MUSCULAR SYSTEM.

The muscles of the dog have nothing remarkable about them, except that they are renewed and wasted faster than in most
13

animals. This has passed into a proverb, and should be known as influencing the time which dogs take to recruit their strength.

THE BRAIN AND NERVOUS SYSTEM.

The nervous system is highly developed in those breeds which have been carefully attended to, that is, where individuals of high nervous sensibility have been selected to breed from. This is therefore remarkable in the bulldog, selected for generations for courage; in the pointer, where steadiness in pointing has been the prominent cause of choice; and in the greyhound, whose characteristic is speed; all requiring a high development of the nervous system, and all particularly liable to nervous diseases, such as fits, chorea, etc. On the other hand, the cur, the common sheep-dog, etc., seldom suffer from any disease whatever.

THE DIGESTIVE SYSTEM.

The stomach of this animal is extremely powerful in dissolving bones, but it is also very liable to sickness, and on the slightest disturbance rejects its contents. This appears to be almost a natural effect, and not a diseased or disordered condition, as there is scarcely a dog which does not wilfully produce vomiting occasionally by swallowing grass. Few medicines which are at all irritating will remain down, and a vast number which are supposed to be given are not retained on the stomach, while others are only partially so. The bowels are extremely liable to become costive, which is in great measure owing to the want of proper exercise, and this also is very apt to produce torpidity of the liver. It may, however, be observed that in almost all particulars, except the tendency to vomit, the digestive organs of the dog resemble those of man.

THE HEART AND LUNGS.

There is nothing whatever remarkable in the heart and lungs; but the blood-vessels, like those of most of the lower animals, are so elastic in their coats that they quickly contract when divided, and a fatal bleeding rarely results.

THE SKIN.

The skin of the dog is said to be quite free from perspiration, but this is a mistake, as I have often seen the short hairs of a smooth-coated dog glistening with fine beads of liquid, poured out on a hot day, when strong exercise was taken. The tongue, however, is the grand means of carrying off heat by evaporation, and its extensive surface, when hanging out of the mouth, is sufficient for the purpose, as the fluid is carried off more rapidly from the air passing over it in expiration. I am persuaded that a considerable amount of insensible perspiration is constantly going on from the surface of the skin, and that nothing ought to be done which is likely to check it. This, however, is contrary to the generally received opinion, which is that nothing of the kind takes place in this animal.

CHAPTER II.

THE REMEDIES SUITED TO THE DOG, AND THE BEST MEANS OF ADMINISTERING THEM.

ALTERATIVES. — ANODYNES. — ANTISPASMODICS. — APERIENTS. — ASTRINGENTS. — BLISTERS. — CAUSTICS. — CHARGES. — CORDIALS. — DIURETICS. — EMBROCATIONS. — EMETICS. — EXPECTORANTS. — FEVER MEDICINES. — CLYSTERS. — LOTIONS. — OINTMENTS. — STOMACHICS. — STYPTICS. — TONICS. — WORM MEDICINES. — ADMINISTRATION OF REMEDIES.

ALTERATIVES.

These are medicines which are given with a view of changing an unhealthy into a healthy action. We know nothing of the mode in which the change is produced, and we can only judge of them by the results. The most powerful are mercury, iodine, hemlock, hellebore, and cod-liver oil, which are given in the following formulas:

  1.—Æthiop's mineral, 1½ to 5 grains.
   Powdered rhubarb, 1 to 4 grains.
    " ginger, ½ to 1½ grain.
Mix and make into a pill, to be given every evening.

  2.—Hemlock extract, or fresh-bruised leaves, 2 to 4 grains.
   Plummer's pill, 1½ to 5 grains.
Mix, and give every night, or every other night.

  3.—Iodide of potassium, 2 to 4 grains.
   Liquid extract of sarsaparilla, 1 drachm.
Mix, and give in a little water, once or twice a day.

  4.—Stinking hellebore, 5 to 10 grains.
   Powdered jalap, 2 to 4 grains.
Mix into a bolus, and give every other night.

  5.—Cod-liver oil, from a teaspoonful to a tablespoonful.
To be given twice a day.

ANODYNES.

Anodynes are required in the dog chiefly to stop diarrhœa, which is a very common disease with him. Sometimes also they are used for the purpose of relieving spasm. Opium is so little objectionable in the dog that it is almost the only anodyne used; but the dose must be far larger than for human beings, and less than a teaspoonful of laudanum for an average dog will be found to be wholly ineffectual.

For slight purging:

  6.—Prepared chalk, 2 to 3 drachms.
   Aromatic confection, 1 drachm.
   Laudanum, 3 to 8 drachms.
   Powder of gum arabic, 2 drachms.
   Water, 7 ounces.

Mix, and give two tablespoonfuls every time the bowels are relaxed.

     or,

  7.—Castor oil, from a dessert to a tablespoonful.
   Laudanum, 1 to 2 drachms.

Mix, and give as a drench, repeating it in a day or two if necessary.

For long standing and severe purgation:

  8.—Creosote, 2 drachms.
   Laudanum, 6 to 8 drachms.
   Prepared chalk, 2 drachms.
   Powdered gum arabic, 2 drachms.
   Tincture of ginger, 2 drachms.
   Peppermint water, 6 ounces.

Mix, and give two tablespoonfuls every time the bowels are relaxed, but not more often than every four hours.

ANTISPASMODICS.

Antispasmodics are useful in allaying cramp or spasm, but, as in the case of Alteratives, we do not know how they act. The chief ones are opium, ether, spirits of turpentine, and camphor, prescribed according to the following formulas:

  9.—Laudanum.
   Sulphuric ether, of each ½ to 1 drachm.
   Camphor mixture, 1 ounce.

Mix, and give in any ordinary spasm, as colic, etc.

An antispasmodic injection:
> 10.—Laudanum,
> Sulphuric ether,
> Spirits of turpentine, of each 1 to 2 drachms.
> Gruel, 3 to 8 ounces.

Mix, and inject with a common clyster syringe.

APERIENTS.

Aperients, opening medicines, or purges, by which several names this class of medicines is known, are constantly required by the dog, though it is a great mistake to give them when they are not absolutely demanded by the necessity of the case. All act by quickening the ordinary muscular action of the bowels, but some also stimulate the lining membrane to pour out large quantities of watery fluid, and others either directly or indirectly compel the liver to increase its secretion of bile. Hence they are often classed in corresponding divisions, as laxatives, drastic purgatives, etc. The chief of these drugs used in the dog-kennel are aloes, colocynth, rhubarb, jalap, ipecacuanha, senna, calomel, and blue pill, all of which act more or less on the liver; while Epsom salts, castor oil, and croton oil open the bowels without any such effect. Syrup of buckthorn is commonly given, but has little effect; and, indeed, the syrup of red-poppies is generally substituted for it by the druggist, who seldom keeps the genuine article, from the belief that it is ineffectual.

A mild bolus:
> 11.—Barbadoes aloes, 10 to 15 grains.
> Powdered jalap, 5 to 8 grains.
> Ginger, 2 or 3 grains.
> Soap, 10 grains.

Mix into one bolus for a large dog, or divide into two or three for small ones, and give as required.

Strong bolus:
> 12.—Calomel, 3 to 5 grains.
> Jalap, 10 to 20 grains.
> Mix with syrup, and give as a bolus.

A good common aperient, when the liver is sluggish :
    13.—Podophyllin, ½ grain.
        Compound extract of colocynth, 12 to 18 grains.
        Powdered rhubarb, 3 to 5 grains.
        Oil of cloves, 2 drops.

Mix, and give as a bolus to a large strong dog, or divide into two or three for smaller dogs.

Very strong purgative when there is an obstruction:
    14.—Croton oil, 1 to 2 drops.
        Purified opium, 1 to 2 grains.
        Linseed meal, 10 grains.

Mix the meal with boiling water into a thick paste, then add the oil and spices, and give as a bolus.

Ordinary castor oil mixture:
    15.—Castor oil, 3 ounces.
        Syrup of buckthorn, 2 ounces.
        Syrup of poppies, 1 ounce.

Mix, and give a tablespoonful to a medium-sized dog.

Very strong purgative mixture:
    16.—Jalap, 10 grains.
        Epsom salts, 2 drachms.
        Subcarbonate of soda, 10 grains.
        Infusion of senna, 1 ounce.
        Tincture of senna, 2 drachms.
        Tincture of ginger, 15 drops.

Mix, and give as a drench. For a small dog, give one half, one third, or one quarter, according to size.

A purgative clyster:
    17.—Castor oil, ½ ounce.
        Spirits of turpentine, 2 to 3 drachms.
        Common salt, ½ ounce.
        Gruel, 6 to 8 ounces.

Mix all together, and inject carefully per anum.

ASTRINGENTS.

Astringents produce contraction in all living tissues with which they are placed in apposition, either directly or by means of absorption in the circulation. Of these, opium, gallic acid, alum, bark, catechu, sulphate of zinc, nitrate of silver, and chloride of zinc are the most commonly used.

An astringent bolus for diabetes or internal hemorrhage:

 18.—Gallic acid, 3 to 6 grains.
  Alum, 4 to 7 grains.
  Purified opium, 1 to 2 grains.

Mix with syrup, and give two or three times a day to a large dog.

or,

 19.—Nitrate of silver, ¼ grain.
  Crumb of bread, enough to make a small pill.
  To be given twice a day.

Astringent wash for the eyes:

 20.—Sulphate of zinc, 5 to 8 grains.
  Water, 2 ounces,—Mix.

or,

 21.—Extract of goulard, 1 drachm.
  Water, 1 ounce.—Mix.

or,

 22.—Nitrate of silver, 2 to 6 grains.
  Distilled water, 1 ounce.—Mix.

Wash for the organ:

 23.—Chloride of zinc, ½ 2 to grains.
  Water, 1 ounce.—Mix.

Astringent application for piles:

 24.—Gallic acid, 10 grains.
  Extract of goulard, 15 drops.
  Powdered opium, 15 grains.
  Lard, 1 ounce.
  Mix, and apply night and morning.

BLISTERS.

Blisters are rarely used for the dog, because unless he has a proper muzzle on he will lick them off, injuring himself very materially. Sometimes, however, as in inflammation of the lungs, they are absolutely necessary. Iodine blisters to reduce local swellings may often be applied with a bandage over them, but even then, unless there is a muzzle on, the dog soon gets the bandage off, and uses his tongue. The chief are cantharides, turpentine, sulphuric acid, mustard, ammonia, tincture of iodine, and biniodide of mercury; the last two having some peculiar effect in producing absorption of any diseased substance lying beneath. In all cases the hair ought to be cut off as closely as possible.

A mild blister:
  25.—Powdered cantharides, 5 or 6 drachms.
    Venice turpentine, 1 ounce.
    Lard, 4 ounces.—Mix, and rub in.

Strong blister:
  26.—Strong mercurial ointment, 4 ounces.
    Oil of origanum, ½ ounce.
    Finely powdered euphorbium, 3 drachms.
    Powdered cantharides, ½ ounce.—Mix.

Very quick blister:
  27.—Flour of mustard, 4 ounces.
    Spirit of turpentine, 1 ounce.
    Strong liquor of ammonia, ½ ounce.
Mix the mustard with water into a paste, then add the other ingredients and rub in.

For bony growths or other tumors:
  28.—Tincture of Iodine.
Painted on every day, by means of a common painter's brush.
      or,
  29.—Biniodide of mercury, 1 to 1½ drachms.
    Lard, 1 ounce.
Mix, and rub in a piece the size of a nutmeg every day, keeping the part wet with tincture of arnica, ½ ounce, mixed with half a pint of water.

CAUSTICS.

This name is given to substances which either actually or potentially destroy the living tissue. The actual cautery is an iron heated in the fire, the potential of some chemical substance, such as corrosive sublimate, lunar caustic, caustic potash, a mineral acid, or the like. The actual cautery, or firing, is not often used for the dog, but in some cases it is of great service. Both kinds are used for two purposes: one to relieve the effects of strains and other injuries of the limbs, by which the ligaments are inflamed, and the other to remove diseased growth, such as warts, fungus, etc.

30.—Firing, when adopted for the dog, should be carried out with a very small thin-edged iron, as the dog's skin is thin, and very liable to slough. No one should attempt this without experience or previously watching others.

31.—Lunar caustic, or nitrate of silver, is constantly required, being very manageable in the hands of any person accustomed to wounds, etc.

32.—Sulphate of copper, or bluestone, is much milder than the lunar caustic, and may be freely rubbed into the surface of fungus or proud flesh. It is very useful in ulcerations about the toes.

33.—Fused potass is not fit for any one but the experienced surgeon.

34.—Corrosive sublimate in powder may be applied, carefully and in very small quantities, to warts, and then washed off. It is apt to extend its effects to the surrounding tissues.

35.—Yellow orpiment is not so strong as corrosive sublimate, and may be used in the same way.

36.—Burned alum and white sugar, in powder, act as mild caustics.

CHARGES.

Charges are plasters which act chiefly by mechanical pressure, being spread on while hot, and then covered with tow. They are not much used among dogs, but in strains they are sometimes beneficial, as they allow the limb to be exercised without injury. The best for the dog is composed as follows:

37.—Canada balsam, 2 ounces.
Powdered arnica leaves, ½ ounce.

Melt the balsam, and mix up with the powder, with the addition of a little turpentine, if necessary. Then smear over the part, and cover with tow, which is to be well matted in with the hand; or use thin leather.

CORDIALS.

Warm stimulating stomachics are so called. They may be given either as a ball or a drench.

Cordial ball:

> 38.—Powdered caraway seeds, 10 to 15 grains.
> Ginger, 3 to 5 grains.
> Oil of cloves, 2 drops.
> Linseed meal, enough to make a ball, first mixing it with boiling water.

Cordial drench:

> 39.—Tincture of cardamoms, ½ to 1 drachm.
> Sal volatile, 15 to 30 drops.
> Tincture of cascarilla, ½ to 1 drachm.
> Camphor mixture, 1 oz.—Mix.

DIURETICS.

Medicines which act on the secretion of urine are called diuretics. They are either employed when the kidneys are sluggish, to restore the proper quantity, or to increase it beyond the natural standard, when it is desired to lower the system.

Diuretic bolus:

> 40.—Nitre, 5 to 8 grains.
> Digitalis, ½ grain.
> Ginger, 2 or 3 grains.

Mix with linseed meal and water, and give all or part, according to the size of the dog.

Diuretic and alterative bolus:

> 41.—Iodide of potassium, 2 to 4 grains.
> Nitre, 3 to 6 grains.
> Digitalis, ½ grain.
> Extract of camomile, 5 grains.

Mix, and give all or part.

EMBROCATIONS.

These external applications, otherwise called liniments, are extremely useful in the dog, for strains, or sometimes to relieve muscular inflammation, or chronic rheumatism of the joints. Mustard, ammonia, laudanum, and turpentine, are the chief agents employed.

Mustard embrocation:
    42.—Best mustard, 3 to 5 ounces.
        Liquor of ammonia, 1 ounce.
        Spirit of turpentine, 1 ounce.
    Mix into a thin paste, and rub into the part affected.

Embrocation for strains or rheumatism:
    43.—Spirit of turpentine,
        Liquor of ammonia,
        Laudanum, of each ½ ounce.
    Mix, and shake well before using, then rub in.

EMETICS.

Emetics are very commonly used in the diseases of the dog, and sometimes act very beneficially; but they have a tendency to weaken the stomach, and should therefore be used with caution. If not frequently resorted to no harm is likely to accrue, as vomiting is almost a natural process in the dog.

Common salt emetic:
    44.—Dissolve a teaspoonful of salt and half a teaspoonful of mustard in half a pint of tepid water, and give it as a drench.

Strong emetic:
    45.—Tartar emetic, 1 to 3 grains.
Dissolve in a tablespoonful of warm water, and give as a drench; following it up in a quarter of an hour, by pouring down as much thin gruel as the dog can be made to swallow.

EXPECTORANTS, OR COUGH MEDICINES.

The action of these remedies is to promote the flow of mucus, so as to relieve the congestion of the air passages.

Common cough bolus:
    46.—Ipecacuanha in powder, ½ to 1½ grain.
    Powdered rhubarb, 1 to 2 grains.
    Purified opium, ½ to 1½ grain.
    Compound squill pill, 1 to 2 grains.
Mix, and give night and morning.

Expectorant draught, useful in recent cough:
    47.—Ipecacuanha wine, 5 to 10 drops.
    Common mucilage, 2 drachms.
    Sweet spirit of nitre, 20 to 30 drops.
    Paregoric, 1 drachm.
    Camphor mixture, ½ ounce.
Mix, and give two or three times a day.

Expectorant draught for chronic cough:
    48.—Compound tincture of benzoin, 8 to 12 drops.
    Syrup of poppies, 1 drachm.
    Diluted sulphuric acid, 3 to 8 drops.
    Mucilage, 2 drachms.
    Paregoric, 1 drachm.
    Camphor mixture, ½ ounce.
Mix, and give twice a day.

FEVER MEDICINES.

Fever medicines reduce fever by increasing the secretions of urine and perspiration, and by reducing the action of the heart to some extent.

Common fever powder:
    49.—Nitre in powder, 3 to 5 grains.
    Tartar emetic, ¼ grain.
Mix, and put dry on the dog's tongue every night and morning.

More active powder:
    50.—Calomel, ½ to 1½ grain.
    Nitre, 3 to 5 grains.
    Digitalis, ½ to 1 grain.
Mix, and give once or twice a day, in the same way; or made into a pill with confection.

Fever mixture :
> 51.—Nitre, 1 drachm.
> Sweet spirit of nitre, 3 drachms.
> Mindererus' spirit, 1 ounce.
> Camphor mixture, 6½ ounces.
> Mix, and give two tablespoonfuls every six hours.

CLYSTERS.

Clysters are extremely useful in the dog, which is liable to constipation from want of exercise, and in that case is mechanically bound. A pint of warm water, in which some yellow soap has been dissolved, will generally have the desired effect.

Turpentine clyster in colic:
> 52.—Spirit of turpentine, ½ ounce.
> Castor oil, 1 ounce.
> Laudanum, 2 to 3 drachms.
> Gruel, 1 pint.

Mix, and throw up, using only half or one third for a small dog.

LOTIONS.

Lotions, called Washes, are intended either to reduce the temperature in inflammation of the surface to which they are applied, or to brace the vessels of the part.

Cooling lotion for bruises:
> 53.—Extract of lead, 1 drachm.
> Tincture of arnica, ½ to 1 drachm.
> Water, ½ pint.

Mix, and apply by means of a bandage or sponge.

For severe stiffness from over-exercise :
> 54.—Tincture of arnica, ½ drachm.
> Strong spirit of wine, whiskey, or brandy, 7½ drachms.

Mix, and rub well into the back and limbs, before the fire.

Lotion for the eyes:
> 55.—Sulphate of zinc, 20 to 25 grains.
> Water, ½ pint.

Mix, and wash the eyes night and morning.

Strong drops for the eyes:
> 56.—Nitrate of silver, 3 to 8 grains.
> Distilled water, 1 ounce.
> Mix, and drop in with a quill.

OINTMENTS.

By means of lard, wax, etc., various substances are mixed up so as to be applied to wounds, chiefly to keep out the air.

A good ointment for old sores:
> 57.—Yellow basilicon,
> Ointment of nitric-oxide of mercury, equal parts.

Digestive ointment:
> 58.—Red precipitate, 2 ounces.
> Venice turpentine, 3 ounces.
> Beeswax, 1½ ounce.
> Lard, 4 ounces.—Mix.

Mange ointment:
> 58a.—Green iodide of mercury, 1 drachm.
> Lard, 8 drachms.
> Mix, and rub in carefully every 2nd or 3rd day.

STIMULANTS—*see* CORDIALS.

STOMACHICS.

The name describes the use of the remedies, which are intended to give tone to the stomach.

Stomachic bolus:
> 59.—Extract of gentian, 6 to 8 grains.
> Powdered rhubarb, 2 to 3 grains.
> Mix, and give twice a day.

Stomachic draught:

    60.—Tincture of cardamoms, ½ to 1 drachm.
    Compound infusion of gentian, 1 ounce.
    Carbonate of soda, 3 grains.
    Powdered ginger, 2 grains.
    Mix, and give twice a day.

STYPTICS.

Styptics are remedies to stop bleeding. In the dog the vessels seldom give way externally, but internally the disease is very frequent, either in the form of a bloody flux, or bloody urine, or bleeding from the lungs, for which the following may be tried:

    61—Superacetate of lead, 2 to 3 grains.
    Tincture of matico, 30 to 50 drops.
    Vinegar, 10 drops.
    Water, 1 ounce.

Mix, and give two or three times a day.

TONICS.

Tonics permanently increase the tone or vigor of the system, being particularly useful in the recovery from low fever.

Tonic pill:

    62—Sulphate of quinine, 1 to 3 grains.
    Extract of hemlock, 2 grains.
    Ginger, 2 grains.

Mix, and give twice a day.

Tonic mixture:

    63—Compound tincture of bark, 2 ounces.
    Decoction of yellow bark, 14 ounces.

Mix, and give three tablespoonsfuls twice or thrice daily to a large dog.

WORM MEDICINES.

By this term we are to understand such substances as will expel worms from the intestines of the dog, their action being either poisonous to the worm itself, or so irritating as to cause them to evacuate. All ought either to be in themselves purgative, or to be followed by a medicine of that class, in order to insure the removal of the eggs, as well as the worms themselves. More detailed directions will be found in the chapter of Worms.

Aperient-worm bolus.
   64—Calomel, 2 to 5 grains.
    Jalap, 10 to 20 grains.
 Mix into a bolus, with molasses.

For general worms. Not aperient, and therefore to be followed by castor oil:
   65—Recently powdered areca nut, 1 to 2 drachms.

Mix with broth, and give to the dog directly, as there is no taste in it until it has been soaked some time, when the broth becomes bitter. If the dog refuses it he must be drenched. Four hours after, give a dose of castor oil. N. B.—The exact dose is 2 grains for each pound the dog weighs.

For round-worms, or maw-worms:
   66—Indian pink, ¼ ounce.
   Boiling water, 8 ounces.

Let it stand for an hour, then strain, and give half to a large dog, a quarter to a middle-sized dog, or an eighth to a very small one. This, however, is a severe remedy, and is not unattended with danger. It should be followed by castor oil in six hours.

Mild remedy, unattended with any danger:
   67.—Powdered glass, as much as will lie on a twenty-five cent piece, heaped up.

To be mixed with butter, and given as a bolus, following it up with castor oil after six hours.

For tape-worm:
   68—Kousso, ¼ to ½ ounce.
   Lemon juice, 1 tablespoonful.
   Boiling water, ½ pint.

Pour the water on the kousso, and when nearly cold add the lemon juice. Stir all up together, and give as a drench. It should be followed up in six or eight hours by a dose of oil.

Another remedy for tape-worm:
   69—Spirit of turpentine, 1 to 4 drachms.

Tie this up firmly in a piece of bladder, then give as a bolus, taking care not to burst the bladder. This also requires a dose of oil to follow. Or mix the turpentine with suet into a bolus.

Another:

   70— Fresh root of male fern, 1 to 4 drachms.
    Powdered jalap, 15 grains.
    Liquorice powder and water, enough to make a bolus.

N. B.—The oil of male fern is better than the dry root, the dose being ten to thirty drops.

ADMINISTRATION OF REMEDIES.

Some considerable tact and knowledge of the animal are required, in order to give medicines to the dog to the best advantage. In the first place, his stomach is peculiarly irritable, and so much under the control of the will, that most dogs can vomit whenever they like. Hence it is not only necessary to give the medicine, but also to insure its being kept down. For this purpose, however, it is generally only necessary to keep up the dog's head, as he will not readily vomit without bringing his nose to the ground, and so it is the regular practice in large kennels, in giving a dose of physic, to put the couples on, and fasten them up to a hook, at such a hight that the dog cannot lower his head, maintaining this position for two or three hours. A single dog may be watched, if such is preferred, but a lot of hounds in physic must be treated with less ceremony.

THE DOG'S SYSTEM RESEMBLES THAT OF MAN.

The effects of remedies on the dog are nearly the same as on man, so that any one who understands how to manage himself may readily extend his sphere of usefulness to the dog. On the other hand, horses require a very different treatment, which accounts for the ignorance of the diseases of the dog so often displayed by otherwise clever veterinary surgeons, who have confined their attention to the more valuable animal. Some remedies affect the dog differently, however; thus laudanum, which is a very dangerous drug in human medicine, rarely does harm to the canine species, and treble the dose for a man will be required for the dog. On the other hand, calomel is quite the reverse, being extremely liable to produce great irritation on the lining membrane of the dog's stomach and bowels.

MODE OF GIVING A BOLUS OR PILL.

If the dog is small, take him on the lap, without harshness, and if inclined to use his claws, tie a coarse towel round his neck, letting it fall down in front, which will muffle them effectually; then with the finger and thumb of the left hand press open the mouth by inserting them between the teeth, far enough back to take in the cheeks. This compels the mouth to open from the pain given by the pressure against the teeth, while it also prevents the dog from biting the fingers. Then raising the nose, drop the pill as far back as possible, and push it well down the throat with the forefinger of the right hand. Let go with the left hand, still hold up the nose, keeping the mouth shut, and the pill is sure to go down. Two persons are required in administering a pill to a large dog, if he is at all inclined to resist. First, back him into a corner, then stride over him, and putting a thick cloth into his mouth, bring it together over the nose, where it is held by the left hand; the right can then generally lay hold of the lower jaw. But if the dog is very obstinate, another cloth must also be placed over the first, and then as they are drawn apart, an assistant can push the pill down. Very often a piece of meat may be used to wrap the pill in, and the dog will readily bolt it; but sometimes it is desirable to avoid this, as it may be necessary to give the medicine by itself. Even large dogs, however, are seldom so troublesome as to require the above precautions in giving pills, though they, as a general thing, obstinately refuse liquid medicine when they have tasted it once or twice.

MODE OF DRENCHING THE DOG.

If a small quantity only is to be given, the dog's head being held, the liquid may be poured through the closed teeth by making a little pouch of the cheek. This, however, is a tedious process, as the animal often refuses to swallow the medicine for a long time, and then struggles until half is wasted. A spoon answers for small quantities; for large quantities a soda-water bottles is the best instrument. Having the dog held on either of the plans recommended in the last paragraph, pour a little of the fluid down his throat, and shut the mouth. This is necessary, inasmuch as the act of swallowing can not be performed with the mouth open. Repeat this, until all the medicine is swallowed. Then watch the dog, or tie up his head until it is certain that the medicine will be retained on the stomach.

CLYSTERS OR INJECTIONS.

When the bowels are very much confined, a pint or two of warm gruel will, if thrown up into the rectum, often be of great service. The dog should be placed on his side, and held in this position on a table by an assistant, while the operator passes the pipe carefully into the rectum, and pumps up the fluid.

CHAPTER III.

FEVERS AND THEIR TREATMENT.

SIMPLE EPHEMERAL FEVER, OR COLD.—EPIDEMIC FEVER, OR INFLU-
ENZA.—TYPHUS FEVER, OR DISTEMPER.—RHEUMATIC FEVER.—SMALL-
POX.—SYMPATHETIC FEVER.

The dog is peculiarly liable to febrile attacks, which have always a tendency to put on a low form, very similar in its nature to that known as typhus in human diseases. This is so generally the case, that every dog is said to have the distemper at some time of his life, that name being given to this low form of fever. An attack may commence with a common cold, or any inflammatory affection of the lungs, bowels, etc.; and on assuming the low form, is followed by a genuine case of typhus fever or distemper. Nevertheless, it does not follow that the one must necessarily end in the other; the dog may have simple fever, known as "a cold," or various other complaints, without being subjected to the true distemper. The fevers occurring in the dog are: 1st, Simple ephemeral fever, commonly called "a cold;" 2d, Simple epidemic fever, or influenza; 3d, Typhus fever, known as Distemper; 4th, Rheumatic fever, attacking the muscular and fibrous systems; and, 5th, Small-pox.

SIMPLE EPHEMERAL FEVER.

Simple Ephemeral Fever, known as "a common cold," is ushered in by chilliness, with increased heat of surface, a quick pulse, and slightly hurried breathing. The appetite is not as good as usual; the eyes look dull; the bowels are costive; the urine is scanty and high-colored. There are often cough and slight run ning at the nose and eyes, and sometimes other internal organs are attacked; or the disease goes on until a different form of fever is established, known as typhus. This often occurs when many dogs are collected together, or when one or two are kept in a close kennel, where there is neither proper ventilation nor cleanliness.

Cause.—Exposure to wet or cold.

Treatment.—Complete rest; a gentle dose of opening medicine: (12) or (13) if the liver is torpid, (15) if acting. After this has acted, give slops, and if there is still much fever, one of the remedies (45) or (51). If there is much cough, give the draught (47) or the bolus (46).

INFLUENZA.

The symptoms of influenza at first closely resemble those of ephemeral fever, but as they depend upon some peculiar condition of the air which prevails at the time, and as they are more persistent, the name influenza is given to the disease. After the first few days, the running at the eyes and nose increases, and a cough is almost always present. These symptoms often continue for two or three weeks, and are followed with great prostration of strength and often a chronic cough, which requires careful treatment.

The cause is to be looked for in some peculiar state of the air, concerning the nature of which nothing is known at present.

Treatment.—In the early stage, the remedies should be the same as for ordinary or simple "cold." Towards the second week, a cough-bolus (46) or draught (47) will generally be required. When the strength is much reduced after the second week, and the cough is nearly gone, give a tonic pill (62) or mixture (63). Great care should be taken not to bring on a relapse by improper food, or by too early an allowance of exercise. Fresh air is of the utmost importance, but it must be taken at a slow pace, as a gallop will often undo all that has been effected in the way of a cure.

TYPHUS FEVER, OR DISTEMPER.

It is now generally admitted that this disease is similar to typhus fever in man, and should be treated in much the same manner.

The essence of the disease is some poison admitted from without, or developed within the blood, by which the various secretions are either totally checked, or so altered as no longer to purify the system. The exact nature of this poison is beyond our present state of knowledge, but from analogy there is little doubt that it resides in the blood. As in all cases of poison absorbed in the system, there is a most rapidly depressing effect upon the muscular powers, which is to be expected, inasmuch as their action requires a constant formation of new material from the blood. As this is retarded in common with all other functions, the muscles waste away rapidly, and their contractions are not performed with any strength. The disease is sometimes conveyed by infection. At others it is developed in the body; just as in the case of fermentation in vegetable substances, there may be a ferment added to a saccharine solution, by which the process is hastened, although if left to itself, it will come on in due course.

The symptoms are various; they may be divided into two classes, one of which comprises those always attending upon distemper; the other may or may not be present in any individual attack. The invariable symptoms are, a low insidious fever, with prostration of strength to a remarkable degree, in proportion to the duration and strength of the attack, and rapid emaciation, so that a thick muscular dog often becomes quite thin and lanky in three days. As a part of the fever, there is shivering, attended by quick pulse, hurried respiration, loss of appetite, and impaired secretions. Beyond these, there are no signs which can be called positively invariable, though the running at the eyes and nose, and the short husky cough, especially after exercise, are very nearly always present. The accidental symptoms depend upon the particular complication which may exist; for one of the most remarkable features in distemper is, that, coupled with the above invariable symptoms, there may be congestion, or inflammation of the head, chest, bowels, or skin. In one case the disease may appear to be entirely confined to the head, in another to the chest, and in a third to the bowels; yet it results from the same cause in each case, and requires the same general plan of treatment, modified according to the seat of the complication.

When distemper is the result of neglect, it generally succeeds some other disease which may have existed for an indefinite period. The ordinary course of an attack of distemper, when epidemic, or the result of contagion, is as follows: general dullness or lassitude, together with loss of appetite are first observed. A peculiar husky cough generally follows in a day or two, with sounds as if the dog were trying to discharge a piece of straw from his throat. It always comes on at exercise after a gallop. With this there is also a tendency to sneeze, but not so marked as the "husk" or "tissuck" which may occur in common "cold" or influenza, and is then usually more severe, and also more variable in its severity; soon going on to inflammation, or else entirely ceasing in a few days. In distemper, the strength and flesh rapidly fail and waste, while in common "cold," the cough may continue for days without much alteration in either; this is one of the chief characteristics of the true disease. There is, also, generally a black pitchy condition of the fæces, and the urine is scanty and high-colored. The white of the eyes is always more or less reddened, the color being of a bluish red cast, and the vessels being evidently gorged with blood. When the brain is attacked, the eyes are more injected than when the bowels or lungs is the seat of complication. The corners of the eyes have a small drop of mucus, and the nose runs more or less, which symptoms, as the disease goes on, are much aggravated, both eyes being glued by brownish matter. The teeth are also covered with a blackish brown fur. These are the regular symptoms of a severe attack of distemper, which gradually increases in severity to the third, fourth, or fifth week, when the dog dies from exhaustion, or from disease of the brain, lungs, or bowels, marked by peculiar signs in each case. In this course the disease may be described as passing through four stages or periods: 1st, that in which the poison is spreading through the system, called the period of inculation; 2nd, that in which nature rouses her powers to expel it, called the period of reaction; 3rd, the period of prostration, during which the powers of nature are exhausted, or nearly so, by the efforts which have been made; and 4th, the period of convalescence. On the average, each of these will occupy a week or ten days, varying with the mildness or severity of the attack.

When the head is attacked, there may or may not be a running from the nose and eyes; but more usually there is some evidence of congestion in these organs, the eyes being weak and glued up with the mucus, and the nose running more or less. A fit is, however, the clearest evidence of brain affection, and, to a common observer, the only reliable one. Sometimes there is stupor without a fit, gradually increasing until the dog becomes insensible, and dies. At other times, a raving delirium comes on, easily mistaken for hydrophobia, but distinguished from it by the presence of the premonitory symptoms, peculiar to distemper. This is the most fatal complication of all, and, if the dog recovers, he is often a victim to palsy or chorea for the rest of his life.

If the lungs are attacked, there is very rapid breathing, with cough, and generally a considerable running from the eyes and nose, accompanied with expectoration of thick frothy mucus. If inflammation of the lungs is established, the danger is as great as when the head is the seat of the malady.

The bowels may be known to be seized when there is a violent purging of black offensive matter, often tinged with blood, and sometimes mixed with patches or shreds of a white leathery substance, which is coagulable lymph. The discharge of blood is, in some cases, excessive, and quickly carries off the dog.

If the skin is attacked, which is a favorable sign, there is a breaking out of pustules on the inside of the thighs and belly, which fill with matter, often tinged with dark blood, and sometimes with blood itself of a dark purple color.

It is not an easy matter for an inexperienced observer to distinguish distemper from similar affections, but the practised eye readily detects the difference. The chief diseases which are likely to be confounded with distemper are, the true canine madness, common cold or influenza, inflammation of the lungs, and diarrhœa. The first of these runs a rapid course, and is ushered in by peculiar changes in the temper, which will be described under the head of hydrophobia. Cold and influenza cause no great prostration of strength. The former comes on after exposure to the weather, while the latter is sure to be prevalent at the time. Inflammation of the lungs must be studied to be known; simple diarrhœa has no fever attending upon it.

The treatment of distemper is twofold; care first, being directed to the safe conduct through the lowering effects of the complaint, and second to the warding off of the fatal results which are likely to be occasioned by the local complications in the brain, lungs, or bowels. It must be remembered that the disease is an effort of nature to rid itself of a poison; and, consequently, the powers of the system must be aided throughout, or they will be incompetent to their task. One great means of carrying off this poison, is to be looked for in the bowels and kidneys. These organs must be restored as far as possible to their natural condition, care being exercised that they are not injured by the remedies used. It is well known, for instance, that aperients, and especially calomel, have the property of restoring the suspended action of the liver. But they also have an injurious effect upon the strength of the general system, and therefore must be used with great caution. The best formulæ is, (13) or (15) given only once or twice, at intervals of two or three days. After the secretions are restored, the next thing is to look out for the complications in the brain, lungs, and bowels, which are to be expected; and, if present, to counteract them by appropriate remedies. A seton placed on the back of the neck, covering the tape with blister ointment, will be likely to relieve the head, together with cold applications of vinegar and water by means of a sponge. At the same time the fever mixture (51) may be regularly administered. For any trifling complication in the lungs the fever powder (49) will generally suffice; but, if severe, blood must be taken from the neck vein; though this, if possible, should be avoided, and the cough bolus or draught (46) or (47) be administered. Diarrhœa must be at once checked by one of the mixtures (6) or (8); or, if very severe, by the pill (19). At the same time, rice-water should be given as the only drink; and beef-tea, thickened with arrow-root or rice, as the sole article of diet, changing it occasionally for port wine and arrow-root. When the stage of exhaustion has commenced, the tonic mixture (63) will generally be required; and it is astonishing what may be done by a perseverance in its use. Dogs which appear to be dying will often recover. No case should be given up as long as there is any life remaining.

The diet should be carefully attended to, little or no food being required on the first four or six days, beyond weak broth or gruel, no solid food from the first being permitted. This restriction must be maintained until the dog is quite recovered. When the state of exhaustion or prostration comes on, good strong beef-tea should be given every three or four hours, and, if the dog will not swallow it, force should be used; a spoonful at a time being given in the manner described elsewhere for drenching. Port wine is often of service at such times, being thickened with arrow-root, and given alternately with beef-tea. For a dog of average size, the plan is to give a teacupful of beef-tea, then, after two hours, the same quantity of arrow-root and wine; then, again, after two hours, a dose of the tonic mixture, and so on through the twenty-four hours. Perseverance in this troublesome plan will generally be rewarded with success, but, of course, it is only a valuable dog which will reward it properly. In less important animals, the beef-tea may be provided, and if it is not voluntarily swallowed, the poor patient often dies for want of the compulsion, so that humanity as well as self-interest counsel the adoption of what often appears a harsh proceeding.

No exercise, even of the most gentle kind, should be allowed, as it invariably tends to bring on a return of the disease. Many a young dog has been sacrificed to the mistaken kindness of his master, who has thought that a "breath of fresh air" would do him good. And so it would, if taken in an easy carriage, at rest; but the muscular exertion necessary to procure it is highly injurious, and should be delayed until the strength is restored. This is one reason why dogs in the country bear distemper so much better than in towns; for, as it is known that they are in the fresh air, no attempt is made to take them to it, and so they are left alone, and are not induced to exert their strength prematurely. Even when the dog appears nearly well, it is better to lead him out to excercise for the first day or two. Otherwise he is almost sure to over-exert himself.

Ventilation should not be neglected; moderate warmth is essential to a cure, and a delicate dog like the greyhound should have a cloth on him in cold weather. The greatest cleanliness should be observed, and as far as possible without making the kennel damp with water. Clean straw must be liberally provided, and all offensive matters removed as often as they are voided.

Summary of treatment.—In the early stage of disease, get the bowels into good order by mild doses of aperient medicine: (11), (13), or (15). Attend to any complications which may come on, using a seton for the head and appropriate remedies for the chest, or mixture for the bowels (6) if there is diarrhœa. For the exhaustion, when the violent symptoms are abated, give the tonic (63); and during the whole period attend to the diet, ventilation, cleanliness, and rest, as previously described.

Vaccination has been recommended as a remedy for distemper, and has been largely tried both in foxhound and greyhound kennels, as well as among pointers and setters. Some people think it a sure preventive, and there is evidence that for years after it has been adopted in certain kennels, distemper, which was previously rife among them, has been held in check. On the other hand, a still more numerous party have found no change produced in the mortality among their dogs, and they have come as a natural consequence to the opposite conclusion. Reasoning from analogy, there is no ground for supposing that small-pox or cow-pox should prevent the access of a disease totally dissimilar to these complaints; inasmuch as experience is the best guide, the appeal must be made to it in order to settle the question. Judging from this test, I can see no reason whatever for the faith which is placed in vaccination, because there are at least as many recorded failures as successes; and as we know that after any remedy there will always be a certain number of assumed cures held out by sanguine individuals, so we must allow for a great many in this particular case. Distemper is well known to be most irrregular in its attacks, and to hit or miss particular kennels, as the case may be, for years together, and as vaccination is used at any of these various periods of change, so it gains credit or discredit which it does not deserve. After trying it myself and seeing it tried, and after also comparing the experience of others, my own belief is, that vaccination is wholly inoperative; but, as others may like to test it for themselves, I here append directions for the operation:

To vaccinate the dog, select the thin skin on the inside of the ear, then with a lancet charged with fresh vaccine lymph, make three or four oblique punctures in the skin, to such a depth as barely to draw blood, charging the lancet afresh each time. If the lymph cannot be procured fresh, the punctures must be made as above described, and then the points charged with dry lymph must be introduced, one in each puncture, and well rubbed into the cut surface so as to insure the removal of the lymph from the points. In four or five days an imperfect vesicle is formed, which, if not rubbed, goes on to maturity and scabs at the end of ten days or thereabout. There are various other methods suggested, such as introducing a piece of thread dipped in the virus, etc., but the above is the proper plan, if any is likely to be effectual.

The treatment of the various sequels of distemper, including fits, palsy, etc., will be given under those heads respectively

RHEUMATIC FEVER.

One of the most common diseases in the dog, is rheumatism in some form, generally showing itself with very little fever, but sometimes being accompanied with a high degree of fever. The frequency of this disease is owing to the constant exposure of the dog to cold and wet, and very often to his kennel being damp, which is the fertile source of kennel lameness, or chest-founder, the latter being nothing more than rheumatism of the muscles of the shoulders. Again, those which spend half their time before a roasting fire, and the other half in the wet and cold, are very liable to contract this kind of fever, but not in so intractable a form as the denizen of the damp kennel. By some writers this affection is classed among inflammations, and it is a debatable point to which of these divisions it should be assigned. But this is of little consequence, so that the fever is properly known and easily recognized by the symptoms. I shall therefore include here, rheumatic fever, which is a general affection, and also the partial attacks known as kennel lameness or chest-founder, and rheumatism of the loins, commonly called palsy of the back.

Rheumatic fever is known by the following signs:—There is considerable evidence of fever, but not of a very high character, the pulse being full but not very quick, with shivering and dullness, except when touched or threatened—the slightest approach causing a shriek, evidently from the fear of pain. The dog generally retires into a corner, and is very reluctant to come out. On being forcibly brought out, he snarls at the hand even of his best friend, and stands with his back up, evidently prepared to defend himself from the pat of the hand, which to him is anguish. The bowels are confined, and the urine highly colored and scanty. The treatment consists in bleeding from the neck, to a moderate extent, if the dog is very gross and full of condition, followed with a smart dose of opening physic: (12) or (13). After this has acted give the following pills:

> Calomel.
> Purified opium, of each 1 grain.
> Powdered root of colchicum, 2 to 3 grains.
> Syrup, enough to make a pill.

This is the dose for an average-sized dog. A hot bath is often of service, care being taken to dry the skin before the fire. Then follow up with a liberal friction by the aid of the liniment (43).

Kennel lameness, or chest-founder, manifests itself in a stiffness or soreness of the shoulders, so that the dog is unable to gallop freely down hill, and is often reluctant to jump off his bench to the ground, the shock giving pain to the muscles. It is very common in the kennels of foxhounds, for these dogs, being exposed to wet and cold for hours together, and then brought home to a damp lodging-room, contract the disease with great frequency. Pampered house pets are also very liable to chest-founder, overfeeding being quite as likely to produce rheumatism as exposure to cold, and when both are united this condition is almost sure to follow. When it becomes chronic there is little or no fever. After it has existed for some months it is generally regarded as incurable, but instances are known in which the stiffness has entirely disappeared. Chest-founder also arises from a sprain of the muscles which suspend the chest between the shoulders.

The remedies for kennel lameness are nearly the same as for general rheumatism, care being taken to remove the cause if it has existed in the shape of a damp cold lodging-room. The food should be light, and composed chiefly of vegetable materials; strong animal food tends to increase the rheumatic affection. The liniment (43) is very likely to be of service, especially if used after the hot bath, as previously described. It has been asserted, by persons of experience, that a red herring given two or three times a week will cure this disease. I have no personal experience of the merits of this remedy, but, according to Col. Whyte, it has recently been discovered that in the herring there is a specific for human rheumatism. It is worth a trial in dogs. It is given with two drachms of nitre and one of camphor. Most dogs readily eat the herring and camphor, and the nitre is added in a little water as a drench. Cod liver oil is also said to be of great service (5). Iodine with sarsaparilla (3) is a preparation which I have known to be of more service than any internal medicines.

A dragging of the hind limbs is common enough in the dog; though often called palsy, it really is, in most cases, of a rheumatic nature. It closely resembles chest-founder in all its symptoms, excepting that the muscles affected are situated in the loins and hips. The causes and treatment are the same as those for kennel lameness.

SMALL-POX.

I reproduce Mr. Youatt's description of small-pox in dogs:

In 1809, there was observed, at the Royal Veterinary School at Lyons, an eruptive malady among the dogs, to which they gave the name of small-pox. It appeared to be propagated from dog to dog by contagion. It was not difficult of cure; and it quickly disappeared when no other remedies than mild aperients and diaphoretics were employed. A sheep was inoculated from one of these dogs. There was a slight eruption of pustules around the place of inoculation, but nowhere else; nor was there the least fever. At another time, also, at the school at Lyons, a sheep died of the regular sheep-pox. A part of the skin was fastened, during four and twenty hours, on a healthy sheep, and the other part of it on a dog, both of them being in apparent good health. No effect was produced on the dog, but the sheep died of confluent sheep-pox. The essential symptoms of small-pox in dogs succeed each other in the following order: the skin of the belly, the groin, and the inside of the fore arm becomes of a redder color than in its natural state, and is sprinkled with small red spots irregularly rounded. They are sometimes isolated, sometimes clustered together. The near approach of this eruption is announced by an increase of fever.

On the second day, the spots are larger, and the integument is slightly tumefied at the center of each. On the third day, the spots are generally enlarged, and the skin is still more prominent at the center. On the fourth day, the summit of the tumor is yet more prominent. Towards the ends of that day the redness of the center begins to assume a somewhat grey color. On succeeding days, the pustules take on their peculiar characteristic appearance, and cannot be confounded with any other eruption. On the summit, is a white circular point, corresponding with a certain quantity of nearly transparent fluid which it contains, and covered by a thin and transparent pellicle. This fluid becomes less and less transparent, until it acquires the color and consistence of pus.

The pustule, during its serous state, is of a rounded form. It is flattened when the fluid acquires a purulent character, and even slightly depressed towards the close of the period of suppuration. The desiccation and the desquamation occupy an exceedingly variable length of time; and so, indeed, do all the different periods of the disease. What is the least inconstant, is the duration of the serous eruption, which is about four days, if it has been distinctly produced and guarded from all friction. If the general character of the pustules is considered, it will be observed, that while some of them are in a state of serous secretion, others will only have begun to appear. The eruption terminates when desiccation commences in the first pustules; and, if some red spots show themselves at that period of the malady, they disappear without being followed by the development of pustules. They are a species of abortive pustules. After the desiccation, the skin remains covered by brown spots, which, by degrees, die away. There remains no trace of the disease, except a few superficial cicatrices on which the hair does not grow.

The causes which produce the greatest variation in the periods of the eruption are, the age of the dog, and the temperature of the situation and of the season. The eruption runs through its different stages with much more rapidity in dogs from one to five months old than in those of more advanced age. I have never seen it in dogs more than eighteen months old. An elevated temperature singularly favors the eruption, and also renders it confluent and of a serous character. A cold atmosphere is unfavorable to the eruption, or even prevents it altogether. Death is almost constantly the result of the exposure of dogs, having small-pox, to any considerable degree of cold. A moderate temperature is most favorable to the recovery of the animal. A frequent renewal or change of air, the temperature remaining nearly the same, is highly favorable to the patient, consequently close boxes or kennels should be altogether avoided. I have often observed that the perspiration or breath of dogs laboring under variola, emits a very unpleasant odor. This smell is particularly observed at the commencement of the desiccation of the pustules, and when the ani mals are lying upon dry straw. The friction of the bed against the pustules destroys their pellicles, and permits the purulent matter to escape; and the influence of this purulent matter is most pernicious. The fever is increased, as also the unpleasant smell from the mouth, and generally the fæces. In this state there is a disposition which is rapidly developed in the lungs, to assume the character of pneumonia. This last complication is a most serious one, and always terminates fatally.

SYMPATHETIC FEVER.

This term is applied to the fever which comes on either before or after some severe local affection, and is, as it were, eclipsed by it. Thus in all severe inflammations there is an accompanying fever, which generally shows itself before the exact nature of the attack is made manifest, and though it runs high, yet it has no tendency in itself to produce fatal results, subsiding, as a matter of course, with the inflammation which attends it. The same occurs in severe injuries; but here also, if there is no inflammation, there is no fever; so that the same rule applies as where there is an external cause.

CHAPTER IV.

INFLAMMATIONS.

DEFINITION OF INFLAMMATION.—SYMPTOMS AND TREATMENT OF RABIES, TETANUS, AND TURNSIDE.—INFLAMMATION OF THE EYE, EAR, MOUTH, AND NOSE.—LUNGS.—STOMACH.—BOWELS.—LIVER.—KIDNEYS, BLADDER, AND SKIN.

DEFINITION OF INFLAMMATION.

Inflammation consists in a retardation of the flow of blood through the small vessels; an increased action of the large ones is required to overcome it. When external and visible, it is characterized by increased heat, swelling, pain, and redness; when internally, by the first three, the last not being discerned, though existing. It may be acute when coming on rapidly, or chronic when slow, and without very active symptoms. In the acute form there is always an increased rapidity of the pulse, with a greater reaction of the heart's pulsations, known as hardness of the pulse. In the dog, the healthy pulsations are from 90 to 100 to the minute. This may be taken as the standard of health. The arterial pulse may be felt on the inside of the arm above the knee; by placing the hand against the lower part of the chest, the contractions of the heart may be readily felt. In different breeds there is, however, considerable variation in the pulsations of the heart.

HYDROPHOBIA, RABIES, OR MADNESS.

This disease has been classed among the inflammations. The symptoms are chiefly as follows: The first is a marked change of temper; the naturally cheerful dog becoming waspish and morose, and the bold fondling pet retreating from his master's hand as if it was that of a stranger. On the other hand, the shy dog becomes bold; in almost every instance there is a total change of manner for several days before the absolute outbreak of the attack, which is indicated by a kind of delirious watching of imaginary objects, the dog snapping at the wall, or if anything comes in his way, tearing it to pieces with savage fury. With this there is constant watchfulness, and sometimes a peculiarly hollow howl. At other times no sound whatever is given, the case being then described as " dumb madness." Fever is always present, but it is difficult to ascertain to what extent on account of the danger of approaching the patient. Urgent thirst accompanies the fever. Mr. Grantley Berkeley strongly maintains that no dog really attacked with rabies will touch water, and that the presence of thirst is a clear sign of the absence of this disease. This theory is so entirely in opposition to the careful accounts given by all those who have witnessed the disease, when it had unquestionably been communicated either to man or to some of the lower animals, that no credence need be given it. Mr. Youatt witnessed more cases of rabies than perhaps any equally good observer, and he strongly insists upon the presence of thirst, as may be gathered from the concluding portion of the following extract:

"Some very important conclusions may be drawn from the appearance and character of the urine. The dog, at particular times when he is more than usually salacious, may, and does diligently search the urining places; he may even at those periods be seen to lick the spot which another animal has just wetted. If a peculiar eagerness accompanies this strange employment, if in the parlor, which is rarely disgraced by this evacuation, every corner is perseveringly examined, and licked with unwearied and unceasing industry, the dog cannot be too carefully watched; there is great danger about him; he may, without any other symptom, be pronounced to be decidedly rabid. I never knew a single mistake about this. Much has been said of the profuse discharge of saliva from the mouth of the rabid dog. It is an undoubted fact that, in this disease, all the glands concerned in the secretion of saliva become increased in bulk and vascularity. The sublingual glands wear an evident character of inflammation; but it never equals the increased discharge that accompanies epilepsy or nausea. The frothy spume, at the corners of the mouth, is not for a moment to be compared with that which is evident enough in both of these affections. It is a symptom of short duration, and seldom lasts longer than twelve hours. The stories that are told of the mad dog, covered with froth, are altogether fabulous. The dog recovering from, or attacked by a fit may be seen in this state, but not the rabid dog. Fits are often mistaken for rabies, and hence the delusion.

"The increased secretion of saliva soon passes away. It lessens in quantity and becomes thick, viscid, adhesive, and glutinous. It clings to the corners of the mouth, and probably more annoyingly so to the membrane of the fauces. The human being is sadly distressed by it. He forces it out with the greatest violence, or utters the falsely supposed bark of a dog, in his attempts to eject it from his mouth. This symptom occurs in the human being when the disease is fully established, or at a late period of it. The dog furiously attempts to brush away the secretion with his paws. It is an early symptom in the dog, and it can scarcely be mistaken in him. When he is fighting with his paws at the corners of his mouth, let no one suppose that a bone is sticking between the poor fellow's teeth; nor should any useless and dangerous effort be made to relieve him. If all this uneasiness arose from a bone in the mouth, the mouth would continue permanently open, instead of closing when the animal for a moment discontinues his efforts. If after a while he loses his balance and tumbles over, there can be no longer any mistake. It is the saliva becoming more and more glutinous, irritating the fauces and threatening suffocation. To this naturally and rapidly succeeds an insatiable thirst. The dog that still has full power over the muscles of his jaws continues to lap. He knows not when to cease, and the poor fellow whose jaw and tongue are paralyzed, plunges his muzzle into the water-dish to his very eyes, in order that he may get one drop of water into the back part of his mouth to moisten and to cool his dry and parched fauces. Hence, instead of this disease being always characterized by the dread of water in the dog, it is marked by a thirst often perfectly unquenchable. Twenty years ago, this assertion would have been peremptorily denied. Even at the present day we occasionally meet with those who ought to know better, and who will not believe that the dog which fairly, or perhaps eagerly, drinks, can be rabid."

My own experience fully confirms the above account, having seen, as I have, seven cases of genuine rabies, in all of which thirst was present in a greater or less degree; in five of the cases the disease was communicated to other dogs. If the rabid dog is not molested he will seldom attack any living object; but the slightest obstruction in his path is sufficient to rouse his fury, he then bites savagely, and in the most unreasoning manner, wholly regardless of the consequences. The gait, when at liberty, is a long trot in a straight line.

The average time of the occurrence of rabies after the bite is, in the dog, from three weeks to six months, or possibly even longer; a suspected case therefore requires careful watching for at least that time; after three months, the animal supposed to have been bitten may be considered tolerably safe, if no unfavorable symptoms have in the meantime shown themselves. The duration of the disease is about four or five days, but I have myself known a case to be fatal in forty-eight hours. No remedy having yet been discovered for rabies, nothing remains but to kill the dog suffering therefrom.

TETANUS.

Resembling rabies in some degree, tetanus differs from it in the absence of any affection of the brain, the senses remaining perfect to the last. It is not common with the dog. It is generally produced by a severe injury, and shows itself in the form known as "lock-jaw." It consists in spasmodic rigidity of certain muscles, alternating with relaxation. The stiffness continues for some length of time, not appearing and disappearing as quickly as in cramp.

If the tetanic spasm affects the muscles of the jaw, the state is called "lock-jaw." When it seizes on all muscles of the back, the body is drawn into a bow, the head being brought in close proximity to the tail. Sometimes the contraction is of one side only, and at others of the muscles of the belly, producing a bow in the opposite direction to that alluded to above. These various conditions exactly resemble the contractions produced by the poison of strychnine. When, therefore, they occur, as the disease is extremely rare, it is fair to suspect that poison has been used. Nevertheless, it should be known that they were witnessed long before this poison was in use; and, therefore, they may arise independently of it.

The successful treatment of tetanus is hopeless, if the case is clearly established. Purgatives and bleeding may be tried, followed by chloroform, which will always relieve the spasm for the time; but, as it returns soon after the withdrawal of the remedy, no permanent good is likely to accrue from its use. Except in the case of highly valued dogs, I should never advise any remedies being tried; the humane course is to at once put the poor animal out of misery, the spasms being evidently of the most painful nature.

TURNSIDE.

Turnside is more frequently seen in the dog than tetanus, still it is by no means common. It consists in some obscure affection of the brain, resembling the "gid" of sheep, and probably results from the same cause. The dog has no fits, but keeps continually turning round and round, until death ensues from exhaustion. Tetanus is more commonly met with in high-bred puppies, whose constitutions are delicate; I have known a whole litter carried off, one after the other by the malady. No remedy to my knowledge is of any avail; bleeding, blistering, and purgatives are said to have restored some few cases. The seton, also, has been recommended, and is, in my opinion, more likely than any other remedy to produce a cure, care being taken to maintain and support the strength of the animal against the lowering effects of this remedy.

INFLAMMATIONS OF THE EYE.

Ophthalmia, or simple inflammation of the eyes, is very common in dogs, especially during the latter stages of distemper, when the condition of this organ is often seemingly, though not really, hopeless. On more than one occasion I have saved puppies from a watery grave, whose eyes were said to be beyond cure. Applying no remedy locally, but simply attending to the general health of the dog, I have secured the recovery of the affected eye to its normal condition. The indications are, an unnatural bluish redness of "the white" of the eye, together with a film over the transparent part, which may or may not show red vessels spreading over it. There is great intolerance of light, with a constant watering. If the eye be opened by force, the dog most strenuously resists, giving evidence of pain from exposure to the rays of the sun. This state resembles the "strumous ophthalmia" of children, and may be treated in the same way, by the internal use of tonics, the pills (62) being especially serviceable. In the ordinary ophthalmia, the "white" of the eye is of a brighter red, and the lids are more swollen, while the discharge is thicker, and the intolerance of light is not so great. The treatment here which is most likely to be of service is of the ordinary lowering kind, exactly the reverse of that indicated above. Purgatives, low diet, and sometimes bleeding, will be required, together with local washes, such as (55) or (56). If the eyes still remain covered with a film, a seton may be inserted in the back of the neck with advantage, and kept open for two or three months.

Cataract may be known by a whiteness, more or less marked in the pupil, and evidently beneath the surface of the eye, the disease consisting in an opacity of the lens, which is situated behind the pupil. It may occur from a blow, or from inflammation, or result from hereditary tendency. No treatment is of avail.

In amaurosis the eye looks clear, and there is no inflammation; the nerve however is destroyed, and there is partial or total blindness. It may be known by the great size of the pupil.

CANKER, OR INFLAMMATION OF THE EAR.

Many dogs, especially of sporting breeds, contract an inflammation of the membrane or skin lining of the ear, from high feeding generally, and exposure to the weather. This causes irritation, and the dog shakes his head continually. This, together with the tendency to spread externally, causes an ulceration of the tips of the ears of those dogs, such as the hound, pointer, setter, spaniel, etc., which have these organs long and pendulous. Hence, the superficial observer is apt to confine his observations to this external ulceration, and I have even known the tips of the ears cut off in the hope of getting rid of the mischief. This heroic treatment, however, only aggravated the malady, because, while the incessant shaking caused the wound to extent, the internal inflammation was not in the slightest degree relieved. The pointer is specially liable to "canker," as shown at the tips of the ears, inasmuch as there is little hair to break the acuteness of the "smack" which is given in the shake of the head. Long-haired dogs, on the other hand, are quite as liable to the real disease, as shown by an examination of the internal surface, owing however to the protection afforded by the hair, the pendulous ear is less ulcerated or inflamed. Whenever, therefore, a dog is seen to continually shake his head, and ineffectually endeavor to rub or scratch his ear, not being able to succeed, because he cannot reach the interior, an examination should at once be made of the passage leading into the head. If the lining be red and inflamed, there is clear evidence of the disease, even though the external ear be altogether free from it. On the other hand, the mere existence of an ulceration on the tips of the ears is no absolute proof of "canker," inasmuch as it may have been caused by the briars and thorns which a spaniel or hound encounters in hunting for his game. Still it should lead to a careful inspection, and, if it continues for any length of time, it may be generally concluded that there is an internal cause for it. The treatment should in every case be chiefly directed to the internal passage; the cap which is sometimes ordered to be applied to the head, with a view of keeping the ears quiet, has a tendency to i.crease the internal inflammation, and should not therefore be employed. The first thing to be done, is to lower the system by purgatives (11), (12), (15), or (16), with low diet, including no animal food. As soon as this has produced a decided effect, the nitrate of silver wash (22), the ointment (58a), melted, or the sulphate of zinc (20), should be dropped into the ear-passage, changing one for the other every second or third day. At the same time the sores on the edges of the ears may be daily touched with bluestone, which will dry them up. In slight cases, this treatment will suffice for a cure, if carried on for three weeks or a month. In long-standing attacks, however, a seton must be put into the back of the neck; this seldom fails to afford relief. If the inflammation in the external ear has been so great as to produce abscesses, they must be slit open with the knife to the very lowest point, as wherever matter is confined in a pouch there can be no tendency to heal. The dog should be muzzled and the head held firmly on a table, whenever any remedial fluid is applied internally to the ear. Deafness may result from canker, or from rheumatic or other inflammation of the internal ear. As no treatment is likely to be beneficial, there is no necessity for enlarging on the subject; the only remedy at all to be relied on, in recent cases, is the seton in the back of the neck.

INFLAMMATION OF THE MOUTH AND TEETH.

Dogs fed on strongly stimulating food, are very apt to lose their teeth by decay, and also to suffer from a spongy state of the gums, attended with a collection of tartar about the roots of the teeth. Decayed teeth are better extracted, but the tartar, when it produces inflammation, may be removed by instruments. By carefully scraping the teeth there is little or no difficulty in removing it if the dog's head is held steadily. If the animal be highly prized, he should be taken to a veterinary surgeon for the operation. Afterwards brush the teeth occasionally with a lotion composed of 1 part of a solution of chlorinated soda, 1 part of tincture of myrrh, and 6 parts of water. When puppies are shedding their milk teeth, frequent soreness in the mouth prevents them from eating. In such cases the old teeth are better removed with a pair of forceps.

Blain is a watery swelling beneath the tongue, showing itself in several large vesicles containing straw-colored lymph, sometimes stained with blood. The treatment consists in lancing them, after which, the lotion, given above, may be effectually applied to the sores.

OZÆNA.

Ozæna is an inflamed condition of the lining membrane of the nose, producing an offensive discharge from the nostrils. This is very common in the pug dog, and also more or less in toy spaniels. There is little to be done in the way of treatment; a solution of chloride of zinc (2 grains to the ounce of water), may be thrown into the nostrils with a syringe.

LARYNGITIS AND BRONCHOCELE.

Laryngitis is inflammation of the top of the wind-pipe, where there is a very narrow passage for the air, and consequently where a slight extra contraction caused by swelling is necessarily fatal. When acute, it is very dangerous, and characterized by quick laborious breathing, accompanied with a snoring kind of noise. There is also a hoarse and evidently painful cough. The pulse is quick and sharp, attended with some fever. The treatment must be active, or it will be of no avail. Large bleedings, followed by a calomel purge (12), and the fever powder (50), will be necessary; but no time should be lost in calling in skilful aid, if the dog's life is valued.

Chronic laryngitis attacks the same part, comes on insidiously, and manifests itself chiefly in a hoarse cough and stridulous bark. It is best treated by a seton in the throat, together with low diet and the alterative pill (1).

Bronchocele is known by an enlargement, often to the size of the fist, of the thyroid body placed on each side of the wind pipe. If this does not press upon the air-passage, there is no inconvenience; but in course of time it generally does this, and the dog becomes wheezy and short-winded. It is chiefly seen in house pets, and may be relieved by the internal use of iodine (3), given for weeks in succession.

INFLAMMATION OF THE LUNGS.

The organs of respiration consist of an external serous and an internal mucous membrane, united together by cellular tissue. Each of these is the seat of a peculiar inflammation (pleurisy, pneumonia, and bronchitis), attended by different symptoms and requiring a variation in treatment. There is likewise, as in all other inflammations, an acute and a chronic kind, so that here we have six different inflammatory disorders of the organs of the chest, besides heart disease and phthisis or consumption. All the acute forms are attended with severe sympathetic fever, and quick pulse; but the character of the latter varies a good deal. The chronic forms have also some slight febrile symptoms; but generally in proportion to the acuteness is the amount of this attendant or sympathetic fever. As these three forms are liable to be easily mistaken for each other, I place the symptoms of each in juxtaposition in the following Table:

INFLAMMATION OF THE LUNGS.

COMPARATIVE TABLE OF SYMPTOMS.

	Acute Pleurisy.	Acute Pneumonia.	Acute Bronchitis.
Early symptoms.	Shivering, with slight spasms of the muscles of the chest; inspiration short and unequal in its depth, expiration full, air expired not hotter than usual; cough slight and dry; pulse quick, small, and wiry.	Strong shivering, but no spasms; inspiration to erably full, expiration short, air expired perceptibly hotter than natural; nostrils red inside; cough violent and sonorous, with expectoration of rusty colored mucus; pulse quick, full, and soft.	Shivering, soon followed by continual hard cough; inspiration and expiration equally full; air expired warm, but not so hot as in pneumonia; cough soon becomes moist, the mucus expectorated being frothy, scanty at first, but afterwards profuse; pulse full and hard.
Stethoscopic sounds.	No very readily distinguishable sound. A practised ear discovers a friction sound or rubbing.	A crackling sound, audible in the early stage, followed by crepitating wheezing.	The sound in this form varies from that of soap bubbles to a hissing or wheezing sound.
Percussion.	Produces at first no result different from a state of health. After a time, when serum is thrown out, there is increased dullness.	Dullness after the early stage is produced by the thickening of the tissue, approaching to the substance of liver, hence called "hepatization."	No change.
Termination.	The symptoms either gradually disappear, or lymph is thrown out, or there is an effusion of serum or matter, with a frequently fatal result.	If the symptoms do not disappear, there is a solidification of the lung, by which it is rendered impervious to air, and in bad cases suffocation takes place, or matter is formed, producing abscess.	The inflammation generally subsides by a discharge of mucus, which relieves the inflammation; or it may go on to the extent of causing suffocation by the swelling of the lining membrane filling up the area of the tubes.
Treatment.	Bleeding in the early stages, in degree according to the severity of the attack. Relieve the bowels by (12) or (13). No blistering, which is actually prejudicial. Try the fever powder (49) or (50), and if not active enough, give calomel and opium, of each 1 grain, in a pill, 3 times a day. Low diet of slops only.	Bleeding in the early stages, in amount according to the severity of the attack. Give an aperient, (12) or (13). Blisters to the chest of service, or the mustard embrocation (42). Give the cough bolus (46) or the draught (47). If the inflammation is very high, give calomel and opium, of each 1 grain, digitalis, ¼ grain, tartar emetic, ½ grain, in a pill, 3 times daily. Low diet of slops.	No bleeding is required. In the early stage give an emetic (44). Follow this up with a mild aperient, (11) or (15). Apply the embrocation (42) to the chest, and give the cough bolus (46) or the draught (47). Low diet in the early stages; afterwards, a little solid food, not meat, may be given.

COMPARATIVE TABLE OF CHRONIC SYMPTOMS.

	Chronic Pleurisy.	Chronic Pneumonia.	Chronic Bronchitis.
Early symptoms.	Inspiration slower than expiration; cough dry; pulse quicker than natural, small and wiry.	Respiration quick and painful; cough troublesome but restrained; expectoration trifling; pulse quick and full.	Respiration quick but free; cough constant and severe, but without pain; pulse scarcely affected.
Termination.	Either in a cure, or else there is an effusion of serum into the chest, and generally also into the belly and limbs, causing suffocation by pressure.	If not ending in a cure, there is great difficulty of breathing, often ending in suffocation. The animal does not lie down, but sits up on his hind legs, supporting himself on his fore legs.	Ends in a cure, or in a permanently chronic state of inflammation. Or, if fatal, there is suffocation from effusion, but this is very rare in chronic bronchitis.
Treatment.	The same as for acute pleurisy, but milder in degree, and the diet is not required to be so strictly confined to slops.	Bleeding will seldom be required. Give the calomel, opium, and tartar emetic, without the digitalis, in the doses ordered for acute pneumonia. After a few days, have recourse to the bolus (46). Diet nourishing, but strictly confined to farinaceous articles. The embrocation is of great service.	Dispense with the emetic, and at once try the cough bolus (46). In very mild cases, give ipecacuanha ¼ grain, rhubarb 2 grains, opium ¼ grain, in a pill, 3 times a day. Apply the mustard embrocation (43). Milk diet, with nourishing slops.

These various forms constantly run into one another, so that we rarely find pleurisy without some degree of pneumonia, or pneumonia without bronchitis. Still, one generally predominates over the other, and, as far as treatment is concerned, the malady predominating may be considered as distinct. So, also, there is every shade between the very acute form, the acute, the subacute, the chronic, and the permanently chronic. For practical purposes, however, the two divisions are sufficient.

SPASMODIC ASTHMA.

What is often called asthma in the dog is nothing more than a chronic form of bronchitis, very common among petted toy dogs or house dogs, which do not have much exercise. The symptoms and treatment are detailed under the head of Chronic Bronchitis. There is, however, a form of true asthma, accompanied with spasms, among the same kind of dogs, the symptoms of which are much more urgent. They comprise a sudden difficulty in breathing, so severe that the dog manifestly gasps for breath; still there is no evidence of inflammation. This malady may be known by the suddenness of the attack, inflammation being comparatively slow in its approach. The treatment consists in the administration of an emetic (45), followed by the cough bolus (46), or the draught (47). If the spasms are very severe, a full dose of laudanum and ether must be given, viz.—1 drachm of laudanum, and 30 drops of the ether, in water, every three hours, until relief is afforded. The mustard embrocation (42), or the turpentine liniment (43), may be rubbed on the chest with great advantage.

PHTHISIS, OR CONSUMPTION.

Though very often fatal among highly-bred animals, phthisis or consumption has not been noticed by writers on dog diseases, neither Blain, Youatt, nor Mayhew making the slightest allusion to it. I have, however, seen so many cases of tubercular diseases in the dog, that I cannot doubt its existence as an ordinary affection. Furthermore, I know that hundreds of canines die every year from it. I have seen the tubercules in almost every stage of softening, and I have known scores of cases in which a blood-vessel has given way, producing the condition known in the human being as spitting of blood.

The symptoms of consumption are, a slow insidious cough, without fever in the early stage, followed by emaciation, and ending, after some months, in diarrhœa, or exhaustion from the amount of expectoration, or in the bursting of a blood-vessel. This last is generally, the termination in those dogs that are kept for use, the work to which they are subjected leading to excessive action of the heart, which is likely to burst the vessel. In the latter stages there is a good deal of constitutional fever, but the dog rarely lives long enough to show this condition, being either destroyed as incurable, or dying rapidly from loss of blood or diarrhœa. Treatment is of little avail. Though the attack may be postponed, the disease cannot be cured, and no phthisical animal should be bred from. Cod-liver oil is of just as much service as in the human subject, but, as before remarked, it can only postpone the fatal result. It is therefore not well to use it except in the case of house pets. The dose is from a teaspoonful to a tablespoonful three times a day.

GASTRITIS, OR INFLAMMATION OF THE STOMACH.

This affection is, like all others of the same kind, either acute or chronic. The former very rarely occurs except from poison, or highly improper food, which has the same effect. The symptoms are a constant and evidently painful straining to vomit, with an intense thirst, dry hot nose, quick breathing, and an attitude which is peculiar—the animal lying extended on the floor, with his belly in contact with the ground, and in the intervals of retching licking anything cold within reach. The treatment consists in bleeding, if the attack is very violent, and calomel and opium pills, of a grain each. These pills are to be given every four hours, to be followed with two drops of the diluted hydrocyanic acid, distilled in a small quantity of water. Thin gruel or arrow-root may be given occasionally in very small quantities, but until the vomiting ceases, they are of little service. If poison has clearly been swallowed, the appropriate treatment must be adopted.

Chronic gastritis is only another name for one of the forms of dyspepsia, the symptoms and treatment of which are given elsewhere.

INFLAMMATION OF THE LIVER.

This is one of the most common of the diseases to which sporting dogs are liable, in consequence of exposure to cold and wet.

It causes congestion of the liver, which runs into inflammation. Dogs deprived of exercise likewise contract it, because their livers first becoming torpid, the bile accumulates, and then, in order to get rid of it, nature establishes an action which ends in inflammation. The symptoms are a yellow condition of the whites of the eye and of the skin generally, from which the disease is commonly called "the Yellows."

Acute hepatitis comes on rapidly, and with a good deal of fever, generally manifesting itself on the day following a long exposure to wet and cold. The dog shivers; his nose is hot. His breathing is more rapid than usual, and his pulse is quick and weak. The bowels are confined; and when moved, the "motions" are clay-colored or slaty. If these symptoms are not immediately attended to, the case ends fatally, sickness coming on, and the strength being rapidly exhausted. The treatment should be, first, a considerable abstraction of blood; then give the bolus (13); and, as soon as it has acted, rub the embrocation (42) or (43) on the right side, over the liver. At the same time, give calomel and opium pills of a grain each, every four hours, taking care to keep the bowels open by the bolus (13), or by castor oil (15). As soon as the proper color returns to the motions, the calomel may be entirely or partially discontinued, small doses of rhubarb and ipecacuanha being substituted. An emetic (45) in the early stages will sometimes act like a charm, unloading the liver, and at once cutting short the congestion. When, however, inflammation has actively set in, it is worse than useless, inasmuch as it aggravates the disease tenfold.

Chronic hepatitis is caused more frequently by improper food than by exposure, and is very different in its symptoms from the acute form. Whenever the fæces are pale, dark, or slate-colored, the approach of this disease may be suspected, and appropriate treatment should be commenced forthwith; but it is not until the liver is perceptibly enlarged, and the dog is evidently out of condition, that it is generally considered to be established. Then scarcely any remedies will be of much service. At this time there is frequently not only a hard enlarged state of the liver—easily felt through and below the ribs on the right side—but also a yield ing watery enlargement of the belly, from a collection of serous fluid, which is thrown out in consequence of the pressure on the veins, as they return through the liver. The skin is "hide-bound," the hair dull and awry, and the dog looks thin and wretched. The treatment consists in the use of small doses of mercury, or podophyllin, according to the state of the liver (1) or (13); or sometimes ipecacuanha may be given instead of the mercury, in half-grain doses. It requires a long time, however, to act, and will suffice only in very mild cases. The red iodide of mercury mixed with lard, may be rubbed into the side, one drachm to one ounce of the lard, or the embrocation (42) or (43) may be used instead. Gentle exercise may be given at the same time, and mild farinaceous food, with a small quantity of weak broth. After a time, as the liver begins to act, shown by the yellow color of the fæces, the disease relaxes, and the mercury may be dispensed with. As a general thing, however, considerable time elapses before the stomach recovers its tone. A strong decoction of dandelion roots boiled in water and strained, may be given for this purpose, the dose being half a teacupful, administered every morning.

INFLAMMATION OF THE BOWELS.

Four varieties of inflammation of the bowels are met with, viz.: 1, acute inflammation of the peritonæal coat; 2, spasms of the muscular coat, attended with congestion or inflammation, and known as colic; 3, inflammation of the mucous coat, attended by diarrhœa; and 4, chronic inflammation, generally followed by constipation. Acute inflammation of the peritonæal coat is known as peritonitis and enteritis, according as its attacks are confined to the membrane lining the general cavity, or to that covering the intestines; but, as there is seldom one without more or less of the other, there is little practical use in the distinction. The symptoms are very severe. They are indicated by shivering, feverishness, cold dry nose, ears, and legs, hot breath, and anxious expression—showing evidence of pain, which is increased on pressing the bowels with

INFLAMMATION OF THE BOWELS. 339

the hand. The tail is kept closely against the body. The attitude is peculiar to the disease, the back being arched, and the legs drawn together. The bowels are costive, and the urine scanty and highly-colored. There is likewise thirst, attended with loss of appetite. Sometimes there is a slight vomiting after food. The disease soon runs on, and, if not relieved, is fatal in a few days. To treat it, take a large quantity of blood; give calomel and opium in grain doses of each, every three or four hours. Place the dog in a warm bath for half an hour, and, after drying him, rub in the embrocation (43), avoiding pressure, and applying it rapidly, but lightly. After twelve hours, the bowels may be moved by means of the castor oil (15); or, if necessary, by the strong mixture (16), repeating the calomel pills until the tenderness ceases. Great skill is required in adapting the remedies to the disease, and a veterinary surgeon should be called in, whenever the dog is worth the expense.

Colic is a frequent complaint among dogs, the signs being intense pain, aggravated at intervals to such a degree as to cause the patient to howl most loudly. The back at the same time is arched as far as possible, and the legs are drawn together. If this shows itself suddenly after a full meal, the colic may at once be surmised to exist, but the howl at first is not very loud, the dog starting up with a sharp moan, and then lying down again, to repeat the start and moan in a few minutes with increased intensity. The nose is of a natural appearance, and there is little or no fever, the evidence of pain being all that directs the attention to the bowels. The treatment should be by means of laudanum (1 drachm) and ether (30 drops) in a little water every two or three hours; or, in very bad cases, croton oil (1 drop) may be given in a pill with three grains of solid opium every four hours until the pain ceases. The embrocation (45) may also be rubbed into the bowels, either at once, or after a very hot bath. The clyster (17) may also be tried with advantage, and sometimes a very large quantity of warm water thrown into the bowels while the dog is in the warm bath, will afford instant relief. Colic sometimes ends in intussusception, or a drawing of one portion of the bowel into the other; but of this there is no evidence during life. If there were, no remedy would avail short of opening the belly with the knife and drawing out the inverted portion with the hand. Diarrhœa, or inflammation of the mucous membrane of the bowels, is a constant visitor to the kennel. The symptoms are too plain to need description, further than to remark that the motions may be merely loose, marking slight irritation, or there may be a good deal of mucus, which is an evidence of great irritation of the membrane; or, again, there may be shreds or lumps of a white substance resembling the boiled white of an egg, in which case the inflammation has run very high. Lastly, blood may be poured out, marking either ulceration of the bowels, when the blood is bright in color, or an oozing from the small intestines, when it is of a pitchy consistence and chocolate color. The treatment varies. If there is reason to believe that irritation from improper food exists, a dose of oil (15) will clear all away and nothing more is needed. In slight cases of mucous diarrhœa, laudanum may be added to a small dose of oil (7). If this does not have the desired effect, try (6), (8), or (9). Bleeding from an ulcerated surface or from the small intestines seldom occurs except in distemper, and can rarely be restrained when severe. Relief may be attempted by the bolus (18) or the pill (19), but the shock to the system is generally too great to allow of perfect health being restored. In case of bleeding from the large intestines, the chalk mixture (6), together with the bolus (18), will often avail. Rice water should be given as the only drink, and well-boiled rice flavored with milk as the only solid food.

Chronic inflammation with constipation is very liable to occur in dogs which are not exercised, and are fed with biscuit or meal without vegetables. The treatment of habitual constipation should be regular exercise and green vegetables with food. Coarse oatmeal will generally act gently on the bowels of the dog, and a costive animal may be fed upon porridge with great advantage, mixed with wheat-flour or Indian meal. It is better to avoid opening medicine as a rule, though there is no objection to an occasional dose of a mild drug like castor oil. If the fæces are impacted, throw up warm water or gruel repeatedly, until they are softened, at the same time giving the aperient (12), (15), or (16). For piles, give every morning to a dog of average size as much brimstone as will lie on a quarter of a dollar.

INFLAMMATION OF THE KIDNEYS AND BLADDER.

The former of these affections, which may be known by a great scantiness of urine, and evident pain in the loins, is not very common in the dog, but it does occasionally occur. The only treatment likely to be of service, is the administration of carbonate of soda (5 grs.), with 30 drops of sweet spirit of nitre, in a little water twice a day. The bladder, and the urethra leading from it for the passage of the urine, are often subject to a mucous inflammation characterized by pain and constant irritation in passing water, and by a gradual dropping of a yellowish discharge from the organ. This is generally the result of cold, and may be treated by giving full doses of nitre (10 grs.), with Epsom salts (half an ounce), in some water twice a week. If the discharge and pain are very severe, balsam of copaiba may be administered, the best form being the " capsules " now sold, of which two form a dose for an average-sized dog. If the discharge has spread to the exterior of the organ, the wash (20) will be of service.

SKIN DISEASES.

Nearly all skin diseases are due to neglect in some form. In the dog, they arise either from improper management, as in the case of " blotch," or " surfeit," or from the presence of parasites, as in mange. These three names are all that are applied to skin diseases in the dog, though there can be no doubt that they vary greatly, and mange itself is subdivided by different writers so as to comprehend several varieties. Fleas, ticks, etc., likewise irritate the skin, and all will therefore be included here, the inflammation produced by them being entitled to be considered a skin disease as much as mange itself.

Blotch, or surfeit, shows itself in the shape of scabby lumps of matted hair, on the back, sides, head, and quarters, as well as occasionally on the inside of the thighs. They vary in size from a ten cent to twenty-five cent piece, are irregularly round in shape, and after about three or four days, the scab and hair fall off, leaving the skin bare, red, and slightly inclined to discharge a thin serum. The disease is not contagious, and evidently arises from gross feeding joined very frequently with want of exercise, and often brought out by a gallop after long confinement to the kennel. The appropriate treatment is to remove the cause by giving mild aperients (11), (13), or (14), with low diet and regular exercise, by the aid of which, continued for some little time, there is seldom any difficulty in effecting a cure.

An eruption between the toes, similar in its nature and cause to "blotch," is also very common, showing itself chiefly at the roots of the nails, and often making the dog quite lame. In bad cases, when the constitution is impaired by defective kennel arrangements, the sores become very foul, and are very difficult to heal. The general health must first be attended to, using the same means as in "blotch" if the cause is the same. Touch the sores with bluestone, which should be well rubbed into the roots of the nails. When the health is much impaired and the sores are in a foul state, give from five to eight drops of liquor arsenicalis with each meal, which should be of good nourishing food. This must be continued for weeks, or even months in some obstinate cases. After applying the bluestone, it is often well to rub in a very little tar-ointment; then dust all over with powdered brimstone.

Foul mange, resembling psoriasis in man, is an unmanageable disease of the blood, requiring a complete change in the blood before a cure can be effected. I am satisfied that it is hereditary, though probably not contagious. For example, I have seen a bitch apparently cured of it, and with a perfectly healthy skin, produce a litter of whelps all of which broke out with mange at four or five months old, though scattered in various parts of the country. The bitch afterwards revealed the impurity of her blood by again becoming the subject of mange. I should therefore never breed from either a dog or bitch attacked by this form of eruption. There is considerable thickening of the skin, with an offensive discharge from the surface, chiefly flowing from the cracks and ulcerations under the scabs on it. This dries and falls off in scales, taking with them a good deal of the hair, which is further removed by the constant scratching of the poor dog, who is tormented with incessant itching. Generally there is a fat unwieldly state of the system for want of exercise, but the appetite is often deficient. Clear the bowels with a brisk aperient, such as (12) or (13). Give low diet without flesh, starving the dog until he is ready to eat potatoes and green vegetables, alternately with oatmeal porridge—in moderate quantities. As soon as the stomach is brought down to this kind of food, but not before, begin to give the liquor arsenicalis with the food, the dose being a drop to each four pounds in weight of the animal. A dog of eight pounds weight, for example, will require two drops, three times daily; taking care to divide the food into three equal portions, and not to give more of this altogether than is required for the purpose of health. The arsenic must be administered for weeks or even months. As soon as the itching abates, and the health is improved, the mangy parts of the skin may be slightly dressed with small quantities of sulphur and pitch ointments, mixed in equal proportions. In two or three months the blood becomes purified, the eruption disappears, and the health seems impaired, a stomachic or tonic, (59) or (62), will often be required. Sometimes the ointment (58a) will be necessary.

Virulent mange, similar to psora and porrigo in the human subject, is of two kinds, one attributable to a parasitic insect, and the other of vegetable origin. In the former case, which is its most common form, it appears in large, unclean, unkempt kennels. The disease is highly contagious. The skin is dry and rough, with cracks and creases, from some of which there is a thin ichorous discharge when the scabs are removed. The dog feeds well, but from want of sleep is languid and listless; likewise shows thirst and some feverishness. The treatment of this form of mange is based upon a belief that it is caused by an insect of the acarus tribe, which has been detected by the microscope in many cases, but which by some people is maintained to be an accidental effect, and not a cause of mange. However this may be, it is found that remedies which are destructive to insect life, are by far the most efficacious, such as hellebore, sulphur, corrosive sublimate, tobacco, etc. The second kind of virulent mange is more rare than that described above, and still more difficult of cure, the vegetable parasite being less easily destroyed than the insect. This parasite is supposed to be of the nature of mould or fungus, which is most obstinately tenacious of life, and is reproduced again and again in any liquid where it has once developed its germs. In outward appearance this variety of mange differs very little from the insect-produced form, but it may be known by its generally attacking young puppies, while the other appears at all ages, but chiefly in the adult animal. The hair falls off in both, but there is more scab in the insect mange, probably from the fact, that it does not produce such violent itching, and therefore the scratching is not so incessant. The treatment is nearly the same in both cases, being chiefly with external remedies, though alteratives, stomachics, and tonics are often required from the loss of health which generally accompanies the disease. In all cases, therefore, it is necessary to attend to this, giving generally a mild aperient first, such as (12) or 13), and subsequently (2) and (3) combined together, or (1) and (59), according to circumstances. At the same time one of the following applications may be tried externally, using a wire or leather muzzle so that the dog does not lick off the ointments, either one of them, as they are highly poisonous when taken into the stomach.

Ointment (or dressing) for virulent mange: Green iodide of mercury, 2 drachms. Lard, 2 ounces. Mix, and rub as much as can be got rid of in this way, into the diseased skin, every other day, for a week; then wait a week, and dress again. Take care to leave no superfluous ointment. A milder ointment: Compound sulphur ointment, 4 oz. Spirits of turpentine, 1 ounce. Mix, and rub in every other day. All applications should be rubbed well into the roots of the hair.

Red mange differs materially from either of the above forms, being evidently a disease of the bulb which produces the hair, inasmuch as the coloring matter of the hair itself is altered. It first shows itself almost invariably at the elbows and inside the arms, then on the front and inside of the thighs, next on the buttocks, and finally on the back, which is attacked when the disease has existed for some weeks or months. The general health does not appear to suffer, and the skin is not at all scabbed, except from the effects of the scratching, which is very frequent, but not so severe as in the virulent or foul mange. Red mange is probably contagious, but it is by no means a settled question, as it will often be seen in single dogs which are in the same kennel with others free from it entirely. Dogs highly fed, and allowed to lie before the fire, are most subject to it, while the poor half-starved cur becomes affected with the foul or virulent forms. The treatment is to lower the diet; give aperients (12) to (13). Following up these with the addition of green vegetables to the food, at the same time using one or other of the following applications every other day. In obstinate cases arsenic may be given internally.

Dressing for red mange:—Green iodide of mercury, 1½ drachm; spirits of turpentine, 2 drachms; lard, 1½ ounce. Rub a very little of this well into the roots of the hair every other day.

Or, use carbolic acid, 1 part; water, 30 parts. Use as a wash.

Canker of the ear has elsewhere been alluded to under the diseases of that organ.

Irritative inflammation of the skin is produced by fleas, lice, and ticks, which are readily discovered by examining the roots of the hair. Dog-fleas resemble those of the human subject. The lice infesting the animal are much larger, but otherwise similar in appearance. Dog-ticks may easily be recognized by their spider-like forms, and bloated bodies, the claws adhering firmly to the skin, so that they are with some difficulty removed. These last are of all sizes, from that of an average pin's head to the dimensions of a ladybird. They suck a great quantity of blood when numerous, and impoverish the animal to a terrible extent, partly by the drain on the system, and partly by the constant irritation which they produce. The remedies are as follows:—

To remove fleas and lice :—

Mix soft soap with as much carbonate of soda as will make it into a thick paste; rub this well into the roots of the hair all over the dog's body, adding a little hot water, so as to enable the operator to completely saturate the skin with it. Let it remain on for half an hour, then put the dog into a warm bath for ten minutes, letting him quietly soak, and now and then ducking his head under. Lastly wash the soap completely out, and dry before the fire, or at exercise, if the weather is not too cold. This, after two or three repetitions, will completely cleanse the foulest skin.

Dry remedies for lice and ticks :—

Break up the lumps of some white precipitate, then with a hard brush rub it well into the roots of the hair over the whole body. Get rid of the superfluous powder from the external surface of the coat by means of light brushing or rubbing with a cloth. Place a muzzle on, and leave the dog with the powder in the coat for five or six hours. Then brush all well out, reversing the hair for this purpose, and the ticks and lice will all be found dead. A repetition at the expiration of a week will be necessary, or even perhaps a third time.

Or, use the Persian Insect-destroying Powder, which seems to answer well.

Or, the following wash may be tried: Acetic acid 3½ ounces; borax, ¼ drachm; distilled water, 4½ ounces. Mix, and wash into the roots of the hair.

CHAPTER V.

DISEASES ACCOMPANIED BY WANT OF POWER.

CHOREA. — SHAKING PALSY. — FITS. — WORMS. — GENERAL DROPSY OR ANASARCA.

Inflammation is attended by increased action of the heart and arteries. The above class of diseases is, on the contrary, accompanied by a want of tone (atony) in these organs, as well as by an irritability of the nervous system. None of them require lowering measures, but, tonics and generous living are demanded. I have included worms in the classification, because these parasites produce a lowering effect, and rarely infest to any extent a strong healthy subject, preferring the delicate and half starved puppy, to the full-grown and hardy dog.

CHOREA.

Chorea, or St. Vitus's dance, may be known by the spasmodic twitches which accompany it, and cease during sleep. In slight cases the spasm is a mere drop of the head and shoulder, or sometimes of the hind quarter only, the nods in the former case, or the backward drop in the latter, giving a very silly and weak expression to the animal. Chorea is generally a consequence of distemper, so that it is unnecessary to describe its early stages. It rarely destroys life, though it is occasionally accompanied by fits, and the sufferer ultimately dies, apparently from exhaustion. Of the exact nature of the disease we know nothing, the most careful examination of the brain and spinal cord leading to no decided result. In the treatment it is desirable to ascertain the existence of worms, and if they are found, no remedy will be likely to be beneficial, so long as they are allowed to continue their attacks. It they are only suspected, it is prudent to give a dose of the most simple worm-medicine, such as the areca nut (65). If this brings away only one or two, the presence of others may be predicated, and a persistence in the proper medicines will be necessary, until the dog is supposed to be cleansed from them. Beyond this, the remedies must be directed to improve the general health, and at the same time to relieve any possible congestion of the brain or spine, by the insertion of a seton in the neck. Fresh country air is very beneficial. If good nourishing animal food, mixed with a proper proportion of vegetables does not avail, recourse may be had to the following tonic, which is often of the greatest service: Sulphate of zinc, 2 to 5 grains; extract of gentian, 3 grains. Mix, and form a bolus. To be given three times a day.

Careful attention must be paid to the state of the bowels, both constipation and looseness being prejudicial to the health, and each requiring the appropriate treatment. Sometimes the tonic pill (62) will do wonders, and often the change from it to the sulphate of zinc and back again will be of more service than either of them continued by itself. A perseverance in these methods, with the aid of the shower-bath, used by means of a watering-pot applied to the head and spine, and followed by moderate exercise, will sometimes entirely remove the disease. In the majority of cases a slight drop will be ever afterwards noticed, and in sporting-dogs the strength is seldom wholly restored.

SHAKING PALSY.

This resembles chorea in its nature, but it is incessant, except during sleep, and attacks the whole body. The same remedies may be applied, but it is an incurable disease, though not always destroying life.

FITS.

Fits are of three kinds: 1st, those arising from irritation, especially in the puppy, and known as convulsive fits: 2ndly, those connected with pressure on the brain, and being of the nature of apoplexy; and, 3rdly, epileptic fits, which may occur at all ages, and even at intervals, through the whole life of the animal.

Convulsive fits are generally produced by the irritation of dentition, and occur chiefly at the two periods when the teeth are cut, viz., during the first month, and from the fifth to the seventh month They come on suddenly, the puppy lying on its side, and being more or less convulsed. There is no foaming at the mouth, and the recovery from them is gradual, in both these points differing from epilepsy. The only treatment at all likely to be of service, is the use of the hot-bath, which in young and delicate puppies may sometimes give relief. Fits arising in distemper, are caused by absolute mischief in the brain, unless they occur as a consequence of worms, which being removed, the fits cease.

In apoplectic fits the dog lies insensible, or nearly so; does not foam at the mouth, but snores and breathes heavily. Take away blood from the neck-vein, afterwards purging by means of croton oil, and inserting a seton in the back of the neck. The attack, however, is generally fatal, in spite of the most scientific treatment.

Epilepsy may be distinguished by the blueness of the lips and gums, and by the constant champing of the jaw and frothing at the mouth. The fit comes on without any notice, frequently in sporting dogs while they are at work, a hot day being specially provocative of it. In the pointer and setter, the fit almost always occurs just after a "point," the excitement of which appears to act upon the brain. The dog falls directly the birds are sprung, after lying struggling for a few minutes, he rises, looking wildly about him, and then sitting or lying down again for a few minutes, is ready to renew work apparently unconscious that anything unusual has occurred. As in chorea so in epilepsy, nothing is known of the cause and the treatment is therefore guided by the most empirical principles. Within the last ten years bromide of potassium has been used with great success in the human subject, but although I have recommended its use in many cases on the dog, I cannot bear testimony as to the result. The dose for a moderate sized animal is 3 grs. twice a day in a pill, continued for a month at least.

WORMS.

Worms are a fertile source of disease in the dog, destroying every year more puppies than does distemper itself; and, in spite of every precaution, attacking the kennelled hound or shooting-dog, as well as the pampered house pet and the half-starved cur. In old and constantly used kennels, they are particularly rife, and I believe that, in some way, their ova remain from year to year, attached either to the walls or to the benches. All of the varieties met with are propagated by ova, though some, as the Ascaris lumbricoides are also viviparous, so that the destruction of the worms actually existing at the time the vermifuge is given does not necessarily imply the after clearance of the animal. He may be infested with them as badly as before, from the hatching of the eggs left behind. Besides the intestinal worms, there are also others met with in the dog, including the large kidney worm, and the hydatid, which is in all probability the cause of turnside. I shall, therefore, first describe the appearance of each kind of worm; then the symptoms of worms in general; and, lastly, the best means for their expulsion.

The Maw-worm is much larger than its representative in the human subject, which is a mere thread, and is hence called the "thread-worm." In the dog it is about an inch in length, having a milky white color. Maws-worms exist in great numbers in the dog, chiefly occupying the large intestines. They do not injure the health to any great degree, unless they exist in very large numbers. They are male and female, and are propagated by ova.

The Round-worm is from four to seven inches long, round, firm, and of a pale pink color. The two extremities are exactly alike, and are slightly flattened in one direction at the point. See engraving. Figure 47 shows a group of three round worms as actually discharged from the intestine of a dog in which they were thus knotted. I have often seen from six to a dozen round worms thus collected together, so as when discharged to form a solid mass as large as an egg. Like the last species, they are propagated by ova, but sometimes these are hatched in the body of the parent, so that a large worm may be seen, full of small ones. This species occasions much more inconvenience than the maw-worm, but still far less than the tape-worm.

Tape-worms in the dog are of five kinds, of which the *Tænia solium* and *Bothriocephalus latus* are common to man and the dog. The other kinds are not readily distinguished from these two, and

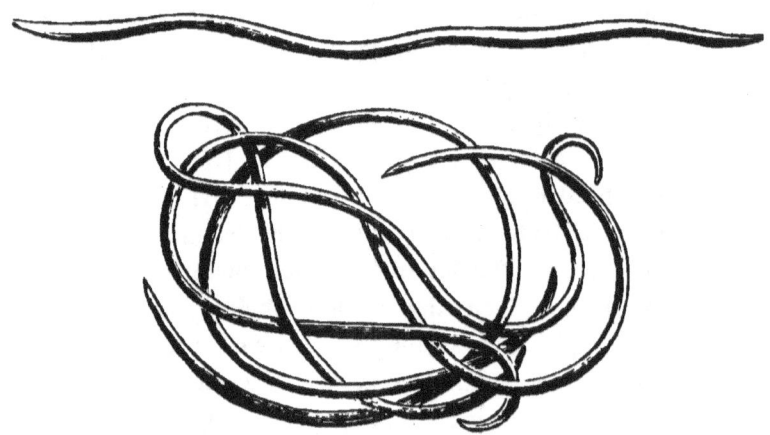

Fig. 47.—MAW-WORM.

all are now said to be developed from the hydatid forms found in the livers of sheep, rabbits, etc. The peculiarity in the bothriocephalus consists in the shape of the head, which has two lateral longitudinal grooves, while that of the true tænia is hemispherical Professor Owen says: "The *Tænia solium* (Fig. 48) is several fcct long. The breadth varies from one-fourth of a line at its anterior part to three or four lines towards the posterior part of the body, which then again diminishes. The head (fig. 49) is small, and generally hemispherical, broader than long, and often as truncated anteriorly; the four mouths, or oscula, are situated on the anterior surface, and surround the central rostellum, which is very short, terminated by a minute apical papilla, and surrounded by a double circle of small recurved hooks. The segments of the neck, or anterior part of the body, are represented by transverse rugæ, the marginal angles of which scarcely project beyond the lateral line. The succeeding segments are subquadrate, their length scarcely

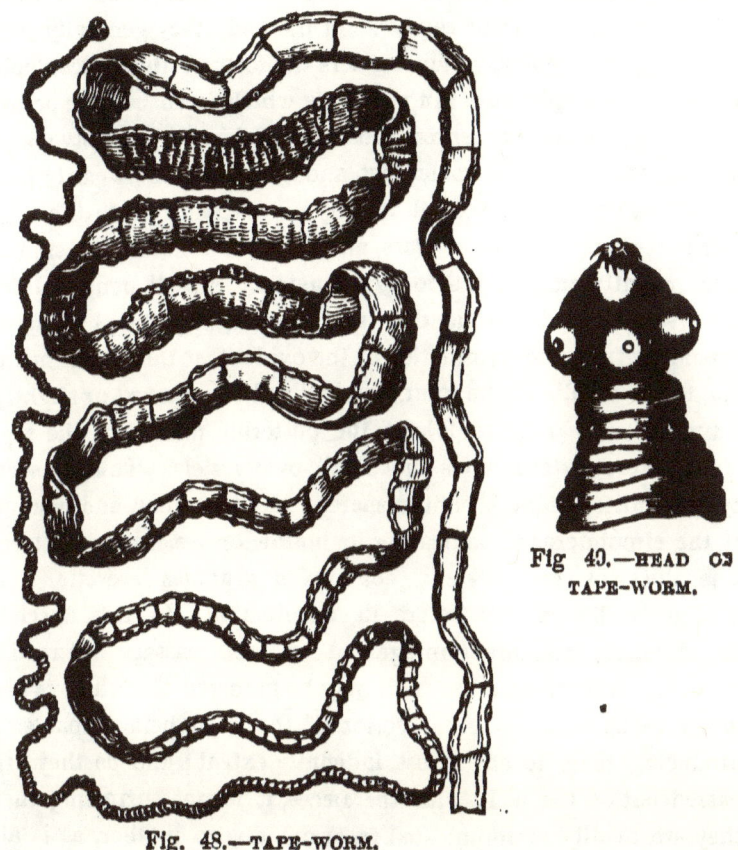

Fig. 48.—TAPE-WORM.

Fig 49.—HEAD OF TAPE-WORM.

exceeding their breadth. They then become sensibly longer, narrower anteriorly, thicker and broader at the posterior margin, which slightly overlaps the succeeding joint. The last series of segments are sometimes twice or three times as long as they are broad. The generative orifices are placed near the middle of one of the margins of each joint, and generally alternate.

The *Tænia solium* is androgynous; that is to say, it produces its ova without the necessity for the contact of two individuals, the male and female organs being contained in each. Professor Owen further describes them: " In each joint of this worm there is a large branched ovarium, from which a duct is continued to the lateral opening. The ova are crowded in the ovary, and in those situated on the posterior segments of the body they generally present a brownish color, which renders the form of their receptacle sufficiently conspicuous. In segments which have been expelled separately, we have observed the ovary to be nearly empty; and it is in these that the male duct and gland are most easily perceived. For this purpose, it is only necessary to place the segment between two slips of glass, and view it by means of a simple lens, magnifying from 20 to 30 diameters. A well defined line, more slender and opaque than the oviduct, may then be traced, extending from the termination of the oviduct, at the lateral opening, to the middle of the joint, and inclined in a curved or slightly wavy line to near the middle of the posterior margin of the segment, where it terminates in a small oval vesicle. This, as seen by transmitted light, is subtransparent in the center, and opaque at the circumference, indicating its hollow or vesicular structure. The duct, or *vas deferens*, contains a grumous secretion; it is slightly dilated just before its termination. In this species therefore, the ova are impregnated on their passage outward " From this minute description, it may be gathered that the ova are in enormous numbers, each section of the worm being capable of producing them to an almost indefinite extent; and as they are passed out of the body with the fæces, it is not surprising that they are readily communicated from one dog to another, as is almost proved to be the case from the fact of their prevalence in certain kennels, and absence from others. The injury caused by these worms is twofold, viz., the abstraction of nourishment, which is absorbed by the worms, and the irritation produced by their presence in the intestines. It is, therefore, of the utmost importance to get rid of so troublesome customers.

The Kidney-worm (*gigas*), Professor Owens says, "inhabits the

354 ATONIC DISEASES.

kidney of the dog, as well as that of the wolf, otter, raccoon, glutton, horse, and bull, (see fig. 50). It is generally of a dark blood-color, which seems to be owing to the nature of its food, which is derived from the vessels of the kidney, as, when suppuration has taken place round it, the worm has been found of a whitish hue. In the human kidney it has been known to attain the length of three feet, with a diameter of half an inch. The head (*a*), is obtuse, the mouth orbicular and surrounded by six hemispherical papillæ (A); the body is slightly impressed with a circular striæ, and with two longitudinal impressions. The tail is incurved in the male and terminated by a dilated point or bursa (B), from the base of which the single intromittent spiculum (*b*), projects. In the female, the caudal extremity is less attenuated and straighter, with the anus (c), a little below the apex." I have been thus particular in inserting descriptions of these worms, because their study is becoming more general, and they present a large field for the microscopic inquirer.

Indications of worms in the dog should be carefully noted and anxiously looked for, if the health of the animal is of any importance. They are, an unhealthy appearance of the coat, the hair looking dead and not lying smoothly and evenly. The appetite is ravenous in proportion to the condition, which is generally low, though worms may exist for months without interfering much with the presence of fat. After a time, however, the fat of the body is absorbed, and the muscles, without being firm and promi-

Fig. 50.—KIDNEY-WORM.

ment, are marked with intervening lines from its absence. The fæces are passed frequently and in small quantities, the separate passage of a small quantity of mucus each time being particularly indicative of worms. The spirits are dull, the nose hot and dry, and the breath offensive. These signs are only present to the full extent when the dog is troubled with tape-worm, or with the round-worm in large quantities; the maw-worm being only slightly injurious in comparison with the others, and rarely being attended with all of these symptoms. The kidney-worm has no effect upon the intestinal secretions, but it produces bloody urine, more or less mixed with pus. Still, as this is often present without the worm, it is impossible to predict its existence during life, with any degree of certainty. When worms are suspected, in order to distinguish the species, it is better to give a dose of calomel and jalap (16), unless the dog is very weakly, when the areca nut may be sustituted (65). Then, by watching the fæces, the particular worm may be detected and the treatment altered accordingly.

The expulsion of the worms is the proper method of treatment in all cases, taking care afterwards to prevent their regeneration, by strengthening the system, and by occasional doses of the medicine suited to remove the worm in question. All vermifuges act as poison to the worms themselves, or as mechanical irritants; the former including the bulk of these medicines, and the latter powdered glass and tin as well as cowhage. These poisons are all more or less injurious to the dog, and in spite of every precaution fatal results will occur after most of them; even the areca nut, innocent as it is said to be, has occasionally nearly destroyed valuable dogs under careful superintendence.

The following is a list of remedies for the various worms:—For round and maw-worms: Betel nut (*Nux areca*). Stinking hellebore (*Helleborus fœtidus*). Indian pink (*Spigelia Marylandica*). Calomel (*Hydrargyri chloridum*). Wormwood (*Artemisia Absinthium*). Santonine, the active principle of wormseed (*Artemisia contra*). Cowhage (*Mucuna pruriens*). Powdered tin and glass.

For tape-worm: Spirits of turpentine (*Spiritus terebinthinæ*)

Kousso (*Brayera anthelmintica*). Pomegranate bark (*Punica Granatum*). Leaves and oil of male fern (*Filix mas*).

The areca nut was first recommended as a vermifuge by Major Besant, who had seen it used in India for that purpose. It has since been very generally adopted, and appears to answer the purpose remarkably well. It should be given every week or ten days, for six or seven times, if the round-worm is present; two or three doses occasionally given will suffice for the maw-worm. Six or eight hours afterwards, a dose of castor-oil should be administered. The dose of the freshly powdered areca nut is about two grains to every pound of the dog's weight. Thus a dog of 30 lbs. will take one drachm, or half an average nut. Stinking hellebore is very innocent, and even useful in other ways. The dose for a 30-lb. dog is five or six grains mixed up with eight or ten of jalap, and formed into a bolus, to be given every five or six days. Indian pink is a very powerful vermifuge; but it also occasionally acts very prejudicially on the dog, and it must never be given without knowledge of the risk which is incurred. I have myself used it in numberless instances without injury; but its employment has so frequently been followed by fatal results in other hands that I cannot do otherwise than caution my readers against it. How, or why, this has been, I have never been able to ascertain; but, that it is so, I have no doubt whatever. If it is determined to use it, half an ounce of the drug, as purchased, should be infused in half a pint of boiling water; and of this infusion, after straining it, from a tablespoonful to two tablespoonfuls should be given to the dog, according to size, followed by a dose of oil. Calomel is a powerful expellant, but it also is attended with danger. The dose is from three to five grains, mixed with jalap. Wormwood may be given with advantage to young puppies, being mild in its operation. The dose is from ten to thirty grains, in syrup or honey. Santonine is an admirable remedy, when it can be procured in a pure state. The brown is the best, of which from one half to three grains is the dose, mixed with from five to fifteen grains of jalap, and given at intervals of a week. Cowhage, powdered tin, and glass, all act by their mechanical irritation, and may be given without the slightest fear. The first should be mixed with molasses, and a teaspoonful or two given occasionally. The second and third are better mixed with butter, the dose being as much as can be heaped upon a twenty-five cent piece. Spirits of turpentine is without doubt the most efficacious of all worm medicines; but, if not given with care, is apt to upset the health of the dog, by irritating the mucous membrane of the alimentary canal, and of the kidneys also. I am satisfied, however, that it is not necessary to give it in its undiluted form, and that by mixing it with oil, its dangerous qualities are altogether suppressed. I have known young puppies, under two months of age, cleared of worms without the slightest injury, by giving them from three to ten drops, according to their size, in a teaspoonful of oil. The old plan was to tie up the turpentine in a piece of bladder, which is then to be given as a bolus; but this is either broken in the throat, causing suffocation by getting into the windpipe, or it is dissolved in the stomach, which is then irritated by the almost caustic nature of the turpentine. The ordinary dose given in this way is from half a drachm to half an ounce, the latter being only adapted to very strong and full-sized dogs. Certainly it is very useful given in this way, if it does not irritate; but I should prefer the mixture with oil, though it is sometimes rejected from the stomach. The leaves and oil of the male fern are both very efficacious remedies, when obtained in a state of purity.

GENERAL DROPSY.

General Dropsy consists, in serum infiltrated into the cellular membrane, beneath the skin of the whole body, as shown by swelling without redness, and "pitting" on the pressure of the finger being removed. The immediate cause is to be looked for either in general debility, by which the serum is not absorbed in due course, or from defective action of the kidneys, by which the blood is overcharged with it. More remotely, improper stimulants or gross food will produce it, especially in foul and dirty kennels, and in old and worn-out dogs when the liver is deficient

ATONIC DISEASES.

In activity. The treatment must vary with the cause, and it is therefore important that this should be ascertained at once. Thus, in case there is merely general debility, tonics (62) or (63) will be the proper remedies. If the kidneys are in fault, but merely torpid, the diuretic bolus (40) or (41) may be relied on; while, if they have been inflamed, the treatment proper to that disease must be resorted to. Sometimes, in a broken down constitution, when the urine is mixed with blood, small doses of cantharides may be found beneficial, as advised by Mayhew; but these cases are so difficult to distinguish, that it is only when veterinary aid cannot be obtained that I should advise the use of this drug. The dose is two to three drops in water twice a day; Tincture of Cantharides, 2 drops; Spirits of Nitric Ether, 15 drops; Water, 1 oz. Mix, and give as a drench twice a day.

CHAPTER VI.

DISEASES ARISING FROM MISMANAGEMENT OR NEGLECT.

ANÆMIA.—RICKETS.—INDIGESTION.

POVERTY OF BLOOD.

When puppies are reared in densely populated parts of cities, or even in the country where they are crowded together in large numbers, they are weakly in constitution; their blood is pale, from being deprived of the red particles which fresh air and good food, with sunlight, will alone produce. The feeding has a good deal to do with this, but not so much as other causes. The signs are clear enough, the young dog looking emaciated and delicate, and his coat staring, while his lips and tongue are of a pale pink, as if washed out. Worms are almost always present, and if so they aggravate the disease tenfold. Give plenty of fresh air, in the country if possible, admitting the sun on all occasions. Administer good nourishing food, composed of the proper proportions of animal and vegetable ingredients. The following mixture of quinine and steel may be used as an internal medicine: Sulphate of quinine; sulphate of iron, of each 1 grain; extract of dandelion 3 grains. Mix, and give three times a day. If worms are present, they must of course be got rid of.

RICKETS AND ENLARGED JOINTS.

By rickets is understood a soft and weak condition of the bones, in which the lime is deficient; the gelatine comprising their framework having no proper support, they bend in any direction which the superincumbent weight may give them. Hence we so often see puppies which are confined to their kennels with bandy legs. This is usually the first sign of rickets. Sometimes the shins bend forward, producing what is called the "buck-shin," but whether the legs bow outwards or forwards the cause is the same. The remedy is country air, exercise, and good food; quinine and steel pills, ordered for poverty of blood, will also prove beneficial. Enlarged joints may be merely a sign of excessive vigor in the formation of the bone. But there is to be met with a scrofulous enlargement of the joints, which is seldom got rid of. This scrofulous enlargement may occur in the knees, hocks, or stifles, but the last-named joints are usually the seats of the disease. Sometimes nature rallies and throws off this tendency to scrofula, but more frequently the joints become larger and larger, the lameness increases, and, in most cases nothing is left but to kill the sufferer.

INDIGESTION.

Among the most common consequences of improper feeding and neglect of exercise is indigestion, attended by its usual concomitant, constipation. If moderate starvation does not soon restore the stomach, care must be taken that the liver is acting properly, the fæces being watched to see if they are of a proper color; if they are not, small doses of calomel or blue pill will be required: (1), (2), or 13). If, on the contrary, the liver acts properly, yet the stomach is out of order, recourse may be had to the stomachic bolus (59), or to the draught (60), which will very seldom fail, if aided by proper management. It should, however, never be forgotten that medicine is of no use, unless, at the same time, the diet is attended to, and sufficient exercise given. In cases of indigestion, it is particularly necessary to change the food every third or fourth day.

CHAPTER VII.

DISEASES AND ACCIDENTS REQUIRING SURGICAL AID.

TUMORS.—CANCER.—ENCYSTED TUMORS.—ABSCESSES.—UNNATURAL PAR‑
TURITION.—ACCIDENTS AND OPERATIONS.

TUMORS.

Bronchocele, or Goitre, is very common among house pets, showing itself in a large and rather soft swelling in the front of the throat. The treatment consists in rubbing in iodine outwardly, and, if this fails, giving it internally also. The internal remedy may be according to the formula (3); but, if the expense is objected to, the sarsaparilla may be omitted. The ointment is as follows: Iodide of potassium, 1 drachm ; Lard, 1 ounce. Mix, and rub in the size of a filbert, night and morning.

CANCER.

Cancer is a malignant disease, that is, it is incapable of a cure by the natural powers, and must be eradicated either by the knife or by caustic. It is, however, very doubtful whether by their means the disease is checked for any length of time, and does not return after the lapse of a few months. The knife is the only remedy, and should be used only by practised hands. When, therefore, a cancer is to be removed, a veterinary surgeon should at once be called.

ENCYSTED TUMORS.

Encysted tumors are sacs or bags of various sizes, just beneath the skin, containing a thick, glairy, and transparent fluid resembling the white of an egg. They are readily detected by their soft yielding feeling, and by their evident want of connection with the surrounding parts. Nothing but the knife is of the slightest use. By cutting through them, the sac may readily be torn out, each half at a time, taking care not to leave a particle behind, as it is sure to grow again into another sac of the same size as before.

ABSCESSES.

Abscesses, the result of inflammation, are very common in the dog. They show themselves in the early stage, as hard painful swellings more or less deep, but gradually coming to the surface, when the skin reddens, and they burst in the course of time. Very often, however, the matter forms so slowly, and has such a tendency to burrow among the muscles, that, if it is let out by the knife in the early stage, it produces great exhaustion from the quantity formed. Matter may be detected as soon as it is thrown out, by the sensation given to the fingers of each hand called "fluctuation." That is to say, on pressing one side of the swelling with the left hand, the other side rises beneath the fingers of the right, in an elastic way, just as happens with a water-pillow, when pressure is made upon it. When, therefore, this fluctuation is clearly made out, a lancet or knife should be inserted, and made to cut its way out, so as to leave a considerable opening, which should be so arranged as to let the matter drain out at all times. This is what in surgery is called a "depending opening."

UNNATURAL PARTURITION.

When, says Mr. Youatt, the time of parturition arrives, and there is evident difficulty in producing the fœtus, recourse should be had to the ergot of rye, given every hour or half-hour, according to circumstances. If after a certain time, some progress, however little, has been made, the ergot must be continued in smaller doses, or perhaps suspended for a while; but, if all progress is evidently suspended, recourse must be had to the hook or the forceps. By gentle but continued manipulation much may be done, especially when the muzzle of the puppy can be brought into the passage. Little force as possible must be used, and the fœtus be but little broken. Many a valuable animal is destroyed by the undue application of force. If the animal seems to be losing strength, a small quantity of laudanum and ether may be administered. The patience of bitches in labor is extreme, says Mr. Blaine; and their distress, if not relieved, is most striking and affecting. Their look at such times is particularly expressive and apparently imploring. When the pupping is protracted, and the young ones are evidently dead, the mother may be saved, if none of the puppies have been broken. In process of time the different puppies may, one after another, be extracted; but when violence has been used at the commencement, or almost at any part of the process, death will surely follow.

PUERPERAL FITS.

Nature proportions the power and resources of the mother to the wants of her offspring. In her wild undomesticated state she is able to suckle her progeny to the full time; but, in the artificial state in which we have placed her, we shorten the interval between each period of parturition, we increase the number of her young ones at each birth, we diminish her natural powers of affording them nutriment, and we give her a degree of irritability which renders her whole system liable to be excited and deranged by causes that would otherwise be harmless. Fits ultimately follow. Place the sufferer in a bath, temperature 96°, and cover her with the water, her head excepted. It will be surprising to see how soon the simple application of this equable temperament will quiet down the erethism of the excited system. In ten minutes, or a quarter of an hour, she may be taken out of the bath evidently relieved, and then, a hasty and not very accurate drying having taken place, she is wrapped in a blanket and placed in some warm situation, a good dose of physic having been previously administered. She soon breaks out in a profuse perspiration. Everything becomes gradually quiet. She falls into a deep and long sleep, and at length awakes somewhat weak, but to a certain degree restored. If, then, all her puppies except one or two are taken from her, and her food is, for a day or two, somewhat restricted, and after that given again in its usual quantity and kind, she will live and do well. Bleeding at the time of her fit, or suffering all puppies to return to her, will inevitably destroy her.

ACCIDENTS AND OPERATIONS.

Cuts, tears, and bites, unless they are very extensive, and therefore likely to occupy a long time in healing, are better left to themselves, the dog's tongue being the best healing remedy. But when a V-shaped flap is torn down, or a very long and straight cut or tear is accidentally made, a few stitches should be put in with a proper curved needle, armed with strong thread or silk. It is only necessary to introduce the needle in two places on exactly opposite sides, and then, an assistant drawing the skin together, the ends are tied in a common knot, and cut off closely. When, however, this plan is adopted, a muzzle must be worn as long as the stitches are kept in, because the dog never rests satisfied until he has licked the knots open, or in some way with his teeth and tongue has got rid of them. Wounds in the dog do not heal "by the first intention," that is, in three or four days, as in man, but fill up by what is called granulation. Of course, in long wounds, more than one stitch is required, but, as perfect union can never be effected by adhesion, the attempt to bring the edges carefully together is a failure; and, provided that anything like an approach to this is effected, all is done which can be desired by a few stitches at short distances. A bandage may be added afterwards and kept on for three days, after which it must be changed daily, the muzzle still being kept on. When the red granulations rise above the level of the skin called then "proud flesh," a piece of bluestone should be rubbed on them daily, or often enough to keep them down to the proper level. When below the level of the skin, they never require caustic of any kind.

In any cuts about the legs or feet, the parts may be protected by collodion painted on rapidly with a camel's-hair brush, and allowed to dry; but a very little friction removes it. Canada balsam, spread on white leather and warmed, will keep its place well enough to bear the rubs of a course in the greyhound, and is, I believe, the best application. A leathern boot may be made to fit the pointer's or setter's foot, or, indeed, that of any dog which requires protection, during work.

Fractures may recur in any of the bones of the dog, but excepting in the legs or ribs, little relief can be afforded by art. They are detected by the deformity which is seen in the part, an angle being presented in the interval between two joints, when occurring in the limb, and a *crepitus* or crackling being heard and felt on handling the part. When the ribs have been broken, the injury is easily detected by the depression which is felt, and the grating sound often produced in breathing. In this case a flannel bandage may be bound tightly round the chest. The dog, after being bled, should be kept quiet, and fed on low diet. A horsegirth passed twice or thrice round and buckled answers the purpose pretty well, but is not equal to a well-applied bandage. Fractures of the limbs may be set by extending the broken ends, and then carefully applying wooden or gutta percha splints lined with two or three thicknesses of coarse flannel.

Dislocations occur in the shoulder and elbow very rarely; in the knee and toes frequently; in the hip very often; in the stifle occasionally, and in the hock very seldom, except in connection with fracture. In all cases, they are detected by the deformity occurring in any of these joints, which is not capable of restoration by gentle handling, and is not accompanied by the crepitus, which marks the fracture. To reduce a dislocation, two persons must lay firm hold of the two parts of the limb on each side of the injured joint, and then extending them strongly, the head of the bone in slight and recent cases will be felt slipping into the socket. Chloroform should be given during the operation, if the attempt is not immediately successful when made directly after the accident, inasmuch as it relaxes the muscles in a remarkable manner, and enables the operator to proceed without being opposed by the struggles of the dog. Dislocated toes are sometimes reduced directly after the accident occurs, but they are very apt to return to their deformed condition immediately, and a small splint should be bound on at once. In dislocations of the knee, also, a bandage should be applied, so as to keep the joint slightly bent, and prevent the foot from being put to the ground. The operations likely to be practised on the dog are somewhat numerous, but the only ones fit to be attempted by any but the professed veterinarian are bleeding, the insertion of a seton, and the closing of wounds by the ligature.

INDEX.

Age to Breed From... 178
Albanian Dog........... ....: 50
American Dogs...................... 31
Anatomy of the Dog:................287
Axioms for Breeders Use ·........175
Barbet, the........................153
Beagles, American * 64
" Dwarf 65
" Rabbit *.................... 66
Bench Show, New York...........367
Bitch, the Duration of Heat 182
" Management of in Season...182
" " " Whelp...183
" Preparation for Whelping...184
Bloodhound, the * 55
Breaking Pointers and Setters.....223
Breaking and Entering Dogs......218
Breed, Time of Year to... 181
Breeding, General Principles of....173
" In-and-In 178
Buffalo Hunter's Camp *..........281
Bulldog, the *..:....................141
Bull Terrier *......................169
Camp, How to Make a.............265
Characteristics of Different Species. 24
Chesapeake Bay Dog *.............124
Cuvier's Divisional Arrangement... 24
Dachshund, the * ...:.............. 85
" Character of........ .. 87
Dalmatian Dog *................... 91
Dandie Dinmonts, Origin of 73
Deer at a Salt-Lick *...............277
Deerhound *........ 32
" Entering of...........218
Deer-Hunting 276
Dhole, the, of India *.............. 28
Digestive System of the Dog.....290
Dingo of Australia *..... ... : 19–27
Diseases of the Dog...............309
Distemper 311
Fevers,................... 309
Influenza........... 310
Rheumatic Fever.......... 317
Smallpox.... 320
Sympathetic Fever.... . .322
Tpyhus Fever........... ..311

Inflammations................823
Hydrophobia...............323
of the Bowels..............338
of the Ear... 329
of the Eye...... 328
of the Kidneys & Bladder. 341
of the Liver......... 336
of the Lungs..............332
of the Mouth and Teeth... 330
of the Nose................331
of the Stomach. 336
of the Throat 331
Tetanus..... 326
Turnside.............. ...327
Asthma, Spasmodic............335
Diseases from Neglect........ ... 359
Indigestion.... 360
Rickets... .... .359
Diseases of the Skin..............341
Blotch..:...................342
Eruption on the Toes.........342
Fleas, etc...................345
Foul Mange..............342
Red Mange...... 344
Virulent Mange.... 343
Diseases of the Nerves............ 347
Chorea.......................347
Fits..........................348
Paley........................348
Worms*. 350
Diseases Requiring Surgical Aid...361
Abscesses..:................362
Accidents and Operations......364
Cancer.......................361
Dropsy.......................357
Fits, Puerperal..............363
Parturition, Difficult...........361
Phthisis....................335
Tumor....................361
Tumors Encysted.... 362
Dog—an Article of Food.... 21
" Descent from the Wolf....... 19
" Varieties of the........ 21
Dogs Used with the Gun..... 88
" Domesticated................ 32
Drenching, Mode of... 309

367

Ears, Cropping. 205	Pariah, The 29
Esquimaux Dogs*. 135	Parturition, Healthful. 184
Faults, Correction of 231	Pastoral Dogs. 125
Feeding before Weaning. 191	Pills, How to Give. 307
Food, Value of Articles of 201	Pointers, Breaking. 223
Foxhound, The*. 57	Pointer, Daisy*. 237
" Colors of. 62	Pointer, English. 88
" Entering of 221	" " Portrait of*. 21
" How to Choose a. 58	" Portuguese. 90
Game in the Far West. 283	Poodle, The*. 152
Greyhound, Choice of a. 47	Pug Dog,*. 158
" Entering of 208	Puppies, Food of. 201
" Grecian. 50	" Amount of Food for. 203
" Irish. 48	" Choice of, after Weaning. 104
" Italian*. 52	" Cropping and Rounding
" Kennels for. 206	Ears 205
" Persian. 51	" Treatment of. 203
" Points of a. 38	" Weaning. 193
" Russian 50	Puzzle Peg, Use of*. 231
" The Rough Scotch. 32	Quail Shooting. 250
" The Smooth *. 36	Quartering Ground, Plan of*. 228
" Turkish. 51	Ranging and Beating. 229
Grouse, Varieties of. 249	Remedies, Administration of. 306
Hare Hunting. 275	Remedies against Disease. 292
Hare-Indian Dog *. 49	Alteratives. 292
Harriers, Entering of. 221	Anodynes. 293
" The 63	Antispasmodics. 293
Hounds, Kennel Management of. . . 213	Aperients. 294
" Feeding 215	Astringents. 295
" Food for. 214	Blisters. 296
House Dogs, Management of. 216	Caustics. 297
Kennels, Benches for* 211	Charges, or Plasters. 298
" Elevation of. 208	Clysters. 202, 308
" for Foxhounds and Har-	Cordials. 299
riers. 209	Diuretics. 299
" for Greyhounds 206	Embrocations. 299
" for Pointers and Setters. 216	Emetics. 300
" Management of. 206	Expectorants 300
" Pavement for. 208	Fever Medicines. 301
" Plan of*. 207	Injections. 302, 308
" Single Dogs. 216	Lotions. 302
" Ventilation for*. 212	Ointments. 303
Labrador Dogs. 132	Stimulants. 303
Lion Dog, The. 155	Stomachics. 304
Maltese Dog, The*. 154	Styptics. 304
Mastiff, English*. 146	Tonics 304
Matins. 24, 48	Vermifuges 355
Muscular System of the Dog. 289	Worm Medicines. 304
Nervous System of the Dog. 290	Remedies, Effects of. 306
Newfoundland Dog*. 132	Retrieve, Breaking to 242
Origin of the Dog. 18	Retriever, The Curly Coated. 167
Otterhound, The. 67	" The Terrier Cross. 167

INDEX.

Retriever, The........ 163
" The Large Black........164
" The Wavy Coated......164
Scotch Colley Dog*........ 126
Setters, Breaking............. 223
Setters 92
" Countess, Pedigree of....... 97
" English*.. 96
" Gordon, The*..............104
" Irish...... 107
* Lang, Pedigree of......... 106
" Laverack................. 96
Sheep Dog, English.............. 126
" " German.............. 130
Shock Dog, The..................155
Shooting Grouse and Quail........218
Sire and Dam, influences of in Breeding.......................174
Skeleton of the Dog...... 287
Snipe Shooting. 255
Spaniel Covert, Breaking... 245
Spaniel, Head of*.......... 123
" Irish Water*...........121
" The Clumber*............112
" The Cocker*... 115
" The English Water*... ..121
" The Field*... ... .111, 155
" The Sussex*......... ...114
" The Water*..............118
Spaniels, Blenheim*.............. 157
" King Charles*............ 156

Spaniels, Toy*.... 155
Spitz Dog*................... ...131
St. Bernard Rough, The*..........148
" Smooth, The*... 150
Springer, The... 112
Teeth of the Dog*............. ...288
Terrier, Bedlington............ .. 80
" Dandie Dinmont*. 72
" English*............. 69
" Fox*... 79
" Halifax, Blue Tan........162
" Scotch................ ... 71
Terrier, Skye*...................... 77
Terrier, Toy, The*.......... 161
Terriers, Varieties of. 68
Terriers, Yorkshire*.............. 81
Thibet Dog, The...................151
Vermin Dogs, Breaking............246
Vermin, Prevention of.............215
Water-fowl, Shooting............262
Water-fowl, Deep, Varieties of.....270
Water-fowl, Shoal, Varieties.......267
Watch Dogs...................... 141
Whelps, Choice of at Birth........ 185
" Management of, in Nest...187
Whelping, Choice of Place for......191
Wild Dogs... 27
" " Of Africa............... 30
" " Of India 29
Woodcock Shooting.................257
Yards, Arrangement for..... 207

* *Illustrated.*

STANDARD BOOKS

..PUBLISHED BY..

ORANGE JUDD COMPANY

NEW YORK   CHICAGO
52 & 54 Lafayette Place   Marquette Building

BOOKS sent to all parts of the world for catalog price. Discounts for large quantities on application. Correspondence invited. Brief descriptive catalog free. Large illustrated catalog, six cents : : :

The Cereals in America

By THOMAS F. HUNT, M.S., D. Agr. If you raise five acres of any kind of grain you cannot afford to be without this book. It is in every way the best book on the subject that has ever been written. It treats of the cultivation and improvement of every grain crop raised in America in a thoroughly practical and accurate manner. The subject matter includes a comprehensive and succinct treatise of wheat, maize, oats, barley, rye, rice, sorghum (kafir corn), and buckwheat, as related particularly to American conditions. First-hand knowledge has been the policy of the author in his work, and every crop treated is presented in the light of individual study of the plant. If you have this book you have the latest and best that has been written upon the subject. Illustrated. 450 pages. 5 1-2 x 8 inches. Cloth. $1.75

The Potato

By SAMUEL FRAZER. A reliable guide on the cultivation of the potato, its development, manuring and fertilizing, planting, tillage, sprays and spraying, breeding new varieties, harvesting, storing, marketing, etc., etc. Takes all in all it is the most complete, reliable and authoritative work on the potato ever published in America. Illustrated. 200 pages. 5 x 7 inches. Cloth. $0.75

Farm Grasses of the United States of America

By WILLIAM JASPER SPILLMAN. A practical treatise on the grass crop, seeding and management of meadows and pastures, description of the best varieties, the seed and its impurities, grasses for special conditions, lawns and lawn grasses, etc., etc. In preparing this volume the author's object has been to present, in connected form, the main facts concerning the grasses grown on American farms. Every phase of the subject is viewed from the farmer's standpoint. Illustrated. 248 pages. 5 x 7 inches. Cloth. $1.00

The Book of Corn

By HERBERT MYRICK, assisted by A. D. SHAMEL, E. A. BURNETT, ALBERT W. FULTON, B. W. SNOW, and other most capable specialists. A complete treatise on the culture, marketing and uses of maize in America and elsewhere, for farmers, dealers and others. Illustrated. 372 pages. 5 x 7 inches. Cloth. $1.50

The Hop—Its Culture and Care, Marketing and Manufacture

By HERBERT MYRICK. A practical handbook on the most approved methods in growing, harvesting, curing and selling hops, and on the use and manufacture of hops. The result of years of research and observation, it is a volume destined to be an authority on this crop for many years to come. It takes up every detail from preparing the soil and laying out the yard, to curing and selling the crop. Every line represents the ripest judgment and experience of experts. Size, 5 x 8; pages, 300; illustrations, nearly 150; bound in cloth and gold; price, postpaid, ... $1.50

Tobacco Leaf

By J. B. KILLEBREW and HERBERT MYRICK. Its Culture and Cure, Marketing and Manufacture. A practical handbook on the most approved methods in growing, harvesting, curing, packing and selling tobacco, with an account of the operations in every department of tobacco manufacture. The contents of this book are based on actual experiments in field, curing barn, packing house, factory and laboratory. It is the only work of the kind in existence, and is destined to be the standard practical and scientific authority on the whole subject of tobacco for many years. 506 pages and 150 original engravings. 5 x 7 inches. Cloth. , . . . , $2.00

The Nut Culturist

By ANDREW S. FULLER. A treatise on the propagation, planting and cultivation of nut-bearing trees and shrubs adapted to the climate of the United States, with the scientific and comman names of the fruits known in commerce as edible or otherwise useful nuts. Intended to aid the farmer to increase his income without adding to his expenses or labor. Cloth, 12mo. $1.50

Cranberry Culture

By JOSEPH J. WHITE. Contents: Natural history, history of cultivation, choice of location, preparing the ground, planting the vines, management of meadows, flooding, enemies and difficulties overcome, picking, keeping, profit and loss. Illustrated. 132 pages. 5 x 7 inches. Cloth. . . $1.00

Ornamental Gardening for Americans

By ELIAS A. LONG, landscape architect. A treatise on beautifying homes, rural districts and cemeteries. A plain and practical work with numerous illustrations and instructions so plain that they may be readily followed. Illustrated. 390 pages. 5 x 7 inches. Cloth. $1.50

Grape Culturist

By A. S. FULLER. This is one of the very best of works on the culture of the hardy grapes, with full directions for all departments of propagation, culture, etc., with 150 excellent engravings, illustrating planting, training, grafting, etc. 282 pages. 5 x 7 inches. Cloth. $1.50

Gardening for Young and Old

By JOSEPH HARRIS. A work intended to interest farmers' boys in farm gardening, which means a better and more profitable form of agriculture. The teachings are given in the familiar manner so well known in the author's "Walks and Talks on the Farm." Illustrated. 191 pages. 5 x 7 inches. Cloth. $1.00

Money in the Garden

By P. T. QUINN. The author gives in a plain, practical style instructions on three distinct, although closely connected, branches of gardening—the kitchen garden, market garden and field culture, from successful practical experience for a term of years. Illustrated. 268 pages. 5 x 7 inches. Cloth. $1.00

Alfalfa

By F. D. COBURN. Its growth, uses, and feeding value. The fact that alfalfa thrives in almost any soil; that without reseeding, it goes on yielding two, three, four, and sometimes five cuttings annually for five, ten, or perhaps 100 years; and that either green or cured it is one of the most nutritious forage plants known, makes reliable information upon its production and uses of unusual interest. Such information is given in this volume for every part of America, by the highest authority. Illustrated. 164 pages. 5 x 7 inches. Cloth. $0.50

Ginseng, Its Cultivation, Harvesting, Marketing and Market Value

By MAURICE G. KAINS, with a short account of its history and botany. It discusses in a practical way how to begin with either seed or roots, soil, climate and location, preparation, planting and maintenance of the beds, artificial propagation, manures, enemies, selection for market and for improvement, preparation for sale, and the profits that may be expected. This booklet is concisely written, well and profusely illustrated, and should be in the hands of all who expect to grow this drug to supply the export trade, and to add a new and profitable industry to their farms and gardens, without interfering with the regular work. New edition. Revised and enlarged. Illustrated. 5 x 7 inches. Cloth. . . . $0.50

Landscape Gardening

By F. A. WAUGH, professor of horticulture, university of Vermont. A treatise on the general principles governing outdoor art; with sundry suggestions for their application in the commoner problems of gadening. Every paragraph is short, terse and to the point, giving perfect clearness to the discussions at all points. In spite of the natural difficulty of presenting abstract principles the whole matter is made entirely plain even to the inexperienced reader. Illustrated. 152 pages. 5 x 7 inches. Cloth. $0.50

Hedges, Windbreaks, Shelters and Live Fences

By E. P. POWELL. A treatise on the planting, growth and management of hedge plants for country and suburban homes. It gives accurate directions concerning hedges; how to plant and how to treat them; and especially concerning windbreaks and shelters. It includes the whole art of making a delightful home, giving directions for nooks and balconies, for bird culture and for human comfort. Illustrated 140 pages. 5 x 7 inches. Cloth. $0.50

Greenhouse Construction

By PROF. L. R. TAFT. A complete treatise on greenhouse structures and arrangements of the various forms and styles of plant houses for professional florists as well as amateurs. All the best and most approved structures are so fully and clearly described that any one who desires to build a greenhouse will have no difficulty in determining the kind best suited to his purpose. The modern and most successful methods of heating and ventilating are fully treated upon. Special chapters are devoted to houses used for the growing of one kind of plants exclusively. The construction of hotbeds and frames receives appropriate attention. Over 100 excellent illustrations, especially engraved for this work, make every point clear to the reader and add considerably to the artistic appearance of the book. 210 pages. 5 x 7 inches. Cloth. $1.50

Greenhouse Management

By L. R. TAFT. This book forms an almost indispensable companion volume to Greenhouse Construction. In it the author gives the results of his many years' experience, together with that of the most successful florists and gardeners, in the management of growing plants under glass. So minute and practical are the various systems and methods of growing and forcing roses, violets, carnations, and all the most important florists' plants, as well as fruits and vegetables described, that by a careful study of this work and the following of its teachings, failure is almost impossible. Illustrated. 382 pages. 5 x 7 inches. Cloth. $1.50

Fungi and Fungicides

By PROF. CLARENCE M. WEED. A practical manual concerning the fungous diseases of cultivated plants and the means of preventing their ravages. The author has endeavored to give such a concise account of the most important facts relating to these as will enable the cultivator to combat them intelligently. 90 illustrations. 222 pages. 5 x 7 inches. Paper, 50 cents; cloth $1.00

Mushrooms. How to Grow Them

By WILLIAM FALCONER. This is the most practical work on the subject ever written, and the only book on growing mushrooms published in America. The author describes how he grows mushrooms, and how they are grown for profit by the leading market gardeners, and for home use by the most successful private growers. Engravings drawn from nature expressly for this work. 170 pages. 5 x 7 inches. Cloth. $1.00

Land Draining

A handbook for farmers on the principles and practice of draining, by MANLY MILES, giving the results of his extended experience in laying tile drains. The directions for the laying out and the construction of tile drains will enable the farmer to avoid the errors of imperfect construction, and the disappointment that must necessarily follow. This manual for practical farmers will also be found convenient for reference in regard to many questions that may arise in crop growing, aside from the special subjects of drainage of which it treats. Illustrated. 200 pages. 5 x 7 inches. Cloth. . . $1.00

Barn Plans and Outbuildings

Two hundred and fifty-seven illustrations. A most valuable work, full of ideas, hints, suggestions, plans, etc., for the construction of barns and outbuildings, by practical writers. Chapters are devoted to the economic erection and use of barns, grain barns, horse barns, cattle barns, sheep barns, cornhouses, smokehouses, icehouses, pig pens, granaries, etc. There are likewise chapters on birdhouses, doghouses, tool sheds, ventilators, roofs and roofing, doors and fastenings, workshops, poultry houses, manure sheds, barnyards, root pits, etc. 235 pages. 5 x 7 inches. Cloth. $1.00

Irrigation Farming

By LUTE WILCOX. A handbook for the practical application of water in the production of crops. A complete treatise on water supply, canal construction, reservoirs and ponds, pipes for irrigation purposes, flumes and their structure, methods of applying water, irrigation of field crops, the garden, the orchard and vineyard, windmills and pumps appliances and contrivances. New edition, revised, enlarged and rewritten. Profusely illustrated. Over 500 pages. 5 x 7 inches. Cloth. $2.00

Forest Planting

By H. NICHOLAS JARCHOW, LL. D. A treatise on the care of woodlands and the restoration of the denuded timberlands on plains and mountains. The author has fully described those European methods which have proved to be most useful in maintaining the superb forests of the old world. This experience has been adapted to the different climates and trees of America, full instructions being given for forest planting of our various kinds of soil and subsoil, whether on mountain or valley. Illustrated. 250 pages. 5 x 7 inches. Cloth. $1.50

The New Egg Farm

By H. H. STODDARD. A practical, reliable manual on producing eggs and poultry for market as a profitable business enterprise, either by itself or connected with other branches of agriculture. It tells all about how to feed and manage, how to breed and select, incubators and brooders, its labor-saving devices, etc., etc. Illustrated. 331 pages. 5 x 7 inches. Cloth. $1.00

Poultry Feeding and Fattening

Compiled by G. B. FISKE. A handbook for poultry keepers on the standard and improved methods of feeding and marketing all kinds of poultry. The subject of feeding and fattening poultry is prepared largely from the side of the best practice and experience here and abroad, although the underlying science of feeding is explained as fully as needful. The subject covers all branches, including chickens, broilers, capons, turkeys and waterfowl; how to feed under various conditions and for different purposes. The whole subject of capons and caponizing is treated in detail. A great mass of practical information and experience not readily obtainable elsewhere is given with full and explicit directions for fattening and preparing for market. This book will meet the needs of amateurs as well as commercial poultry raisers. Profusely illustrated. 160 pages. 5 x 7 1-2 inches. Cloth. . $0.50

Poultry Architecture

Compiled by G. B. FISKE. A treatise on poultry buildings of all grades, styles and classes, and their proper location, coops, additions and special construction; all practical in design, and reasonable in cost. Over 100 illustrations. 125 pages. 5 x 7 inches. Cloth. $0.50

Poultry Appliances and Handicraft

Compiled by G. B. FISKE. Illustrated descriptions of a great variety and styles of the best homemade nests, roosts, windows, ventilators, incubators and brooders, feeding and watering appliances, etc., etc. Over 100 illustrations. Over 125 pages. 5 x 7 inches. Cloth. $0.50

Turkeys and How to Grow Them

Edited by HERBERT MYRICK. A treatise on the natural history and origin of the name of turkeys; the various breeds, the best methods to insure success in the business of turkey growing. With essays from practical turkey growers in different parts of the United States and Canada. Copiously illustrated. 154 pages. 5 x 7 inches. Cloth . . . $1.00

Animal Breeding

By THOMAS SHAW. This book is the most complete and comprehensive work ever published on the subject of which it treats. It is the first book which has systematized the subject of animal breeding. The leading laws which govern this most intricate question the author has boldly defined and authoritatively arranged. The chapters which he has written on the more involved features of the subject, as sex and the relative influence of parents, should go far toward setting at rest the wildly speculative views cherished with reference to these questions. The striking originality in the treatment of the subject is no less conspicuous than the superb order and regular sequence of thought from the beginning to the end of the book. The book is intended to meet the needs of all persons interested in the breeding and rearing of live stock. Illustrated. 405 pages. 5 x 7 inches. Cloth. . . $1.50

Forage Crops Other Than Grasses

By THOMAS SHAW. How to cultivate, harvest and use them. Indian corn, sorghum, clover, leguminous plants, crops of the brassica genus, the cereals, millet, field roots, etc. Intensely practical and reliable. Illustrated. 287 pages. 5 x 7 inches. Cloth. $1.00

Soiling Crops and the Silo

By THOMAS SHAW. The growing and feeding of all kinds of soiling crops, conditions to which they are adapted, their plan in the rotation, etc. Not a line is repeated from the Forage Crops book. Best methods of building the silo, filling it and feeding ensilage. Illustrated. 364 pages. 5 x 7 inches. Cloth. $1.50

The Study of Breeds

By THOMAS SHAW. Origin, history, distribution, characteristics, adaptability, uses, and standards of excellence of all pedigreed breeds of cattle, sheep and swine in America. The accepted text book in colleges, and the authority for farmers and breeders. Illustrated. 371 pages. 5 x 7 inches. Cloth. $1.50

Profits in Poultry

Useful and ornamental breeds and their profitable management. This excellent work contains the combined experience of a number of practical men in all departments of poultry raising. It forms a unique and important addition to our poultry literature. Profusely illustrated. 352 pages. 5 x 7 inches. Cloth. $1.00

Cabbage, Cauliflower and Allied Vegetables

By C. L. ALLEN. A practical treatise on the various types and varieties of cabbage, cauliflower, broccoli, Brussels sprouts, kale, collards and kohl-rabi. An explanation is given of the requirements, conditions, cultivation and general management pertaining to the entire cabbage group. After this each class is treated separately and in detail. The chapter on seed raising is probably the most authoritative treatise on this subject ever published. Insects and fungi attacking this class of vegetables are given due attention. Illustrated. 126 pages. 5 x 7 inches. Cloth. $0.50

Asparagus

By F. M. HEXAMER. This is the first book published in America which is exclusively devoted to the raising of asparagus for home use as well as for market. It is a practical and reliable treatise on the saving of the seed, raising of the plants, selection and preparation of the soil, planting, cultivation, manuring, cutting, bunching, packing, marketing, canning and drying, insect enemies, fungous diseases and every requirement to successful asparagus culture, special emphasis being given to the importance of asparagus as a farm and money crop. Illustrated. 174 pages. 5 x 7 inches. Cloth. . $0.50

The New Onion Culture

By T. GREINER. Rewritten, greatly enlarged and brought up to date. A new method of growing onions of largest size and yield, on less land, than can be raised by the old plan. Thousands of farmers and gardeners and many experiment stations have given it practical trials which have proved a success. A complete guide in growing onions with the greatest profit, explaining the whys and wherefores. Illustrated. 5 x 7 inches. 140 pages. Cloth. $0.50

The New Rhubarb Culture

A complete guide to dark forcing and field culture. Part I—By J. E. MORSE, the well-known Michigan trucker and originator of the now famous and extremely profitable new methods of dark forcing and field culture. Part II—Compiled by G. B. FISKE. Other methods practiced by the most experienced market gardeners, greenhouse men and experimenters in all parts of America. Illustrated. 130 pages. 5 x 7 inches. Cloth. $0.50

Successful Fruit Culture

By SAMUEL T. MAYNARD. A practical guide to the cultivation and propagation of Fruits, written from the standpoint of the practical fruit grower who is striving to make his business profitable by growing the best fruit possible and at the least cost. It is up-to-date in every particular, and covers the entire practice of fruit culture, harvesting, storing, marketing, forcing, best varieties, etc., etc. It deals with principles first and with the practice afterwards, as the foundation, principles of plant growth and nourishment must always remain the same, while practice will vary according to the fruit grower's immediate conditions and environments. Illustrated. 265 pages. 5 x 7 inches. Cloth. $1.00

Plums and Plum Culture

By F. A. WAUGH. A complete manual for fruit growers, nurserymen, farmers and gardeners, on all known varieties of plums and their successful management. This book marks an epoch in the horticultural literature of America. It is a complete monograph of the plums cultivated in and indigenous to North America. It will be found indispensable to the scientist seeking the most recent and authoritative information concerning this group, to the nurseryman who wishes to handle his varieties accurately and intelligently, and to the cultivator who would like to grow plums successfully. Illustrated. 391 pages. 5 x 7 inches. Cloth. . . . $1.50

Fruit Harvesting, Storing, Marketing

By F. A. WAUGH. A practical guide to the picking, storing, shipping and marketing of fruit. The principal subjects covered are the fruit market, fruit picking, sorting and packing, the fruit storage, evaporating, canning, statistics of the fruit trade, fruit package laws, commission dealers and dealing, cold storage, etc., etc. No progressive fruit grower can afford to be without this most valuable book. Illustrated. 232 pages. 5 x 7 inches. Cloth. $1.00

Systematic Pomology

By F. A. WAUGH, professor of horticulture and landscape gardening in the Massachusetts agricultural college, formerly of the university of Vermont. This is the first book in the English language which has ever made the attempt at a complete and comprehensive treatment of systematic pomology. It presents clearly and in detail the whole method by which fruits are studied. The book is suitably illustrated. 288 pages. 5 x 7 inches. Cloth. $1.00

Coburn's Swine Husbandry

By F. D. Coburn. New, revised and enlarged edition. The breeding, rearing and management of swine, and the prevention and treatment of their diseases. It is the fullest and freshest compendium relating to swine breeding yet offered. Illustrated. 312 pages. 5 x 7 inches. Cloth. $1.50

Home Pork Making

The art of raising and curing pork on the farm. By A. W. Fulton. A complete guide for the farmer, the country butcher and the suburban dweller, in all that pertains to hog slaughtering, curing, preserving and storing pork product-- from scalding vat to kitchen table and dining room. Illustrated. 125 pages. 5 x 7 inches. Cloth. . . . $0.50

Harris on the Pig

By Joseph Harris. New edition. Revised and enlarged by the author. The points of the various English and American breeds are thoroughly discussed, and the great advantage of using thoroughbred males clearly shown. The work is equally valuable to the farmer who keeps but a few pigs, and to the breeder on an extensive scale. Illustrated. 318 pages. 5 x 7 inches. Cloth. $1.00

The Dairyman's Manual

By Henry Stewart, author of the "Shepherd's Manual," "Irrigation," etc. A useful and practical work, by a writer who is well known as thoroughly familiar with the subject of which he writes. Illustrated. 475 pages. 5 x 7 inches. Cloth. $1.50

Feeds and Feeding

By W. A. Henry. This handbook for students and stockmen constitutes a compendium of practical and useful knowledge on plant growth and animal nutrition, feeding stuffs, feeding animals and every detail pertaining to this important subject. It is thorough, accurate and reliable, and is the most valuable contribution to live stock literature in many years. All the latest and best information is clearly and systematically presented, making the work indispensable to every owner of live stock. 658 pages. 6 x 9 inches. Cloth. . . $2.00

Bulbs and Tuberous-Rooted Plants

By C. L. ALLEN. A complete treatise on the history, description, methods of propagation and full directions for the successful culture of bulbs in the garden, dwelling and greenhouse. The author of this book has for many years made bulb growing a specialty, and is a recognized authority on their cultivation and management. The cultural directions are plainly stated, practical and to the point. The illustrations which embellish this work have been drawn from nature and have been engraved especially for this book. 312 pages. 5 x 7 inches. Cloth. . . . $1.50

Fumigation Methods

By WILLIS G. JOHNSON. A timely up-to-date book on the practical application of the new methods for destroying insects with hydrocyanic acid gas and carbon bisulphid, the most powerful insecticides ever discovered. It is an indispensable book for farmers, fruit growers, nurserymen, gardeners, florists, millers, grain dealers, transportation companies, college and experiment station workers, etc. Illustrated. 313 pages. 5 x 7 inches. Cloth. $1.00

Prize Gardening

Compiled by G. BURNAP FISKE. This unique book shows how to derive profit, pleasure and health from the garden, by giving the actual experiences of the successful prize winners in the American Agriculturist garden contest. Every line is from actual experience based on real work. The result is a mine and treasure house of garden practice, comprising the grand prize gardener's methods, gardening for profit, farm gardens, the home acre, town and city gardens, experimental gardening, methods under glass, success with specialties, prize flowers and fruits, gardening by women, boys and girls, irrigation secrets, etc., etc. Illustrated from original photos. 320 pages. 5 x 7 inches. Cloth. $1.00

Spraying Crops—Why, When and How

By CLARENCE M. WEED, D. Sc. The present fourth edition has been rewritten and reset throughout to bring it thoroughly up to date, so that it embodies the latest practical information gleaned by fruit growers and experiment station workers. So much new information has come to light since the third edition was published that this is practically a new book, needed by those who have utilized the earlier editions, as well as by fruit growers and farmers generally. Illustrated. 136 pages. 5 x 7 inches. Cloth. $0.50

Farmer's Cyclopedia
of Agriculture 🗡 🗡

A Compendium of Agricultural Science and Practice on Farm, Orchard and Garden Crops, and the Feeding and Diseases of Farm Animals : : : :

By EARLEY VERNON WILCOX, Ph.D.
and CLARENCE BEAMAN SMITH, M.S

Associate Editors in the Office of Experiment Stations, United States Department of Agriculture

THIS is a new, practical, and complete presentation of the whole subject of agriculture in its broadest sense. It is designed for the use of agriculturists who desire up-to-date, reliable information on all matters pertaining to crops and stock, but more particularly for the actual farmer. The volume contains

Detailed directions for the culture of every important field, orchard, and garden crop

grown in America, together with descriptions of their chief insect pests and fungous diseases, and remedies for their control. It contains an account of modern methods in feeding and handling all farm stock, including poultry. The diseases which affect different farm animals and poultry are described, and the most recent remedies suggested for controlling them.

Every bit of this vast mass of new and useful information is authoritative, practical, and easily found, and no effort has been spared to include all desirable details. There are between 6,000 and 7,000 topics covered in these references, and it contains 700 royal 8vo pages and nearly 500 superb half-tone and other original illustrations, making the most perfect Cyclopedia of Agriculture ever attempted.

Handsomely bound in cloth, $3.50; half morocco (very sumptuous), $4.50, postpaid

ORANGE JUDD COMPANY, 52 Lafayette Place, New York, N Y
Marquette Building, Chicago, Ill.

SENT FREE ON APPLICATION

Descriptive Catalog of Rural Books

CONTAINING 112 8vo PAGES, PROFUSELY ILLUSTRATED, AND GIVING FULL DESCRIPTIONS OF THE BEST WORKS ON THE FOLLOWING SUBJECTS : : : : :

Farm and Garden
Fruits, Flowers, etc.
Cattle, Sheep and Swine
Dogs, Horses, Riding, etc.
      Poultry, Pigeons and Bees
      Angling and Fishing
      Boating, Canoeing and Sailing
      Field Sports and Natural History
Hunting, Shooting, etc.
Architecture and Building
Landscape Gardening
Household and Miscellaneous

...PUBLISHERS AND IMPORTERS...

Orange Judd Company

52 and 54 Lafayette Place, NEW YORK

Books will be Forwarded, Postpaid, on Receipt of Price

www.ingramcontent.com/pod-product-compliance
Lightning Source LLC
Chambersburg PA
CBHW030358230426
43664CB00007BB/648